KU-781-182

3/94

UNIVERSITY OF
WOLVERHAMPTON

LIB/LEND/001

Dudley Campus Library

Castle View
Dudley DY1 3HR

Wolverhampton (01902) 323559

This item may be recalled at any time. Keeping it after it has
been recalled or beyond the date stamped may result in a fine.
See tariff of fines displayed at the counter.

	1 5 NOV 1999	
−5. FEB 1997	**1 0 NOV 1999**	
	2 4 NOV 1999	
	− 1 DEC 1999	
19. MAY 1998		
27 NOV 1998	**1 4 JAN 2000**	
29. JAN. 1999	− 3 APR 2000	

WITHDRAWN

WP 0876803 X

Putting the Family First

Putting the Family First
Identities, decisions, citizenship

Bill Jordan
University of Exeter

Marcus Redley
University of Surrey

Simon James
University of Exeter

UNIVERSITY OF WOLVERHAMPTON
LIBRARY

Acc No.
876803

CONTROL
1857281659

DATE
31 AUG 1994

SITE
DY

CLASS
306.
85
JOR

UCL
PRESS

© Bill Jordan, Marcus Redley, Simon James 1994

This book is copyright under the Berne Convention.
No reproduction without permission.
All rights reserved.

First published in 1994 by UCL Press

UCL Press Limited
University College London
Gower Street
London WC1E 6BT

The name of University College London (UCL) is a registered trade mark
used by UCL Press with the consent of the owner.

ISBN:
1-85728-165-9 HB
1-85728-166-7 PB

British Library Cataloguing in Publication Data.
A catalogue record for this book is available from the British Library.

Typeset in Photina
Printed and bound by
Biddles Ltd., Guildford and King's Lynn, England.

Contents

Acknowledgements

The authors would like to thank the ESRC for funding of the research project on which this book is based (Grant no. RG00232124).

We are also extremely grateful to Martin Hollis, Andrew Travers, Ali de Regt and David Morgan for their helpful comments on earlier drafts of the book. They were generous with their time, and encouraging as well as constructively critical, as we struggled to present our work in a way that was acceptable to a commercial publisher.

Also, many thanks to Gill Watson for skilfully typing and retyping count-less versions of the book. We are sure that she will be heartily glad that it has finally reached its destination.

Finally, we are grateful to the interviewees who worked so hard to make sense of the questions asked, and gave up a good deal of time to talk to us.

CHAPTER 1

Introduction

It is seldom easy to explain the obvious; yet understanding the everyday and taken-for-granted is one of the most important tasks for social scientists. All of us could, at a pinch, give an account of who we are, how we decided to do the things that we have done, and how all this relates to the political community in which we live. But how do we do it? Social scientists have difficulty in agreeing how ordinary people produce selves, make decisions, and play the rôles of citizens.

This book is about the contribution that a research study can make to the theory of identity, decision making and citizenship. We analyze interviews with a sample of ordinary people – 36 higher-income British couples with children – about their choices of employment and how they coordinated their decisions, to see what light they shed on key issues in economic and social theory. Hence it is also about what the everyday theorizing of these lay people, in reconstructing their decisions and trying to make sense of their lives, can contribute to social scientific theorizing about agency, rationality and membership of a political community.

Our methods of analysis are interdisciplinary. In many social scientific texts, this means that there are separate chapters (or sections of the book) written by authors from different disciplines. In our case, we have tried to use our theoretical backgrounds – respectively in economics, sociology and social policy – to discover a method of relating interview data to major issues. The most interesting of these issues occur on the borderlines between the social sciences or in territory that is contested between them. As in our earlier study of decision making in low-income households, *Trapped in poverty?*,[1] we seek to demonstrate our method through the analysis itself, using substantial quotations from the interview transcripts.

In once sense, therefore, the whole book is about methodology. However, it is probably useful for readers if we collect together some accessible infor-

1

Table 1.1 The research study.

Funded by	ESRC (Grant no. R000232124)
Nature	Qualitative research. Tape-recorded interviews, using open-ended questions, transcribed for analysis
Sample	36 higher-income couples with children (details in Appendix A)
Form	Individual interview with each of the couple, followed by joint interview, usually on a separate occasion
Duration	Between half an hour and one hour per interview
Date	1990–91
Interviewers	Marcus Redley and Bill Jordan
Contact	By telephone, followed up by letter explaining the project
Location	Medium-sized city in SW England

mation about the research study, for reference at various points in the text. Table 1.1 and Appendix A give succinct summaries of the research project, and the sample of interviewees (how this was gathered, and the economic and social characteristics of the couples). Appendix B summarizes the interviewees' pseudonyms – for the sake of anonymity we called them after trees – and the composition of their households.

Although the analysis continuously addresses theoretical issues, it also presents our research "findings" about these issues. In this sense, it is a *case study* of decision making by couples in the material comfort zone in contemporary Britain. We make no apologies to readers from other countries for the Britishness of our research study, because of the pivotal position of Britain in the development of new social relations in the West. For the decade before our study was undertaken, the Thatcher government espoused a programme of American-style economic liberalization while simultaneously – and often contradictorily – trying to exploit the benefits of membership of the European Community. The former required a process of bold institutional innovation, designed to realign the links and loyalties of large groups of citizens, replacing an order based on public services and communal solidarities by one founded on property ownership, commercial systems and family responsibilities. The latter involved a reorientation of trade and consumption patterns towards a Continent where corporatist institutions remained dominant, and welfare states retained support. Our research method was designed to provide evidence about the effects of these changes on social relations that could not emerge from other kinds of studies – evidence that was thus equally relevant for the analysis of societies in North America and in Continental Europe.

We encouraged the interviewees to tell their stories – to account for their decisions and to reflect on their relative good fortune (compared with older and younger generations, or with the poor people we interviewed in our earlier study). Our questions allowed them to describe their lives in their own terms, holding themselves accountable by the standards they saw as applying to an interview about economic decisions, family relationships and community membership. In this way, our qualitative research complements and supplements the vast bulk of quantitative evidence now available about how mainstream British people live their lives.

This introductory chapter collects together the major theoretical issues and substantive findings of the book. It sets out the way we have organized our analysis in its three parts, and provides a guide to the structure of what follows.

Identities

Our research study was primarily about decision making. However, the first set of theoretical puzzles that exercised us concerned the nature of the agents making these decisions. The interviewees sought, through their accounts, to establish individual identities, constituted through life stories. Yet they were chosen to reflect (by their combinations of occupations – see Appendix A) the characteristic configurations of higher-income households with children in this city: what differentiated them, giving them individual identities, and what made them "typical" or "normal", and hence like each other? "Born originals, how come we to be copies?" enquired an 18th-century philosopher; conversely, we wanted to analyze the common cultural practices through which better-off people established their identities.

The programmes of economic liberalization championed by Margaret Thatcher drew their inspiration from the United States, influenced social change in western Europe, and eventually contributed to the political collapse of the Soviet bloc. These forms of liberalism emphasized the diversity of human aspirations and the impossibility of planning for social needs. Hayek (Thatcher's favourite philosopher) distinguished strongly between "spontaneous" and "constructed" order, insisting that markets and families allowed individuals to adapt to each other's divergent preferences in flexible ways, given how little it was possible to chart or predict complex processes.[2] State planning and allocation, by contrast, relied on crude generalizations to construct an order that was necessarily rigid, authoritarian, inefficient and intrusive.[3] The idea that markets and families should provide the basic elements in the social order was enormously influential in the 1980s; it would scarcely be an exaggeration to say that it underpinned a programme for the global restructuring of social relations.

Yet the theory of the human agent from which this programme is derived is remarkably thin. The denizen of the market place – *homo economicus* – is a somewhat emaciated, desiccated being, all appetite and little substance, an abstract opportunist with an eye for a bargain and a nose for a killing. In such agents, the only identifying trait is their *consistency* in choosing under constraint.[4] *Homo sociologicus*, meanwhile, has deserted the wilder shores of community and become domesticated. The agents of contemporary sociological theory are exponents of "lifestyle politics" that give material forms to their identities. They continually reconstruct themselves in fireside chats and therapeutic sessions ("narratives of self-identity") in Giddens' recent analysis of modernity.[5]

Our study aims to give some substance to the economic agents of rational choice theory, and to locate the lifestyles of self-constructing narrators in the wider context of social and political relations. In Chapter 2, we analyze the common cultural framework of the interviewees' identities in terms of Durkheim's *individualism*.[6] In claiming to be distinctive selves, they all adopted a form of accountability in which they told us "what they had made of themselves" through their decisions, and how they had "put the family first". In this way, they sought to give *morally adequate*[7] versions of their life choices (over work and welfare), trying to provide coherent accounts of how they had developed themselves and prioritized the family within the structures of economy and society, but all within the cultural resources and requirements of this mode of being.

It has become something of a cliché that the cultures of present-day societies are becoming more individualistic, and that British society has been in the vanguard of these changes. Hence our study is of particular interest for its evidence on individualism-in-action – how the adoption of this form of accountability affects people's perceptions of their responsibilities, how they prioritize their commitments to others, how they reconcile conflicting demands arising from these priorities, and the extent to which they recognize the wider social relevance of their actions. These are the topics of Chapter 2.

The claim that both markets and families provide "spontaneous" order, arising – without conscious effort – from the actions of individuals, is even more shadowy than the identities of the agents themselves in neo-liberal theory. In the Scottish Enlightenment tradition of Adam Smith and David Hume, the invisible hand ordered market exchanges, but the family's success as an institution was attributed to natural instincts and sympathies. In these interviewees' accounts, family rôles and responsibilities were as much constructed out of *choices* as were their material lifestyles: they insisted that their self-making and their household obligations were consistent, and tried to give coherent versions of how they reached decisions that reconciled them.

With only one couple as exceptions, the interviewees accounted for their decisions within strongly gendered requirements of family responsibility – men as main providers of income, women as primarily responsible for child care and domestic organization. Furthermore, their interpretation of "family" was in most cases a narrow, nuclear one. Only those who had regular involvement with older kin saw themselves as responsible for their care.[8] The rest described their elderly parents in terms of "indomitable independence", or as being the responsibility of other kin. This links with their accounts of their own provision for retirement and old age, described in terms of men's occupational or private pensions. Only one woman gave a version of how she had provided for her post-employment income that included the possibility of the breakup of her marriage.

Hence one paradox of the individualism of choice was the predominance of strongly gendered versions of responsibility within parallel accounts of what men and women had made of themselves. Decisions were very seldom described in terms of a feminist repertoire. Furthermore, this form of accountability made it difficult for *public issues* to emerge from narratives of self. In the final section of Chapter 2 we analyze the claim that individualism leads to a culture of "narcissism"[9] (because its discourses filter out the shared, public aspects of experience), by examining women's descriptions of their child care arrangements. These supply important evidence that issues were not recognized as ones of public choice (only one woman addressed the collective implications of individual decisions) within the repertoires of individualism. Instead, these women constructed playgroup participation as a step towards returning to the labour market, and (again with one exception) described child-minding without reference to its possible elements of power and exploitation.

Thus interviewees used the repertoires of individualism to construct identities that bore the hallmarks of a distinctive culture – one that prioritized the family as a private, self-responsible setting for the pursuit of self-making in clearly gendered rôles. But these interviews were also *presentations* of the speakers' selves in interaction. Selves were accomplished through tape-recorded performances, negotiating the hazards of giving a public version to a research interviewer. To attempt such a performance is also to risk incoherence, inconsistency, and various forms of social embarrassment. At worst, both interviewee and interviewer, while trying to achieve the appearance of socially valuable selves, hazarded the humiliation of not being able to sustain poise and communication.

Having defined the common culture of accountability in these interviews – the serious attempt to achieve an individualist version of moral adequacy – we turn in Chapter 3 to the processes of interview interaction. It was through these, rather than the individualism of their reconstructions, that interviewees accomplished identities *as individuals*. For our analysis of how they produced themselves within the interview interaction, we draw on the work of Erving Goffman. The achievement of a morally adequate account involved "face work" – the mobilization of the interviewee's socially valued attributes within a reciprocal exchange of ritual respect between the interview participants.[10] This in turn demanded *interactional competence* – the capacity to hook these accounts into the contingencies (incidents and impressions) of the immediate situation.[11] This combination of ritual exchanges and improvised connections establishes a local interactional order[12] in which selves are produced and meaning communicated. We contend that it is the analysis of this informal, *ad hoc* order, and not of some specious "spontaneous" order of the marketplace and the family, that can provide an understanding of the emerging social relations of modernity.

Both the presentation of a morally adequate self and the accomplishment of interactional competence are aspects of the interviewees' identities. Some male respondents (whom we call "heretics") used interactional manoeuvres and ploys (including sexist jokes), or were "carried away" by their own rhetorical practices. Others ("fundamentalists") focused on the management of morally adequate answers in a minimalist way, sacrificing interactional competence. These features of the interviews provide important clues about the nature and purpose of the interactional order. Speakers dealt with threats to the selves they were presenting by creating the appearance of order, stability and normality. They did this through their management of accounts (demonstrating their awareness of "known facts" as well as their accountability for their own actions) and their capacity to improvise in response to unpredictable contingencies.

The last two sections of Chapter 3 analyze in detail two such improvisations. One couple gave a version of their elder son's recent schooling (an "unmitigated disaster", including an expulsion from a private school); another reconstructed their reactions to the threat of his redundancy (including the plan to sell their house and live in a caravan, in order still to be able to have their daughter privately educated). By accounting for their alarming circumstances, using the cultural resources at their disposal, they created a sense of moral obligation, and of objective reality itself, that is exterior and constraining.

Living through a period of rapid and unpredictable change, these interviewees faced the threat of situations in which available cultural resources (in their case, the interpretative repertoires of individualism) were overstretched. In the two examples analyzed, they improvised original accounts, weaving together elements of that repertoire in new combinations. Such "artful practices" indicated interviewees' pressing need to find a way of accounting for their circumstances, even when they were confronted with forces far outside their control. It was their own improvisations, accomplishing an interactional order with the interviewer, that allowed them to experience stability, normality and moral obligation – reality itself – as exterior to themselves and constraining their actions.[13] Thus they felt the sense of a "collective conscience", and avoided "anomie" (in Durkheim's terms) through their own cobbled-together accounts, constructed on the hoof (so to speak) from recycled bits of the individualist repertoire. This seems to be the "spontaneous order" of everyday life.

The question therefore is how this informal, *ad hoc* order relates to the formal, institutional order of social structures, political systems and academic theories. This is one of the major themes of the whole book. The improvisations that give rise to the interactional order are responsive to the needs of selves – for identity, social value, and reciprocity in communication.[14] But speakers such as these interviewees are also accountable in terms of the formal, institutional context of their actions. They used institutional terminology to describe the external frameworks in which their decisions were made. These included accounts of the global economy and the structures of businesses and government departments, as well as local agencies and enterprises.

Hence accounting selves became interacting selves, and used cultural resources for skilful improvisation in ritual exchanges that sustained the sense of local moral order and objective reality. In Chapter 4, we analyze the specifically individualistic features of this order, through an examination of how interviewees use interpretative repertoires[15] to account for the variety in their circumstances. The same range of terms were used to justify apparently incompatibly different decisions, both in giving versions of what they have made of themselves and in showing how they have put the family first. We examine the accounts of the few women who described their labour-market moves as following a "career", to see how their use of this repertoire differs from that in "standard" accounts (by women who disclaimed "careers" and by men whose "careers" consisted in the incremental pursuit of advantages within employment).

These variations imply that the individualistic ethic does not provide prescriptive rules to guide behaviour. Speakers must use judgement to interpret their responsibilities in complex situations, and then create the sense of moral order and institutional constraint by adapting the available cultural resources to their particular circumstances. The terms of the individualist repertoire are "indexical" (as Garfinkel[16] suggests): like "career", "family" has no determinate meaning until it is defined by use in context.[17] Thus one couple gave an account of how they took over the care of a nephew and niece (straight after the death of their father). They reconstructed their assumption of responsibility for these kin – "it's family, you have to do something" – by interpreting the term quite differently from other interviewees. Indeed, for most, the term "family" was used to prioritize the nuclear household and exclude responsibility for other kin – for example by the woman who said she would emigrate if her father came to need her care.

Three other sets of interviewees – a recently reconstituted family and two couples sharing a house and pooling their resources – gave accounts that used terms from the individualist repertoire – "parent" and "family" – to describe a powerful sense of commitment to the welfare of fellow members of these "non-standard households". Thus individualism allows a strong morality of mutual concern (the sanctity of the individual and the responsibility of members to each other) to be sustained in ambiguous, fluid and unpredictable situations that do not correspond to the "nuclear family" pattern. The sense of order and obligation is created by the skilful improvisations of artful practitioners. These *ad hoc* accounts (always provisional and requiring frequent repair) are then used by members to regulate themselves and each other, notwithstanding the indeterminate nature of the expressions from which they are composed.

As a source of identity (narrative coherence) in their accounts, the individualist repertoire was therefore both troublesome and valuable for these agents. They had trouble accounting for what they had made of themselves and how they put the family first in many of the more fluid situations that were characteristic of a society experiencing accelerated change through a programme of economic liberalization. Yet it was in those fluid situations that some such account was most insistently needed as a basis for identity and for the sense of moral order and exterior reality. Couples relied on each other for the maintenance of this stability and for mutual moral regulation; they accomplished it through the creation (sometimes under the threat of anomie) of an improvised interactional order. The "indexical" terms of the individualist repertoire facilitated these processes of improvisation by allowing variable interpretations of their responsibilities. Thus they could legitimate "strange" or even "daft" innovations under the guise of individualist orthodoxy.[18] Above all, they could accomplish morally adequate and interactionally competent performances of themselves in the midst of the potentially alarming and unpredictable contingencies of a research interview.

Decisions

Our research study was about how *couples* reached decisions over work. This implied that individual agents co-ordinated their choices – that each one took account of the other's actions in deciding upon his or her own. In the second part of the book, we analyze what our data can contribute to theory about the co-ordination of decisions in households, and especially about economic and normative reasoning in the process of decision making.

Our starting point is the theoretical model that most impressively defines rationality, explains problems of co-ordination, and sets out an analysis of how they may be overcome. In rational choice theory, agents have complete and consistent preference ordering and can calculate perfectly the probability of events. The way they take account of other agents' actions is represented as a game, in which each chooses a strategy that treats the strategies open to the other as events, and calculates the probability of the other adopting each strategy.[19] The best reply (called a Nash equilibrium) that each strategy can make to the other is when each agent maximizes his or her expected utility, given the other's strategy. A number of problems of co-ordination are represented in the form of games.[20] One of these, called Battle of the Sexes, in which there are two possible equilibria, seemed a promising way of analyzing issues of co-ordination between couples.

In Chapter 5 we show that the interviewees sometimes talked about the difficulties of establishing co-operation (for instance, over household chores) or co-ordinating career and family decisions in ways that could be represented as games. Some even appeared to use the language of strategic bargaining theory in their accounts. However, at other points in the same accounts, they indicated that their expectations of each other were based not on calculations of probabilities, but on mutual commitments – they were normative.

Economic and social theory overlap (and disagree) over the part played by calculative strategies and normative expectations in decisions that are orientated towards others' actions. The theoretical foundations of the modern social sciences were constructed on the notion of a single universal concept of rationality, as the meaningful social action that links means to ends.[21] The edifice of social action was then conveniently divided, employing Weber's distinction between instrumental rationality – the use of calculated expectations of the behaviour of people and things to achieve the actor's purposes – and value rationality – pursuing ethical, aesthetic or religious ends, regardless of consequences.[22] Some modern theorists (such as Elster) retain this distinction, seeing social norms as an independent category, not conditional on consequences or determined by self-interest, but charged with emotion and providing the "cement of society".[23] This neatly separates calculative from normative decisions in a way that might allow us to distinguish between economic and ethical reasoning in the interview accounts.

Yet the interviewees did not appear to make such a distinction. Their expectations of each other, as revealed in the joint interviews, seemed to mix material and moral elements, through calculative and normative discourses. In the concluding section of this chapter, we draw on new theoretical developments in economics that refocus attention on the importance of communication and deliberation in commercial relations. Whereas rational choice theory eliminates these factors from its analysis, Levy argues that ordinary people's talk about decisions is important, because markets and production require a normative framework of self-restraint, respect for property distinctions and contractual obligations, which have to be discursively created and maintained.[24] People would be no more able than rats are to trade, produce or accumulate property if they could not reason about fairness and legality.

Sociologists, too, have argued for a closer study of the conceptual tools used by actors in making decisions, their links with other discourses, and the surrounding conditions.[25] The process of decision making is thus regarded as a specialized technique for connecting beliefs, desires and actions, worthy of investigation in its own right. In Chapter 6 we look in detail at the way that interviewees constructed their answers to questions over decisions. Weber defined rational social action as meaningful, publicly recognizable activity, orientated to such activity by others, and linking means to ends.[26] Analyzing the transcripts of these interviews, we noticed that we as interviewers seemed to be "convinced" by accounts of decisions that gave both "quantity" (economic) and "quality" (value) reasons for decisions. When respondents answered questions in a form that combined these in non-contradictory (albeit often pithy or cryptic) ways, we seemed culturally predisposed to "accept" these and move on to a different question.

The interviewees' reasoning supplied the links between the two elements in the individualistic ethic – the requirements to make something of themselves and to put the family first – and allowed them to co-ordinate their actions with each other's. It provided a sense of order and stability, which was adequate for the practical purposes of everyday life, through a "code"[27] of partnership, whose terms were "indexical" (elaborated in talk and defined only in context). So long as partners' interpretations were reciprocal, this gave them the means to sustain the sense of predictability in their actions and to regulate their own and each other's decisions.

Part of this code was that decisions should be discussed and agreed between them. Yet, in the joint interviews, they had great difficulty in defining what had been agreed, or how this provided a guide to everyday choices. In the following section, we look at what they said about budgeting and household expenditure: many couples claimed that they had no system for keeping account of what they spent, and therefore by implication no way of making the kinds of joint decisions that partnership might require. Those who said they did budget carefully none the less gave examples of where they had reinterpreted the "rules" of their system ("stretching" their budgets) where an item of expenditure could be shown to be "reasonable" in terms of value for money and its contribution to the quality of family life.

Hence the indeterminate, non-prescriptive nature of the partnership code allowed couples the flexibility and individual autonomy to make on-the-spot everyday decisions, while retaining the sense that their actions were part of a stable order and co-ordinated with each other's. The mode of reasoning that linked "quantity" with "quality" factors was well suited to preserve the sense of a meaningful, publicly recognizable co-ordination between the wider world of economic activity and the intimacies of domestic life, as well as between each other's choices.

In the final section of Chapter 6, we analyze decisions that all the couples saw as important – whether to send their children to state or to private schools. Their reasoning over this issue used cultural resources to evaluate their offspring's long-term labour-market prospects, and their psychological and social needs, within each of these systems. It was in this context that several interviewees insisted that, when there was a clash between their political principles and the best interests of their children, they should put the family first.

Where couples favoured state education, their reasoning for it was made up of the same elements (cultural particulars) as those used in accounts of decisions to choose private schooling – long-term economic advantage and the child's individual and social needs. Yet several interviewees described changing their decisions in line with contingencies and circumstances, suggesting that these choices were more provisional than the carefully reasoned (often "more than morally adequate") accounts of others suggested. Thus both the code of partnership and the modes of articulating publicly recognizable "rational" action required interpretation and reinterpretation in line with the changing configuration of everyday family situations.

Chapter 7 provides the crux of our analysis of couples' decisions and hence of our study's contribution to the theory of decision making. Our aim is to find a way of combining the explanations of co-ordination issues derived from strategic bargaining games (chapter 5) and our understanding of the reasoning that constitutes the everyday order of partnership. We do this by analyzing individual strategies within partnerships in terms of *investments*. As anthropological research (such as Popkin's[28]) has shown, agents make choices between allocating their time and energy to communal, shared systems (family, kin, community) or commercial activities (paid employment or private enterprise) as if they were calculating the expected returns (both short term and long term). Hence an economic explanation of decisions, in terms of alternative uses for scarce resources, has more predictive power than a theory that postulates a non-calculative "moral economy" of sharing (in households or communities) with its own different and separate rationality. Thus we start from the hypothesis of partners with long-term investment strategies that take account of each other, and aim to maximize each one's utility, given the other's.

Among these interviewees, men appeared to invest much more in their careers than women (given the similarity of their educational qualifications), and women more in the family than men. Even those men who gave "non-career" accounts of their decisions accumulated more job assets than women, and in only two households was the woman earning more than the man at the time of the interviews. Conversely, women gave a larger proportion of their time and energy to care and the organization of the household. This required women to settle for lesser material benefits in the short and medium term. Being "supportive" of their partner's career could oblige them to move home and disrupt their networks of paid and unpaid activity. This looked like choosing the Nash equilibrium solution in a bargaining game of Battle of the Sexes that gave the man the larger pay-off.

However, if we treat them as agents with the calculative and predictive capacities of those in rational choice theory, these two strategies might be the best replies to each other in a "supergame" played over a life-time. This is because each might be taking account of such factors as women's earlier retirement age and greater longevity compared with men, and the structural characteristics of the labour market. Thus women might get a better return on their investments in their partner's pension (for example) than on the resources that might be required to generate one of their own, where pay-offs are calculated on a lifetime basis. If their partner's career foundered, they could reinvest in one of their own – as two women among these interviewees were doing.

However, it was not clear that such an analysis in terms of bargaining strategies took account of the risks of divorce. Women's reliance on men's income during their children's dependence made them vulnerable during this stage of the life cycle.[29] In the final section of Chapter 7 we show how the moral regulation of partnership and decision making, using the discursive rationality analyzed in Chapter 6, facilitated trust and mutuality within a relationship of asymmetric power during the family life cycle. It also precluded discussion of the possibility of divorce in all but two of the interviews with women.

Feminist theory challenges both economists and sociologists to study partnership and the domestic division of labour in terms of male domination and female subordination.[30] Using the insights of another anthropologist, James C. Scott,[31] we show how the interactional order of partnership permits a degree of autonomy for the pursuit of women's "resistance practices" and for divergent interpretations according to interests. In these partnerships, the mutual commitment necessary for trust and communication required that power and resistance to it were managed within reciprocal exchanges of ritual respect.[32] But women used such ploys as mock conventionality or shows of wifely gratitude to create the domestic order in which they could pursue self-developmental, creative or recreational agendas of their own. Thus the interactional order sustains and is sustained by the practices of partnership, and creates possibilities of autonomous action within structurally unequal rôles. Our detailed examination of the partnership code and couples' reasoning over decisions complements economic analysis using strategic bargaining theory.

Citizenship

In the third part of the book, we shift from the analysis of the decision-making process in partnership to a consideration of how our research study can contribute to theory of citizenship. As a case study of individualism-in-action, it can shed light on how these comfortably-off couples constructed their relations with their fellow citizens, and how their moral priorities and partnership practices influenced their interpretations of their entitlements and obligations as members of a political community. In accounting for their decisions over public or commercial welfare systems and describing their membership of voluntary organizations and their informal co-operative arrangements, the interviewees provided evidence of how individualistic repertoires relate such choices and actions to issues of justice, democracy and solidarity.

Although citizenship has recently become a major topic in social and political theory,[33] social scientists have had difficulty in devising empirical methods for investigating their hypotheses about the origins of order and the consequences of political restructuring.[34] The radical policies of the British government have made British society into something of a laboratory for a social experiment. Theory of citizenship develops ambitious (but largely untested) analyses of the consequences of these programmes on individuals' perceptions of their identities, interests and membership. Our study shows how better-off couples accounted for their relative good fortune and how they interpreted their responsibilities towards others. It also allows us to analyze the longer-term implications of individualistic decision making and some of the perverse consequences of the priorities displayed in these accounts.

In Chapter 8, we look at what the interview accounts can tell us about the "property-owning democracy". This is the version of the liberal tradition of citizenship espoused by the British government under Margaret Thatcher. Protagonists argue that property entitlements and the "spontaneous order" of markets and families provide a more reliable basis for stable social relations than can be achieved through planned distributions in the name of "social justice".[35] In the first section of the chapter, we analyze how interviewees described their "job assets", showing how they treated well paid employment as conferring entitlements in the form of property rights.[36] Individualist repertoires helped them to take for granted their rights to the advantages that flowed from these assets, because they could describe how they got their jobs or businesses in terms of their own efforts and skills – as part of what they have made of themselves. This interpretation also served to exclude consideration of inequalities of opportunity from their accounts: they were in no way responsible for the failure of others to make something of themselves in the labour market.

This leads to an analysis of the forms of political discourse and participation appropriate for a "property-owning democracy". Tocqueville's *America*[37] supplies a possible version of how property-owners might come to perceive their own interests as requiring them to participate in democratic processes to determine the public interest. The nearest thing to such accounts within the interviews consisted of job-holders' descriptions of their attempts to influence decisions within their firms or agencies. But respondents had trouble linking the terms of the individualist repertoire to any political activity, and some acknowledged that their family priorities sometimes contributed to unfairness in society.

Some interviewees did use a *collectivist* repertoire in answer to certain questions. This repertoire drew on the social democratic traditions of the welfare state and trade unionism. Public sector employees in particular interpreted their decisions on commercial welfare systems (such as health insurance) by using this repertoire. However, they too had trouble in linking these decisions with actions to influence the political process. Even those few who clearly stated that they would prefer to pay more in taxes, or who justified their use of public services in terms of political principle, found it difficult to say what this could do to strengthen collectivist structures. Only teachers were able to link a rhetoric of collectivism with a programme of action to resist government reforms of public education.

We next analyze how interviewees used individualistic repertoires to describe changes in the labour market and in social relations, through focusing on their talk about their children's futures. Their lengthy descriptions of their attempts to gain educational advantages for their offspring were legitimated by reference to increased competition for jobs. Although several of the men in highly paid posts themselves had few educational qualifications, they and their partners insisted that a degree would be a necessary condition for success in the labour market conditions of the future. The accountability framework of individualism required them to show how they were equipping their children for increased competition, but not how this took account of the needs of others. Equality of opportunity and equality of citizenship did not emerge as public issues in these version of how they had sought to gain advantage for their children in access to higher education and good jobs.

In the last section of Chapter 8, we analyze how interviewees constructed the combinations of commercial, public and informal welfare sources that they chose. Here we demonstrate that individualistic accountability for their actions did not include a responsibility to account for the effects of their decisions on others, and hence that any reflections upon these consequences (in terms of public policy) were "optional extras". Their choices were legitimated in terms of their entitlements to job assets (in the case of occupational welfare) or their obligations to put the family first. Thus, without wishing any harm to "less fortunate others", and while still giving broad support to the principles of the welfare state, their interpretative repertoires and cultural practices led them to prioritize "family responsibility" over any public issues.

In Chapter 9, we analyze the collective consequences of the individual and household decisions that these interviewees described. Their individualistic and family-orientated quest for advantage (job assets and other forms of property giving advantages to themselves and their offspring), though rational for each household, sum together to give perverse and wasteful outcomes. Drawing on Fred Hirsch's theory of *positional goods* in *Social limits to growth*,[38] we show how the attempt to gain advantage over others (by securing well paid jobs, houses in superior districts and higher education for their children) can trap higher-income couples in a cycle of mutually frustrating choices. Like individuals in a crowd who stand on tiptoe to get a better view, their decisions produced the desired result only if others did not do likewise; if all act similarly, the result is collectively inefficient.

Competition for higher-paid jobs like the ones held by the (predominantly male) interviewees with these positional advantages has driven up their "price" (in terms of educational qualifications). Several respondents recognized that the positions they – often with few examination passes – now held would be accessible only by people with degrees and professional accreditations from the next generation. This led them (as parents) to strive more strongly to get their children into higher education, and those who saw private schooling as giving them an edge over others were willing to pay for this. All were willing to support their offspring through university or college, even if this involved considerable sacrifices. Yet, paradoxically, job-holders were forced to stay in work for longer to provide the income for this extended dependence, thus blocking the access of the next generation (including their own children) to the very job assets they sought for them. A similar phenomenon can be recognized in the housing market.

If men were "trapped in advantage", women's willingness to adopt "supportive" rôles rather than challenge male positional advantage also had some perverse consequences. Using Robert Solow's game-theoretical analysis of *The labour market as a social institution*,[39] we show that women as "outsiders" in employment, but "insiders" in higher-income households, had an apparent stake in preserving the *status quo*. However, in so far as their offspring (and especially their daughters) were also labour-market outsiders, this strategy was perpetuating the new generation's disadvantages. Collectively their decisions not to compete or challenge male advantages, together with their sacrifices for the sake of their children's future job assets, could be seen as producing wasteful results.

In our conclusions, we show that individualist repertoires of choice and family responsibility obscure the perversities of these collective outcomes, and the issues of equality of opportunity, democratic citizenship and public welfare they raise. They pose problems for the politics of collective choice – whether this concerns the obligations of the poor or the contributions of the better-off – because no coherent version of social responsibility or democratic participation can emerge from such accounts. Thus the debate about the future of the welfare state in Britain is being conducted in a dangerous political climate – one recently characterized as "a mood of baffled, shrugging individualism . . . [of] problems without solutions, to be passively accepted and endured, with no faith in any political answers".[40] Our research study traces some of the origins of this culture of apathy and cynicism to the interpretative repertoires and cultural practices of better-off households.

In such a political climate, it is common for social scientists simultaneously to acknowledge the urgent need for institutional innovation yet to bemoan its inevitable impossibility, because of the fragmentation of the coalition that favoured progressive reforms. Yet social research has hitherto done little to uncover the economic discourses and social practices that contribute to apathy and cynicism, or to trace the cultural consequences of social change and government programmes. Nor has it clarified the self-defeating and anti-democratic features of the pervasive individualism of those who are supposed to have benefited from the economic shifts of the 1980s. Our study is intended to contribute to the debates about the future of social justice, institutional reform and the welfare state, as well as to theory about economic decision making and household responsibilities. Research on citizenship should surely explore the links between these two fields more systematically in future.

References

1. B. Jordan, S. James, H. Kay, M. Redley, *Trapped in Poverty? labour-market decisions in low-income households* (London: Routledge, 1992).
2. F. A. Hayek, *Rules and order* (London: Routledge & Kegan Paul, 1973), Ch. 1.
3. F. A. Hayek, *The mirage of social justice* (London: Routledge & Kegan Paul, 1976), Ch. 10; *Rules and order*, Ch. 2.
4. S. Hargreaves Heap, M. Hollis, B. Lyons, R. Sugden, A. Weale, *The theory of choice: a critical guide* Oxford: Blackwell, 1992), Part I, pp. 3–90; M. Hollis & R. Sugden, "Rationality in action", *Mind*, **102**, no. 405 (1993), 1–35.
5. A. Giddens, *Modernity and self-identity: self and society in the late modern age* (Oxford: Polity, 1991), pp. 80–87.
6. E. Durkheim, *The division of labour in society* (1893; New York: Free Press, 1933); "Individualism and the intellectuals", *Revue Bleu*, 4th Series, No. 10 (1898), 7–13.
7. D. Silverman, *Qualitative methodology and sociology* (Aldershot, England: Gower, 1985); E. C. Cuff, "Some issues in studying the problem of versions in everyday situations", Department of Sociology, Manchester University, Occasional Paper No. 3, 1980.
8. J. Finch, *Family obligations and social change* (Oxford: Polity, 1989); J. Finch & J. Mason, *Negotiating family responsibilities* (London: Routledge, 1993.
9. R. Sennett, *The fall of public man* (Cambridge: Cambridge University Press, 1977); C. Lasch, *The culture of narcissism* London: Abacus, 1980).
10. E. Goffman, "On face-work: an analysis of ritual elements in social interaction", in *Interaction ritual: essays on face-to-face behaviour* (London: Penguin, 1972).
11. M. Redley, "Interview moments: how is it that some respondents appear to have more personality than others?" Paper given to the 13th Discourse Analysis Workshop, Exeter University, September 1991.
12. A. Warfield Rawls, "An ethnomethodological perspective on social theory", in *The interaction order*, D. T. Helm et al. (eds), 4–20 (New York: Irvington, 1989).
13. R. Hilbert, "Anomie and the moral regulation of reality: the Durkheimian tradition in modern relief", *Sociological Theory*, **4** (1986), 1–19; and *The classical roots of ethnomethodology: Durkheim, Weber and Garfinkel* Chapel Hill, NC: University of North

REFERENCES

Carolina Press, 1992).

14. A. Warfield Rawls, "Language, self and social order: a reformulation of Goffman and Sacks", *Human Studies* **12** (1989), 147–72.

15. M. Wetherell & J. Potter, "Discourse analysis and the identification of interpretative repertoires", in *Analysing everyday explanation*, C. Antaki (ed.), 168–83 (London: Sage, 1988).

16. H. Garfinkel, *Studies in ethnomethodology* (Englewood Cliffs, NJ: Prentice Hall, 1967), pp. 4–7.

17. J. F. Gubrium & R. J. Lynott, "Family rhetoric as social order", *Journal of Family Issues* **6** (1985), 129–52.

18. A. Travers, "Strangers to themselves: how interactants are other than they are", *British Journal of Sociology* **43**, (4) (1992), 601–37.

19. Hollis & Sugden, "Rationality in action", p. 9; T. C. Schelling, "An essay on bargaining", *American Economic Review* **46** (1956), 281–306; B. Lyons, "Game theory" and "Bargaining", in Hargreaves Heap et al., *The theory of choice*, pp. 93–143.

20. Lyons, "Game theory", pp. 107–12.

21. S. Turner, "Rationality today", *Sociological Theory* **9** (2) (1991), 191–4; M. C. Agodi, "Rational fools or foolish rationalists? bringing the meaning back in", *Sociological Theory* **9** (2) (1991), 199–205.

22. M. Weber, *Economy and society* (1922); ed. G. Roth and C. Wittich (New York: Bedminster Press, 1968), p. 25.

23. J. Elster, *The cement of society: a study of social order* (Cambridge: Cambridge University Press, 1989), especially p. 125.

24. D. M. Levy, *The economic ideas of ordinary people: from preferences to trade* (London: Routledge, 1992).

25. B. Hindess, "Rationality in modern society", *Sociological Theory* **9** (2) (1991), 216–27.

26. Weber, *Economy and society*, p. 5.

27. D. L. Wieder, *Language and social reality: the case of telling the convict code* (The Hague: Mouton, 1974).

28. S. Popkin, *The rational peasant: the political economy of rural Vietnam* (Chicago: University of Chicago Press, 1979).

29. J. Burgoyne, "Change, gender and the life course", in *Social change and the life course*, G. Cohen (ed.) 33–66 (London: Tavistock, 1987); P. Allatt, T. Keil, A. Bryman, W. Bytheway, *Women and the life cycle: transitions and turning points* (London: Macmillan, 1987); J. Finch & D. Morgan, "Marriage in the 1980s: a new sense of realism?" in *Marriage, domestic life and social change: writings for Jacqueline Burgoyne*, D. Clark (ed.), 55–82 (London: Routledge, 1991).

30. See, for instance, S. Walby, *Theorising patriarchy* (Oxford: Blackwell, 1990).

31. J. C. Scott, *Weapons of the weak: everyday forms of peasant resistance* (New Haven, CT: Yale University Press, 1988); and *Domination and the arts of resistance: hidden transcripts* (New Haven, CT: Yale University Press, 1990).

32. B. Jordan, "Framing claims and the weapons of the weak", paper given at International Seminar on Social Welfare Theory, Aylmer, Quebec, Canada, 29 September, 1992.

33. See, for instance, B. S. Turner, "Outline of a theory of citizenship", *Sociology* **24** (2) (1990), 189–217; G. Andrews (ed.), *Citizenship* (London: Verso, 1991); J. Barbalet,

Citizenship (Milton Keynes: Open University Press, 1988); R. Lister, *The exclusive society: citizenship and the poor* (London: CPAG, 1990); D. Marquand, *The unprincipled society* (London: Fontana, 1988); A. Oldfield, *Citizenship and community: civic republicanism and the modern world* (London: Routledge, 1990); R. Plant, "Citizenship, rights and welfare", in *The welfare of citizens: developing new social rights*, A. Coote (ed.), 15–30 (London: IPPR/Rivers Oram Press, 1992).

34. B. S. Turner, "Prolegoma to a general theory of social order" in *Citizenship, civil society and social cohesion*, B. S. Turner (ed.), 1–65 (Swindon: ESRC, 1991).

35. See, for instance, A. Shand, *Free market morality: the political economy of the Austrian school* (London: Routledge, 1990); F. A. Hayek, *Individualism and economic order* (Chicago: Chicago University Press, 1980).

36. P. Van Parijs, "A revolution in class theory", *Politics and Society*, **15** (4) (1987), 453–82; B. Jordan, *The common good: citizenship, morality and self-interest* (Oxford: Blackwell, 1989), Ch. 4.

37. A. de Tocqueville, *Democracy in America* (1836; ed. J. P. Mayer and M. Lanner, London: Collins, 1968).

38. F. Hirsch, *Social limits to growth* (London: Routledge & Kegan Paul, 1977).

39. R. M. Solow, *The labour market as a social institution* (Oxford: Blackwell, 1990).

40. Leader, *Guardian*, 24 July 1993.

PART I: IDENTITIES

CHAPTER 2

Making Something of Oneself

Every day, millions of comfortably off couples with children have breakfast, together or separately, with varying degrees of haste or leisure, and set about their daily tasks. Their subsequent activities reflect decisions that they have made, individually or jointly, with varying degrees of planning and co-ordination. We interviewed 36 British couples with children, living in the material comfort zone in southern England, about how they decided what work to do and the division of labour between them. Our aim was to contribute to theory of labour-market decision making through an interdisciplinary analysis of what they told us.

An important issue for this part of the book is the status of interview research of this kind within the theory of decision making. What could these interviewees' retrospective reconstructions of their moves and motives tell us that was relevant to the strategic bargaining theory developed by economists? Why might the rather abstract social theory that is fashionable nowadays be interested in these diverse and detailed accounts of the everyday world of the provincial bourgeoisie? And how is an interdisciplinary analysis of such data possible, given the many different models of human behaviour employed by economists, sociologists, psychologists and political theorists?

Our starting point is the link between the action of reporting and what is reported – the agent. This chapter is about the nature of the agents whose decisions we are analyzing. We wanted to be able to use these accounts to address issues about rationality (in the second part) and citizenship (in the third). The only theory of decision making that extends across the social sciences – rational choice theory – makes assumptions about its agents that reduce them to stern abstractions, shorn of any social, psychological or political characteristics.[1] At first sight, it seemed unlikely that we could discover a method of analysis that borrowed something from those who explained decisions in terms of games between such ideally rational play-ers, and something from critics of this theory, who insisted that choices must be understood in a context of identity, meaning, communication and social order.

However, there do seem to be some signs of a narrowing of the gap between *homo sociologicus* (taken as a shorthand for the latter models of social agents) and *homo economicus*. Theory of identity in "late modernity" emphasizes choice and risk, rather than kinship and community. For in-stance, Giddens' recent work sees identity as constructed within the "puz-zling diversity of options and possibilities" in a "risk culture".[2] He argues that the risks derived from global social systems are drawn into individu-als' organization of their social world via biographical narratives of the self. "The reflexive project of the self, which consists in the sustaining of coher-ent, yet continuously revised, biographical narratives, takes place in the context of multiple choice, as filtered through abstract systems".[3] Giddens describes "lifestyles" as the set of actions chosen by individuals to give material form to a particular narrative of self-identity.[4]

The *coherence* of a biographical account of the self is therefore analyzed in terms of choice, based on risk assessment, producing a "more or less integrated set of practices" (lifestyle).[5] This sounds surprisingly compatible with the model of decision-making agents in rational choice theory. These choose in accordance with a given set of preferences: rationality is under-stood in terms of the *consistency* of the agent's decisions with one another. An agent whose decisions are consistent chooses as if calculating utility and probability in the face of uncertainty and risk, so as to reckon the expected utility of each of the actions from which choice is made.[6] Giddens' analy-sis of identity in terms of narrative coherence thus sounds not unlike a retrospective commentary – or attempt "to police [their] own decisions for consistency"[7] – by the agents of economic theory, with expected utility reflected in "lifestyles". Interview research offers examples of such retro-spective reconstructions, fleshing out the hypothetical agents of this theo-retical convergence.

How is coherence (or consistency) achieved in these narratives? Our analysis demonstrates that the interviewees accounted for their decisions by showing how they enabled them to "make something of themselves" and "put the family first". They justified all their choices in relation to these two criteria, which provided the accountability framework of the interviews. In adopting these standards for the retrospective legitimation of their decisions, they revealed a shared culture of what constituted a morally adequate version[8] of decision making in higher-income British partnerships. We argue that this culture can be understood through Durkheim's concept of individualism:[9] interviewees described their decisions as if they were morally accountable for the self that they had made through their choices, and for prioritizing the welfare of the domestic units they had chosen to form. Paradoxically, it is this shared culture of individualism that makes their accounts not only comparable, but similar.

This allows us to use this study as a way of analyzing aspects of social relations in comfortable British society. What Giddens calls the "reflexive narrative biographies" of the interviewees are framed within the same requirements of responsibility for self and family; hence they reveal the cultural features of British social relations as much as their "lifestyle" choices. In this chapter, we analyze the kind of selves that interviewees construct, the aspects of their biographies for which they assume critical responsibility, the commitments they prioritize, the way they reconcile conflicting demands arising from these priorities, and the extent to which they recognize the wider social relevance of their actions.

In describing the accounts as "individualistic" in Durkheim's sense, we are characterizing the type of accountability that gives these versions of decision making their coherence or consistency. To make oneself accountable for "what one has made of oneself" is to accept a form of narrative ordering of the self; to prioritize the family over other social units is to adopt the moral requirements of a particular set of social relations. However, the specific features of personal responsibility for steering, choosing and prioritizing within this individualistic framework vary over time and between groups in society, and it is the nature of these specifics (cultural particulars) that we want to analyze in this chapter. Our analysis of individualism-in-action among higher-income British couples sheds light on how similar values can be mobilized in other cultural contexts.

In the next section, we will define individualism and show how this common framework of accountability is revealed in the interviews. Although men and women account for what they have made of themselves within this same overall framework, their narratives of identity are strongly gendered. All but one of the men take primary responsibility for providing the couple's income, and most do so by pursuing a "career" – seeking incremental gains in salary and fringe benefits. Conversely, all but one of the women take primary responsibility for child care and the domestic sphere, and their versions of labour-market decisions have a more self-developmental agenda in the narrative of what they have made of themselves.

24

The moral requirements of "putting the family first" are all gendered along similar lines. In the following section we show how responsibility for income for retirement is incorporated into men's accounts of their labour-market decisions but absent from all but a few accounts by women. The provision of occupational or private pensions thus becomes an element in a morally adequate male narrative, and those men who have not made such arrangements do a good deal of rhetorical work to justify their lack of provision. Only one woman gives a detailed account of providing for her own, independent retirement income, in terms of the possibility of the breakup of her marriage.

The concept of "family" is mobilized by the interviewees to indicate priority in choices over responsibilities. However, as other qualitative studies have indicated, "family" is a term whose meaning is determined by use in particular contexts.[10] Those couples who are geographically distant from elderly kin use the word to denote the nuclear family, and construct their own parents as "indomitably independent" or the responsibility of other members of the kinship network. Those whose older relatives live locally, and who are closely involved with them, include them (and especially their parents) within the ambit of their family responsibilities.

The final section analyzes the extent to which narratives framed in terms of individualism and lifestyle choices give rise to discourses of the public sphere. Do such accounts reveal awareness of the wider social significance of individual decisions or identify public issues? Here we use the example of women's construction of their child care responsibilities to show how individualistic agents describe participation in various systems in terms of self-development; only one identifies child care as an issue for public policy.

In this chapter, therefore, we seek to establish what is common to these apparently very diverse accounts of identity-constructing decisions – the way in which the interviews seek consistency and coherence in their versions of choices from a multitude of options, in several spheres. It is aimed to make sense of a number of the more surprising aspects of the narratives of self given by the interviewees, such as the decision by Mrs Oak, a research scientist with a higher degree, to be a sex therapist (see p. 32), or Mr Hawthorn's description of his purchase of an old mill in France as "a kind of private pension fund" (see p. 35). Our analysis will show how, in the name of "family" responsibility, Mr Larch sees his elderly mother every day (see p. 40), while Mrs Laburnum (p. 49) says she would emigrate if her father needed care in her home; and how Mrs Beech can describe her child-minder as "part of the family", while Mrs Hazel recounts with a laugh how her very active daughter "seems to have exhausted two of the child-minders. One had a bad back from lifting her so much eventually, and the other had a nervous breakdown" (see pp. 46 and 47).

Individualism, identity and social relations

A research interview is both a public account by an interviewee to a researcher, and a piece of social interaction. The interactive elements in the interviewees' production of themselves will be analyzed in the next chapter; this one is concerned with their accounts of their decisions, and what these revealed of their identities and their social relations. Agreeing to give an account of themselves to a researcher showed that they were willing to be answerable to the standards that they took to apply to responsible selves like themselves (and implicitly ourselves) in British society. They made serious efforts to answer questions about how they related their actions to the formal world of economy and polity. They tried to explain their decisions in terms of rates of pay, job security, tax rates, fringe benefits, the return on investments, property values, educational opportunities, and the relative advantages of public and private welfare systems. This involved them in constructing a relationship between the everyday world of their lived experience and the formal, abstract systems of markets and public administration.

The interviewees produced and managed descriptions of their choices of work and how they co-ordinated them with those of their partner. They did this in such a way as to try to achieve the appearance of competent, aware, higher-income members of British society. Silverman[11] and Cuff[12] define the attempt at giving such accounts in terms of "moral adequacy". They display their awareness of culturally accepted standards (of the moral requirements of their rôles) among such members, and use "artful practices" to justify their decisions, in line with these public understandings.

Making themselves accountable to the researcher in this way, the interviewees give versions of events and choices through which they try to present a self that is responsible for steering a course through complex pathways of constraint and opportunity, fate and chance. Identity is established by the continuity not of events but of discursive ordering and reconstruction: it is *the self as reflexively understood by the person in terms of his or her biography*.[13] The common framework of accountability adopted by the interviewees, giving their decisions coherence within this narrative, is to show "what they have made of themselves" and how they have "put the family first".

Consider the following passage from Mr Hemlock's account of how he came to take his current post as a university teacher in this city.

Mr Hemlock: . . . I was living in London, and Hilary, my wife, had a very interesting job in London at the time, a children's book publisher, so I didn't want to leave London because I knew she wouldn't be able to work anywhere else. But at the same time, in a small field like mine [. . .] you had to go wherever there was a job, especially as Hilary wasn't all that well paid. So when a job came up here I applied for it.   (Mr Hemlock, p. 1 of transcript)

Mr Hemlock's account of the decision implicitly accepts responsibility for developing his abilities and capacities through his job – he was morally required to seek a job in his field. He also recognizes his wife's equal accountability for making something of herself, and that her job in London met this requirement very well. However, the specific responsibility on him as a man in their partnership, his account reveals, was to provide the main income for the family, especially as her job was not well paid. Hence in taking the job he was – within his accountability as a male university teacher – justified in moving out of London and asking her to accompany him, because it allowed him both to make something of himself *and* to put the family first.

Mrs Hemlock's account of her subsequent choices of employment reveals a female version of these gendered requirements. She acknowledges a conflict between the demands of his "career" and hers, because job opportunities in her field were all in London, and in his all outside; but she goes on to say, "it wasn't really appropriate" for him to do another kind of job, and to describe some freelance and part-time work that she did after the move. After she had her two children, her working arrangements are described in terms of their compatibility with child care responsibilities.

Mrs Hemlock: So I carried on working until I got pregnant with my second one, and then I decided it was just too much to keep it going, so I stopped working then. [. . .] And then I went to the National Childbirth Trust and became a natal teacher [. . .] And so I was doing that from the time when Sam was very small, which again was only very part time. I carried on with that when I stopped the other and then when Sam was 3 or 4, we went to America for a year because we'd got a fellowship. When we came back I did a [teachers' training certificate]. And I was still carrying on with the NCT teaching. And then it was also in that time that I got interested in [craft work].   (Mrs Hemlock, 13)

The features that differentiate this narrative from her husband's are her implicit acceptance of primary obligations to care for the children, and her account of developing her capacities within the constraints imposed by these responsibilities and the demands of her partner's career (the move from London and the year in America). Mrs Hemlock's version of what she has made of herself is more diverse and self-developmental than his – she has fulfilled more work rôles and developed more of her capacities – but it is framed by her gendered duty to care, which is the woman's part of what it is to "put the family first".

In women's accounts this duty is embedded within a narrative of *choice*, not tradition, biology or social convention. Women give a sense of meaning and purpose to their biographies by describing how they "fitted together" self-development and family responsibility. It is their artful reconciliation of stimulating work experiences and chosen caring obligations that gives coherence to these post-traditional female identities.

Mrs Hemlock: . . . I wanted to be able to spend the time, rather than have someone else looking after the children, I wanted to do it. So that was a very positive and conscious decision to do it. But at the same time I was very aware when I left [employment] that I was stopping, you know cutting off something in my life [. . .] and that was coming to an end whatever I did later on. I do remember feeling that very strongly even though I also wanted to do it. And so when I picked up things again, I was picking up lots of threads of things and starting new things – I was juggling lots of things together in the hope that one of them would develop into something because I think that is something that is common, certainly to a lot of women that I know who've given up work. [. . .] And yet, looking back, there's a coherence to it all, because all of it helped to bring me to where I am [. . .] So it's just been a mixture of certain very conscious decisions and other things that seemed to be juggling around, which I think all follow from having that break.

(Mrs Hemlock, 21–2)

To make oneself accountable for what one has made of oneself, and to prioritize these particular responsibilities within the nuclear family, is to accept a form of narrative ordering of the self that is characteristic of higher-income groups in contemporary Britain. The cultural particulars which will be analyzed in this chapter are specific to British society since the early 1980s, but the accountability framework is common to a far wider spectrum of modern societies. Durkheim called this form of accountability "individualism", and saw it as the dominant moral order of post-traditional communities.[14]

The accounts reflect a collectively shared and collectively enforced morality,[15] which will be further analyzed in Chapter 4. Individualism is not the same as selfishness: individualists may impose on themselves high standards of concern for others, or even of self-sacrifice. What is characteristic of such accounts is their ethic of self-reliance and self-responsibility, and the prioritization of relationships with particular others over membership of the wider community.

Durkheim wrote that the tradition of individualism derived from Kant and Rousseau, embodied in the Declaration of the Rights of Man, had become in modern times "the basis of our moral catechism"[16] because the human person "is considered sacred in the ritual sense of the word".[17] Individualism became "a religion in which man is at once the worshipper and the god";[18] it "penetrates our institutions and our mores".[19]

> The cult, of which he is both the object and the agent, does not address itself to the particular being which he is and which bears his name, but to the human person wherever it is to be found, and in whatever form it is embodied . . . It springs not from egoism but from sympathy for all that is human, a broader pity for all suffering, for all human miseries, a more ardent need to combat them and mitigate them, a greater thirst for justice.[20]

One defining characteristic of individualism in Durkheim's sense is that a person is required to depend on his or her own efforts to fulfil his or her goals – however difficult or unattainable – and hence is morally accountable for what is made of his or her life. This is in marked contrast with the interviewees in our low-income study,[21] who spoke as members of their small community, and were heavily involved in mutual assistance, and hence emphasized interdependence. But Durkheimian individualism should not be confused with egoism. Durkheim specifically rejected egoistic "utilitarianism" – which he described as an "abusive exploitation of individualism" – as a vulgar economic term, and part of an "impoverished moral philosophy."

29

Durkheimian individualism is a sociological concept, which is used to explain the experience by individuals of an external and constraining moral reality (a "social fact"), through which individuals understand their world and within which they feel obliged to act. These interviewees account for their employment histories in the way they do because they interpret their experiences of deciding, choosing, changing and caring within a framework of moral individualism – as what they do, and are required to do, as the owners of themselves and the authors of their destinies. What their accounts have in common, therefore, is a shared sense that they are accountable for making something of themselves and putting the family first.

Mr Chestnut is one of the interviewees without educational qualifications, but he has worked his way up from a manual job as a heating engineer to being recently appointed the site manager of a large transport company, handling £9 million worth of goods each week. When asked, near the start of his interview, how he reached this position, he replies as follows:

Mr Chestnut: I'd been looking for another job for about two years, I suppose, so I'd been for maybe ten interviews with various companies [. . .] I got several jobs and turned them down because I felt I wasn't really achieving what I was looking for. I couldn't see I was actually bettering myself [. . .] Until I applied for the job I've got now . . . I could suddenly see I was working for a big company as regards training employees, the incentives to do well there were quite good.

(Mr Chestnut, 2)

Mr Chestnut's notion of "bettering himself" by moving into a managerial job is an explicit example of this universal feature of these interviewees' accounts of their decisions. Those who come from middle-class family backgrounds seldom make explicit reference to an ethic of self-development, but it is implicit in everything they say about their education and the work experiences. Those from working-class backgrounds, or who did poorly at school, are more likely to be explicit about what they have done to develop their abilities. Mr Cedar, like Mr Chestnut, works in distributive services, in a high-pressure managerial rôle: he now earns over £40,000 a year, as divisional manager of a car parts distribution network with an annual turnover of £40 million. When he is asked about the fact that he has such a responsible and well paid job without formal qualifications, he replies:

Mr Cedar: It's part luck. With a formal education . . . when I was at school the problem with me was that I didn't like being at school, and I didn't like the school I was at, which was a very good school, and really I left way before time, much to the disgust of my father, who was very upset with me at the time, and I don't blame him [. . .] So in effect it was always there, it was just a case that I didn't use it, and it actually took me until I was about 22 to settle down, and then once I settled down at about 22, that's when I thought, "Well, I'd better take life a bit seriously", and then applied for the job I was doing.

Q: So has your father forgiven you now you've reached a sort of . . . ?

Mr Cedar: Yes, now he's pleased with me, he's very pleased . . .

(Mr Cedar, 4)

Mr Cedar adopts a form of accountability in which he requires himself to explain his failure to get educational qualifications despite the opportunities, but goes on to show that once he "settled down" and started to "take life a bit seriously", he was able to develop abilities that were "always there" but had not been used. The choice of the term "seriously", and his father's pleasure in his subsequent achievements, indicate the high moral stakes here: Mr Cedar sees himself as accountable to the interviewer and to his father for "making something of himself". Furthermore, he has the same expectation of his son: he says he was quite lucky to get his foot on the first rung of the ladder (branch manager) without qualifications, but "I work on my son because you can't do that now, I've been very lucky". His son will have to settle down and take life seriously sooner – when he is still at school.

Women too give accounts of education, training and work experience, but most of them do not describe "careers" with promotions, perks and pensions. Instead they talk about how they have developed their abilities through a number of activities – paid and unpaid – that they could combine with child care responsibilities. Mrs Oak (whose children are now 14, 16 and 18) is currently employed as a part-time research assistant in a science department at the university, but she gives a long and detailed account of what led up to her taking this post, only part of which is reproduced below:

Mrs Oak: Well after the children were born [. . .] I got into breast-feeding counselling, because I had quite a few problems breast-feed-ing the first two children, and I decided because of that I wanted to help and do some of that. So I got into counselling in that way – I've got a little bit of training there with counselling, and I just took an interest in it [. . .] So through that I got an interest in counselling, marital counselling [. . .] and just walked in [to voluntary agency] and said I was interested in doing that. And I helped in the office for a bit and through that I got into training and just got into that. And the sex therapy I got into because I just think it's a very important area of relationships, and I liked the area of work they were doing and it seemed to tie up very, very well with the basic counselling [. . .] And then it started paying its counsellors [. . .] but I used to find the amount I did earn would vary quite a bit from month to month [. . .] And I think I saw that I would actually like a job with a little bit more financial security . . .   (Mrs Oak, 3–5)

The main differences between this account and the two men's quoted previously are that Mrs Oak's development of her abilities as a counsellor arise from personal experiences and voluntary work rather than through employment, and that when she does take on paid work it does not come in the form of a "career" with promotion and fringe benefits. However, she is equally concerned to explain how she has used her abilities (she is a graduate with a higher degree by research) in a number of fields, before returning to a post in line with her qualifications.

Selves and responsibilities

To attempt a morally adequate account of one's decisions is to reveal those features of one's life over which one accepts critical responsibility. At the same time as accounting for what they had made of themselves at work, men and women required themselves to show how they had put the family first. As with their labour-market choices, so in responsibility for family matters their versions of a morally adequate account were strongly gendered. This section selects the topic of income for retirement to show how family responsibility is constructed within an individualistic account of the self, and what this tells us about the social relations of better-off British households.

Retirement is an institutionally constructed economic status; it is a product of employers' personnel policies, state regulations, benefits systems (statutory and commercial), insurance schemes and so on. Although a few

of the interviewees in our earlier study of poor people were members of occupational pension schemes, none described themselves as personally responsible for providing an adequate income during retirement, either by
planning ahead, saving, contributing or insuring, nor did any see the timing of retirement as something that required an individual decision. By
contrast, the men among these higher-income interviewees saw it as a
necessary feature of a morally adequate account to explain what provision
they had made for income during retirement, and in many cases to show
that they had thought about when best to retire; with three exceptions,
the women did not. The cultural particulars of individualism in higher-income British households in 1990 prescribed provision for income in retirement as a man's responsibility and hence as a feature of a morally adequate biographical account of what he had made of himself.

For many of the men, the provision of such an income is an intrinsic
part of the job assets they have accumulated by pursuing a career in their
chosen occupation. Mr Willow, an insurance manager, is modest about his
abilities and achievements – partly because, with a salary over £40,000,
he can afford to be. He points out that a good pension is one of the ways
that his employer of the past 35 years has been able to retain his services
in a fairly unexciting job.

Mr Willow: . . . the subsidized mortgage and non-contributory pension scheme, things like that tended to lock people into a situation
of course, and therefore you become . . . your whole attitude of mind
is against moving out of that comfortable situation . . .

(Mr Willow, 11)

Because his occupational scheme makes relatively generous provision,
he can plan to retire at 60 – thus legitimating the precedence he has given
to security over stimulation and self-development in employment. With his
fine house and civilized lifestyle, Mr Willow's high post-retirement income
allows him to achieve moral adequacy despite the fact that he has, on his
own account, made little of himself (in terms of intellectual development,
travel or wider social awareness) in his job. His retirement rôle will be to
enable his wife to continue her (highly self-developmental) work as a nurse,
trainer and writer: her "career" (his term) does not include a responsibility for providing income for retirement.

Mr Willow: . . . Because of my vast length of service I shall qualify for
almost the maximum payment under that [non-contributory

scheme] when I retire. [. . .] But as to having a definite plan, I mean there are lots of things I would like to do now but I'd be able to do more of because I shan't have to go to work. [. . .] But also, again, my wife being that much younger, she will probably want to continue to work, and she's got her own career now, and our children will still be of an age where they'll . . . one's family goes on for ever anyway [laughs]. (Mr Willow, 17–18)

Even so, Mr Willow criticizes the company's pension scheme for its lack of adequate provision for widow's benefits, and says he must do something about this himself. Even after death he is responsible.

Mr Willow: . . . The only area where it doesn't come up to scratch is in the event of my death after retirement, particularly in view of my . . . the disparity in age between myself and my wife . . . so she's likely to live for years and years after I died and so to that extent I'm making some provision to meet that gap now. (Mr Willow, 17)

For men who are directors of companies or self-employed professionals, the issue of how to provide an adequate replacement income for their retirement is more complex, and their accounts reflect a concern to demonstrate awareness of the need to plan for the future proactively. Mr Box is paid a salary as an architect, but is also a director of his company. He is asked why he has started to top up his contribution to his company's pension scheme with a policy of his own.

Mr Box: The feeling that the company one was inadequate, I suppose, and I don't necessarily look forward to retirement or feel it's something I've waited years to tick away until it arrives, but we began to feel that we ought to make better provision, and that's what we've done . . . (Mr Box, 19)

Success in business, on the other hand, is being able to scorn pension schemes. Mr Mahogany, a farmer whose previous year's income was £100,000, can claim that investments in such funds cannot compete with the return on his own enterprise, a point reinforced by his wife.

Mr Mahogany: We would prefer to invest our money in our own business really, and expand our own business, which should bring us some good assets should we need them when we retire, by either letting it or selling it; and I would rather have control over our own money where I can see it and use it than I would investing in something such as pensions, where just a lot of people in pinstripe suits passing money from one organization to another [. . .]

Mrs Mahogany: . . . the growth in our business has been higher than any pension fund would be anyway.   (Mr and Mrs Mahogany, 42)

So strong is the moral requirement to show that one has provided for household income in retirement that men use a rhetoric of prudent planning for this period – Mr Mahogany's "good assets" – even when they are justifying *not* spending money on pension schemes. Similarly Mr Hawthorn, who openly flaunts his contempt for the idea of an incremental career or job security (see p. 78), justifies his speculative investment in an old mill in France (which he is struggling to convert into a holiday home) in terms of its potential for retirement income. After criticizing the system under which people (like himself) who changed employment lost pension benefits, and claiming that he prefers to control his own finances, he admits that he has only belatedly started to contribute to a pension fund in the past three to four years. However, the French venture represents a substitute.

Mr Hawthorn: . . . Basically that was an investment, one of the reasons for going in was that I was having trouble getting work here, so I thought, if I can't get work in this country I might as well go and do something else [indistinct], get out of this country. And the other thing is, you could say it's a kind of private pension fund, that I figure out that if it's going all right by the time I'm 60, and I don't have anything else to do, then I shall go down there and look after the tourists in the summer, clear the place up and whatever and get a bit of money from it.   (Mr Hawthorn, 20)

Thus the male interviewees saw the moral adequacy of their accounts of what they had made of themselves as depending on showing that they had taken personal responsibility for providing household income for retirement. The specific form of individualism displayed in their biographical narrative required the retrospective legitimation of decisions (Mr Mahogany's long-term investment to build up his farm from some 70 acres to over 230, Mr Hawthorn's impulsive purchase of an old mill in France) in terms of such an income. The self that emerges from their version of these decisions displays an important aspect of social relations in higher-income British households – that a creditable male identity involves financial responsibility for retirement.

Although some of the women – for instance, those who work full time in the public sector – do qualify for pensions, they do not construct the provision of post-retirement income as part of the moral requirements of an adequate account of what they have made of themselves. Whereas men make no mention of the state scheme (National Insurance pensions), women refer to it as part of an explanation of why they have made no individual provision for themselves.

Q: Do you pay into a pension scheme?

Mrs Pear: No, it's very basic. I pay my National Insurance and I pay my tax. (Mrs Pear, 6)

Q: Are you paying into a pension scheme?

Mrs Laburnum: No, I'm not [. . .] Well it's just a, well I don't pay a pension scheme. Just a National [Insurance], ordinary pension stuff that you pay. You never think that you're going to grow old you see.
(Mrs Laburnum, 7)

Two women, Mrs Box and Mrs Sycamore, mention that they subscribe to private pensions. Only Mrs Fieldmaple among the women in the sample explains (at some length) that she is making provision for herself for retirement income, even though her husband (a university lecturer) is a member of an adequate occupational pension scheme. Mrs Fieldmaple has had various part-time and voluntary posts and is currently training as an occupational therapist, so she has no earnings. Even so, she explains why she has decided to take out a private pension.

Mrs Fieldmaple: Well yes, I have got a pension, it's funny I started that when I was at [voluntary agency] because there was this thing that if you opted out of the government pension scheme you would actually take some of your payments and get more put into a private pension scheme so I have got a minute private pension [. . .] and Jonathan obviously has one which he pays into through the university. But yeah, I would like to have a bigger private pension. I would like to feel more independent in that respect, I think.

Q: This is independent of the state, you're sort of saying . . . ?

Mrs Fieldmaple: Well, independent of Jonathan in a way, because I mean I'm not suggesting I'm going to rush off next week or anything, but if there came a situation where we weren't together then

I mean he will have contributed to his university pension for years and have a really good income when he's retired whereas I shall be there with my little [bank's name] pension [laughs] and also perhaps not having started working until my forties and actually contributing in pensions there so that I would like to feel that I could be separate and have a reasonable income . . .   (Mrs Fieldmaple, 14–15)

Mrs Fieldmaple has to do quite a lot of rhetorical work to justify her account of herself as a woman who has so little trust in the future of her partnership that she provides for her own retirement income. Some other women explicitly discount the form of decision making that takes account of the possibility of divorce.

Mrs Ash: Well, I know of some marriages where you go in on a basis that you've signed an agreement saying that if you break or divorce, it will be all split half and half, or it won't, or the house will, or something; I mean, I think you've got to be very pessimistic to enter anything like that.   (Mrs Ash, 7)

Mrs Fieldmaple's version of her decision is constructed around a specific contingency, and is not part of her accountability as a woman, a partner and a parent. This in itself reveals much about household relations – that her discourse of "independence" is constructed around the possible breakdown of her marriage and not around her responsibility for income provision within it or indeed her autonomy within it. She then links the possible future trajectory of her life with the story of friends whose marriages have dissolved, discursively legitimating what she is making of herself as a prudent provider with an appeal to fairness.

Mrs Fieldmaple: I mean I don't think that if circumstances arose and I thought I don't want to stay, then I don't think that would actually be a consideration; but I . . . there's just something about it which doesn't seem quite fair [laughs].

Q: Actually, you're the first person to say anything like that, but I can see what you're saying, yes.

Mrs Fieldmaple: It's just, you know, it just annoys me, I mean friends of mine who have divorced, I know the solicitor for the wife has said about this university pension, you know, that she should actually be entitled to some of it because it's quite a . . . it comes at the end when you finish, I think you end up with 50 per cent of your earnings when you finish actually teaching. Now if you have actually been a wife, I don't know, for 20/30 years or something, then I think maybe you have some sort of entitlement to that. But I mean . . . [laughs]

(Mrs Fieldmaple, 15)

Prioritizing commitments

A second form of ordering of their biographical narratives that revealed cultural particulars was the way the interviewees prioritized their commitments to others. Their identities were constructed out of a series of rôles – son or daughter, student, friend, partner, neighbour, employee, parent – but the moral adequacy of their accounts of themselves depended on demonstrating that they had offered these commitments their appropriate priorities. A central feature of all the stories was that they gave precedence to "the family" over other forms of association; but the definition of "the family" was usually one in which partnership and parenthood were given much greater priority than other kinship relationships. The purpose of this section is to show what their versions of themselves as sons and daughters of ageing parents revealed about kinship relations in comfortable Britain.

Recent research has focused on the differential expectations of men and women over caring for elderly relatives.[22] Whereas men see themselves as accountable for some general oversight of the dependency needs of frail parents, women regard it as part of their rôle to provide the physical care that is needed.[23] However, only a minority of households become directly involved in care-giving, and fewer still actually take an elderly relative into their homes.[24] Our study reveals the discursive processes by which most sons and daughters exclude themselves from direct caring rôles (often leaving these tasks to other kin), and how a minority – both men and women – identify themselves as care-givers, and accept this accountability as part of their biographical construction of themselves.

To prioritize partnership and parenting within a context of "making something of oneself" is to construct the nuclear family as one's primary unit of account. The selves whose stories were told in these interviews were showing how they accumulated household assets and provided care for household members; others within their kinship network were constructed in similar terms. Hence questions about the possible frailty and dependency of ageing parents usually elicited descriptions of their "indomitable independence", even in the face of disability and often right up to death. These

38

were elders who in their time had made something of themselves and prioritized their nuclear families, and who neither expected nor needed the care of kin, it was implied.

Mr Redwood: . . . my father has been suffering increasingly over the last two or three years with what's basically senile dementia, which isn't a totally galloping kind at the moment, but is getting bad enough. And my mother is one of those totally indomitable people who would almost rather die than ask for help [. . .] As I say, my mother for her age is amazingly fit and is very capable of looking after and sorting my father out . . .   (Mr Redwood, 25)

Mrs Teak: . . . My mother's 70 and she leads a very active life. She lives in Sussex on her own, and we see her from time to time – she comes here and we go up there – but she's fiercely independent. [. . .] Yes, she's emphatic that she doesn't want to come and live with us. So she's making provision for going into some sort of home or something like that.   (Mrs Teak, 14)

Mrs Laburnum: . . . well one of them's dead, so [. . .] I mean my father is 70 [indistinct], he's got a wife who's younger. [. . .] No, I think he's got adequate means, and I'm sure he'd want to be as independent until he dropped dead really . . .   (Mrs Laburnum, 10)

Mrs Oak: They're both married again [after divorce]. They come in and out of our lives, without any great sense of responsibility [. . .] and everybody seems fairly fit and independent and responsible for themselves at the moment.   (Mrs Oak, 11)

The interviewees who describe their parents in these terms do not accept accountability for care-giving; indeed, some are horrified by the possibility that it could be seen as their responsibility. Willingness to provide care is not a necessary feature of a morally adequate account of themselves in the way that being a supportive partner or a concerned parent is.

Mr Redwood: . . . because they live nearly 200 miles away, I tend to go up there, not as often as I should, but perhaps about every six weeks or something like that over the weekend.   (Mr Redwood, 25)

Mrs Laburnum: . . . I mean I can't see him [coming to live with them], I can't see that happening but . . . God, I'd leave the country [laughs],
                                    (Mrs Laburnum, 10)

Mrs Hemlock: But as far as looking after my parents, there's now no way I'm going to be able to . . . [indistinct] . . . there's only my father – fortunately I think it's unlikely he's going to need looking after anyway – but there isn't any way I would be able to . . .

(Mrs Hemlock, 19)

But this is not the whole story. Some interviewees do provide care, though only one has a parent living in the same house. Those who regularly meet the dependency needs of ageing relatives clearly see this as part of the identity they construct through their narrative account; one of the reasons they have continued to live and work in the area is to be available to do this.

Mr Larch: Well, I see my mother every day, don't I?

Q: Presumably she's in [city's name]?

Mr Larch: Yes.

Q: So this is sort of to keep an eye on her to make sure she's alright?

Ms Plum [partner]:   Yes, that's the reason Michael won't move away from [city's name]. I mean one of your little things is that you would like to live in [nearby town], but there's no way he would go and live [there] while his mother's alive.

(Mr Larch and Ms Plum, 40)

Mr Alder: I've been here for 39 years. Yes, my mother lives in [city's name] and perhaps that is one of the reasons why we do stay here.

Q: In what sort of sense?

Mr Alder: To be near her, yes, but I think we actually like it down here.

(Mr Alder, 28)

Giving priority to parents' needs (and involving them in the care of children) is something that a minority of respondents build into their biographical narrative as part of its continuity, as well as their personal accountability. Geographical proximity is certainly an important part of this: kin who are nearby, and seen frequently, are constructed as part of the family that is put first, whereas kin who are distant are expected to be independent. Living close and being regularly involved seems to be more important than being closely related.[25] In Ms Plum's case, she makes explicit the division of responsibility between herself and her brother, which is accounted for in

40

terms of geography and personal involvement.

Ms Plum: I've got a mother in [home counties], but she's quite a few years off needing to be cared for, isn't she?

Mr Larch: Yes, and you have got an aunt, Gladys, at [village's name] which is 7 miles away from here. She's actually come to live down here because Melissa [Ms Plum] is down here.

Ms Plum: She's probably the relative that I'll look after and my brother will probably look after my mother.

(Mr Larch and Ms Plum, 40)

Perhaps the clearest distinction between the two kinds of kinship relations – those based on proximity and involvement, and those on distance and independence – is provided by Mr and Mrs Box. Mrs Box describes her parents as excluded from her biographical account of family responsibility and commitment by the accidents of geographical mobility: they come within her brother's ambit.

Mrs Box: . . . because we've moved further and further down the motorway from them. We don't live anywhere near our parents. That's not because we don't like them, it's just the way life is. My parents live in [home counties] and my parents aren't that elderly . . . I say not that elderly, I mean my father's, I suppose he's 66 this year [. . .]. And my mother is I think 69 this year [. . .] And I'm afraid that really isn't just something we'll have to face when it happens. My brother lives near them and I have to say that we have actually . . . I have said to my parents, "There is no way I could live with you", and they said, "And there's no way I could live with you either", so that's a pretty upfront conclusion we've got there.

(Mrs Box, 11)

By contrast, Mr Box has been confronted with increased proximity and involvement with his mother following his father's death, and is adjusting to the change in his perception of his responsibilities and commitments. The new self that he presents in his revised autobiography still feels strange.

Mr Box: So, my father died, last September, and she's managed to sell her house and bought a flat in [nearby suburb] and moved down, she's just been here probably four to six weeks I suppose, and it's worked out so far as well as anybody could hope, you know, she's lively, she's fit, she's energetic, she can look after herself and she's

41

starting a new life for herself in [suburb] which is great. What'll happen when she becomes more frail and such like, time will tell [. . .] we've never lived close to either of our sets of parents, so it's a peculiar experience having one just down the road.   (Mr Box, 23)

Other couples' accounts reveal the same distinctions between the narratives of involvement and responsibility, and those that construct elderly kin as being within the sphere of others' accountability. Mrs Fieldmaple says, "I've got a sister who lives nearer to my parents who actually does help out if for some reason my father is ill and he can't go on". "Family" serves as an index of priority. "Independent" old people are seen as outside the "family", or their dependence is the responsibility of another family, where there is geographical distance and rather infrequent contact. The needs of the older generation are included in the prioritization of "family" only when they are part of the narratives of identity and responsibility.

Public and private

In telling what they had made of themselves and how they had prioritized the nuclear family over other forms of association, interviewees accepted moral accountability for the critical success of their life-course in certain aspects and spheres. The selves that emerged from their biographies revealed a certain kind of moral order of individualism that – after a government programme of American-style economic liberalization – characterized British social relations in 1990. This included taking personal responsibility for some issues that might in Continental European countries still be regarded as collective concerns (such as income for retirement), but giving low priority to other commitments (such as those to geographically distant parents) that there and elsewhere might be seen as morally important sources of self-identity. This section looks at another dimension of the accounts – the extent to which the interviewees saw their individual actions as having wider social significance. Here the issue chosen to illustrate this dimension is child care. To what extent did the respondents construct their decisions over the way their pre-school children were cared for as purely individual, personal choices, or how much did they link them with discourses about women's employment rôles, the state's responsibilities for care provision, or the political relevance of the domestic division of labour?

The feminist slogan that "the personal is political" implies that domestic relations have relevance in the public sphere: women seeking political emancipation should first be conscious of oppression in their closest relationships.[26] This gives rise to discourses of the self in which rôles and tasks traditionally constructed as "natural" or "duties" are seen instead to reflect patriarchal domination – the internalization of power-laden texts of subordination.[27] But other social analyses of modernity argue that there is a pervasive tendency for individuals to deny the public significance of their actions, as part of a process of privatization of experience. What authors such as Sennett[28] and Lasch[29] have called "narcissism" consists of a quest for self-identity that focuses on personal needs and feelings at the expense of the public life of membership, participation, community and democracy. The self and its narrative biography lose the very vocabulary of association in the common good.[30] If experiences are significant only in terms of "what they mean to me", then the whole public sphere becomes impoverished and collective life meaningless.[31]

Giddens has criticized the "narcissism" thesis and argued that "late modernity" marks the emergence of "life politics" (a politics of choice over life decisions) as a discourse that transcends the emancipatory political discourses of the early modern era.[32] He suggests that the focus on lifestyles reflects the need for the individual to adapt the narrative of self-identity to rapidly changing circumstances on a local and global scale, connecting future projects with local experiences. "Life politics from this perspective concerns debates and contestations deriving from the reflexive project of the self."[33]

These interviewees certainly present their child care experiences in terms of the narrative of a developmental self that personalizes social experience and focuses on lifestyle choices. What seems more questionable is Giddens' assertion that such life-political discourses "call for a remoralising of social life and demand a renewed sensitivity to questions that the institutions of modernity systematically dissolve".[34] In this section, we will argue that the social relations of child care revealed in these accounts display many of the features of Sennett's "narcissism": they obscure, omit or deny the collective significance of individual choices, and both depersonalize and personalize relations (such as those between employer and child-minder) in such a way as to distort their social relevance. The few exceptions to this generalization are important because they indicate what is lacking in most of the accounts.

Giddens' analysis is right to draw attention to the emphasis on *choice* in accounts of reproductive issues (see Mrs Hemlock's account, p. 28).

Those women who left the labour market to look after their children full time at home describe this as a positive decision. Mrs Linden, who was a highly-paid manager, earning more than her husband, says that she had planned to be a full-time mother (up to when her children went to school) since she herself was a child.

Mrs Linden: I think probably part of it is being very self-centred and influencing my own children and not wanting somebody else to . . . and then on my own head be it if it goes wrong [laughs]. I just like the close links with the children, and doing as much for them as I can when I can still do it. They grow up so quickly.

(Mrs Linden, 49)

Mrs Elm, a graduate and trained teacher, runs a small two-hour weekly nursery class in her home and gives some secretarial help to her husband's home-based accountancy practice, but otherwise is a full-time mother.

Mrs Elm: I would rather be at home with [the children]. In fact, I wouldn't really want to work full time until they were quite a lot older. Anyway, I wouldn't want to work full time with the ages they are [. . .] I don't really like the child-minding set-up very much. I don't think that's the best that we can do for the children really.

(Mrs Elm, 5)

Mrs Pine left her job as a social worker to have children, and waited until her youngest was at school before training as a teacher.

Mrs Pine: . . . when I thought the children were at a stage of being able to cope without having a full-time parent at home [. . .] in fact she was 8 when I started to do teacher training. (Mrs Pine, 15)

Many women describe involvement in playgroups: several became organizers, and used this as a stepping stone in their gradual return to the labour market, often making a change towards a more human-service rôle. Their accounts of their involvement emphasize its self-developmental aspects, rather than the collective significance for women of co-operation in child care provision.

Ms Whitebeam: Well I taught for about seven years before I had the children, and I was very involved with my children's playgroups, and I didn't particularly want to go back into schools, but I did do quite a lot of supply work for quite a few years, but I was wondering what else I could do, and heard about a job that involved doing literacy/ numeracy work with YTS trainees . . .   (Ms Whitebeam, 1)

Mrs Fieldmaple: . . . I was aware when my children were very little that I needed things to do that weren't connected with home, because I didn't feel very confident about being sort of a homemaker/housewife type person, so I had always been involved in playgroups and as I was involved in playgroups and doing the sorts of stuff to do with them I sort of talked about doing teaching as a sort of logical extension . . .
                                                    (Mrs Fieldmaple, 5–6)

Mrs Box: I'm a development worker [. . .] I don't have a title of social worker [. . .] I don't have a social work background [. . .] obviously stemming from when I had my own two children: but most of my life after children has been with the Pre-School Playgroups Association, and that's where I really learned everything that I know today really [. . .] I was the Area Organiser for [City] PPA.
                                                    (Mrs Box, 1–2)

What is absent from these accounts can be gauged by Ms Blackthorn's version of her experiences of child care. Unlike the other interviewees, Ms Blackthorn was a single parent for some of her children's pre-school years. She insists that child care is a political issue and demands collective measures. Both her personal experiences and her work as an employment consultant (advising women who are returning to the labour market) convince her that child care cannot be left to individuals and employers.

Mrs Blackthorn: . . . Then it gets into a political situation of not enough nursery provision, not enough child care provision, so it's a wider issue I think [. . .]. I believe very firmly in a voucher system, so that every individual has the choice. But I think that without a doubt there should be more state provision. Very, very few children in this country, a very small proportion, get nursery education. It should be available to all. And then you choose if you want a private nursery, or a state nursery, or child-minders.   (Ms Blackthorn, 34–5)

Her emphasis on choice and her advocacy of a voucher scheme indicate that her insistence on the political significance of child care does not stem from doctrinaire collectivism; yet nor is it the personalized discourse of lifestyle politics with its framework of accountability for self-development and family priority. She is asked about the origins of her convictions.

Q: Have you always had those principles, or is it something that experience has led you to?

Ms Blackthorn: I suppose I have to say that it's since I've had children, because until you have children you don't give it any thought. But my son's 11, and I've always felt it from then. And he was very fortunate because he actually went into a state nursery for a year, his school had a state nursery, that was only at the age of 3½. So since I've had children it's something I've thought a lot about, and feel very strongly about.   (Ms Blackthorn, 35–6)

This reflective dimension is more present in the narratives of child-minding: more women's accounts extend beyond the self-developmental relevance of the experience for their lifestyle choices and include an acknowledgement of the significance of the work for the child-minder. However, very few transcend this personal aspect and go on to reflect on the wider relevance of the social relations of child-minding in terms of power and life chances. This seems to be partly because they manage the ambiguous relationship of child-minding through a combination of familizing the care element (constructing the child-minder as a family member) and depersonalizing the commercial element (bracketing the human causes and consequences of low pay).

Mrs Beech: Yes, "supergran", not a real granny but we call her "supergran" and she's 60 and she's widowed, and she answered an advert for "help from home". So she comes to the house whenever I am working [. . .]. Yes, respect and a lot of affection, it goes both ways, and we've both helped each other enormously [. . .] mm, she's part of the family.   (Mrs Beech, 2)

Mrs Lime: Well Rachel's obviously happy there, because I went to a child's party and the child-minder was there with other children and her own, and Rachel and I turned up and all Rachel wanted to do was go and sit on this woman's knee, and she got all embarrassed because she said, "That's your mother over there". And Rachel preferred this woman to me at that time, and I thought that can't be a bad thing because she obviously gets on well with her.
                                          (Mr and Mrs Lime, 38)

Mrs Ash: . . . I'm supposed to work 17½ hours a week: in fact I tend to work more like 20, 21 [. . .]

Q: Does the child-minder have any limits? Does she ever say, "No, hang on, I can't do that"?

Mrs Ash: No, I think she's fairly short of money, which is handy [. . .]. So if I need to, thankfully, 'cause my job demands that . . .

(Mrs Ash, 7–8)

Mrs Hazel: We're very lucky in [city], there's a very professional group of child-minders, a lot of them are professional women, and they are registered and vetted quite heavily, and they've got an association [. . .] and they've all been terrific, absolutely fantastic people [. . .]. I've chosen them for their interests and compatibility . . . they're all people with their own children, compatibility of personality and ages, and convenience of where they live, and health. Because the little one's so extraordinarily active, they have to be active people, and when I interview them I make sure of that [. . .]. Unfortunately the little one seems to have exhausted two of the child-minders. One had a bad back from lifting her so much eventually, and the other had a nervous breakdown [laughs] . . . But while they were on top form it was great, and the children seem to have adapted to each one extraordinarily well.

(Mrs Hazel, 22–3)

Mrs Hemlock: . . . We had someone who looked after her one day a week who was a former student of [husband's] who dropped out of university to have a baby. She used to come to the house with her son who was an infant and look after Jane. That didn't last very long . . . and that was not really very satisfactory at all because, although I didn't realize it at the time, it was a disastrous thing to have done for her . . . to have these two small children . . . and she obviously found it difficult to cope. So that carried on for a while but we gave that up.

(Mrs Hemlock, 14)

Finally, although the domestic division of labour over child care will be much more fully analyzed in Chapters 5 and 6, it is important to note at this stage that women construct their "supportive" rôle in partnership as including taking overall responsibility for these tasks, whereas men construe "supportiveness" to mean occasional assistance. In only one household (Mr and Mrs Palm) is the domestic division of labour seen as a political issue and any systematic effort made to share tasks equally in the name of fairness. Mr and Mrs Hazel display the dominant version of male and female "supportiveness" over child care.

Mrs Hazel: . . . I got to the point, 11 years ago, when the first one was born, when I was just going to take off and go up the promotion scale and do much more interesting type of teaching and lecturing, and so I had to at that point decide whether to give up any career and just stop, full stop, for a while, and then just do part time or whatever, and I find that supporting David in his work, so he can work full tilt, and keeping the houses we've had going, has been very, very demanding, much more demanding than I realized, even with one child [. . .]. But now I've got the two younger ones, I was just talking today about going back to work at Christmas full time as David will be working at home, but with [his] writing you can't really just stop and start, and go and fetch and carry four times a day across town, which is what I'm doing at the moment, for all three of them . . .

(Mr and Mrs Hazel, 35)

Mr Hazel: . . . I don't mind pottering around because I actually . . . I decide to potter in the garden, come back and do some writing, then potter, and [. . .] you have to get into a working-writing rhythm [. . .] and you can actually include other things in the rhythm such as doing lots of housework, you know, as a natural break. [. . .] I cannot take over the running of two little children. That is a full-time job *per se*, there's no argument about that whatsoever [. . .] it is very difficult to do any real work in the context academically, looking after young children, you can't do it, it's impossible.

(Mr and Mrs Hazel, 38)

Only one couple analyze the domestic division of labour (including child care) as a *political* issue. Mr and Mrs Palm see the sharing of child care and domestic tasks as part of their political commitment as socialists. For Mrs Palm, her decisions not to employ a child-minder, to share unpaid tasks equally with her husband, and eventually to swap rôles (successfully applying for the senior teaching post he gave up to look after their daughters) all had a political dimension. Mrs Palm rejects employing a low paid child-minder; both see his responsibility for child care as a choice with implications beyond the domestic sphere.

Mrs Palm: . . . I suppose it must have been more political – it wasn't on the principle that I didn't want to leave the children with anybody, but I didn't want to employ anybody to, yes, I suppose it was political. I didn't want to employ anybody to do that [. . .] The idea was we had always taken joint domestic responsibility because it seems to me a lot of women, you know, say, "My husband's good, he does this, this and this", but basically the full domestic responsibility falls on the woman in the partnership, um, and I, well, we didn't want that to happen. (Mrs Palm, 12–13)

Mr Palm: . . . I can remember in 1981 going to the Labour Party Conference in Brighton and talking to some of the fringe groups there on, um, male and female rôles, and I suppose being a little big-headed [laughter] rather saying, "Well look I've done it", um, I look back and sort of slightly shudder to . . . [laughter] (Mr Palm, 14–15)

Conclusion

In this chapter, we have analyzed how interviewees' accountability for their decisions gave coherence to their narratives of identity. They told us their versions of what they had made of themselves and how they put the family first. Focusing on their quest for moral adequacy, we have shown how the accountability adopted in the narrative reconstruction of decisions displays the cultural particulars of individualistic social relations. By analyzing their accounts of their critical responsibility for income in retirement, care of frail kin and child care, we have shown what these display about the moral order of comfortable Britain. The specific forms of individualism – which commitments are prioritized, how conflicting demands are reconciled, which actions are seen as socially relevant and how – are revealed in their narratives.

Our analysis implies that the versions of themselves and their decisions given by the interviewees were not arbitrary. Although they might have given other accounts in different contexts,[35] their narrative reconstructions of their decisions had far too many common features (and common omissions) to be "merely" subjective or personal. In this chapter we saw how certain phrases – "adequate provision" for retirement, "fiercely independent" aged parents, "supportive" partners – kept recurring in the accounts. While these are often adopted from the public discourses of the pension fund brochure, the government paper or the therapeutic textbook, they have been woven into these biographical narratives in ways that discursively construct the social order. If Ms Whitebeam, Mrs Fieldmaple and Mrs Box describe playgroups in terms of their self-developmental potential as a labour-market stepping stone, this constitutes an important aspect of the social relations of women's playgroup involvement.

However, moral adequacy was only one aspect of the achievement of selves in these interviews. Even the most coherently constructed identities had also to be communicated within the interactive context of the interview exchange. It is to these processes that we turn in the next two chapters.

References

1. M. Hollis, "Moves and motives in the games we play", *Analysis* **50** (1990), 49–62.
2. A. Giddens, *Modernity and self-identity: self and society in the late modern age* (Oxford: Polity, 1991), p. 3.
3. Ibid., p. 5.
4. Ibid., p. 81.
5. M. Hollis & R. Sugden, "Rationality in action", *Mind* **102** (405) (1993), 1–35.
6. L. J. Savage, *The foundations of statistics* (New York: Wiley, 1954).
7. Ibid., p. 20.
8. E. C. Cuff, "Some issues in studying the problem of versions in everyday situations", Department of Sociology, Manchester University, Occasional Paper 3, 1980, pp. 34–5. See also G. Baruch, "Moral tales: parents stories of encounters with health professionals", *Sociology of Health and Illness*, **3** (3) (1981), 275–96.
9. E. Durkheim, *The division of labour in society* (1893; New York: Free Press, 1933); "Individualism and the intellectuals", *Revue Bleu*, 4th Series, No. 10 (1898), 7–13.
10. J. F. Gubrium & R. J. Lynott, "Family rhetoric and social order", *Journal of Family Issues* **6** (1985), 129–52.
11. D. Silverman, *Qualitative methodology and sociology* (Aldershot, England: Gower, 1985).
12. Cuff, "Some issues in studying the problem of versions".
13. Giddens, *Modernity and self-identity*, p. 53.
14. Durkheim, *The division of labour in society*.
15. Durkheim, *The division of labour in society*, and "Individualism and the intellectuals".
16. R. N. Bellah (ed.), *Emile Durkheim on morality and society* (Chicago: University of Chicago Press, 1973), from "Individualism and the intellectuals", p. 45.
17. Ibid., p. 46.
18. Ibid.
19. Ibid.
20. Ibid., pp. 48–9.
21. B. Jordan, S. James, H. Kay & M. Redley, *Trapped in poverty? Labour-market decisions in low-income households* (London: Routledge, 1992).
22. C. Ungerson, *Policy is personal: sex, gender and informal care* (London: Tavistock, 1987).
23. G. Dalley, *Ideologies of caring: rethinking community and collectivism* (London: Macmillan, 1988).

24. J. Finch, *Family obligations and social change* (Oxford: Polity, 1989); J. Finch & J. Mason, *Negotiating family responsibilities* (London: Routledge, 1993).
25. Ungerson, *Policy is personal.*
26. G. Pascall, *Social policy: a feminist analysis* (London: Tavistock, 1986).
27. Walby, *Theorising patriarchy* (Oxford: Blackwell, 1990).
28. R. Sennett, *The fall of public man* (Cambridge: Cambridge University Press, 1977).
29. C. Lasch, *The culture of narcissism* (London: Abacus, 1980).
30. R. Bellah, R. Madson, W. D. Sullivan, A. Swidler & S. M. Tipton, *Habits of the heart: individualism and commitment in American life* (Berkeley, CA: University of California Press, 1985).
31. Sennett, *The fall of public man*, p. 219.
32. Giddens, *Modernity and self-identity*, Chs 5–7.
33. Ibid., p. 215.
34. Ibid., p. 224.
35. J. Potter & M. Mulkay, "Scientists' interview talk: interviews as a technique for revealing participants' interpretative practices", in *The research interview: uses and approaches*, M. Brenner, J. Brown, D. Canter (eds), 241–71 (New York: Academic Press, 1985).

CHAPTER 3

Selves in Interaction: Heretics, Fundamentalists and Improvisers

In the previous chapter, we analyzed the identities of the interviewees in terms of their attempts to give morally adequate accounts of their decisions. We showed that they gave coherence to their choices within an accountability framework of individualism – their responsibility for making something of themselves and putting the family first – and illustrated the cultural particulars of this morality through their accounts.

If this were all we had to say about the identities of the agents in our study, we could be justifiably accused of reducing them to "cultural dopes".[1] Although it is true that their responses were often "typical" of individualism (for instance, many used similar images and phrases to describe their pension plans, their elderly relatives and their involvement in playgroups) and much of what they told us could be captured within the standard repertoires of careerism, self-development and gaining advantages for their children, a whole dimension of the interviewees' selves has been left out of our analysis so far.

To tell one's story to a stranger – in this case a research interviewer – is an achievement, requiring effort and skill. To accomplish such an account requires *interactional competence*.[2] This relates to the specific context in which selves are produced and sustained, under what we argue to be essentially hazardous and unstable conditions. Moral adequacy is never a sufficient condition for a successful account of oneself; skills are also needed to negotiate a meaningful and coherent version with one's listeners or co-participants. Selves are as much a product of the interactive theatre of everyday life as they are reconstructions of the moral continuities in a life story. As well as describing choices in a risk environment, the selves of the "late modern age" must also be able to anchor themselves into particular situations, producing actions that are intelligible and identities that are meaningful within the local context and the circumstances of the moment – the temporary, locally produced order of everyday contingency.

In this chapter, we focus on this *interactional order*, to analyze how interviewees produce and sustain themselves in a particular context, achieving an impression of stability and order, and communicating meaning. We analyze this through interactions in the interviews themselves, between the interviewers and the respondents. This should not be read as a chapter "about methodology" or the problems of the research interview as an instrument. Its purpose is far more fundamental to our study of decision making. This is because we will argue – following the work of Anne Warfield Rawls[3] and Richard Hilbert[4] – that the interactional theatre of everyday life is where the wider social order is produced and reproduced. Thus the moral requirements of individualism, which interviewees experience as external and constraining, and within which they frame their accounts, are in practice the products of interactants' own efforts to create the appearance of stability, normality and reliability in their daily lives.

Some readers may find our approach frustrating; it may indeed reawaken criticisms of ethnomethodology as a theoretical cul-de-sac. However, we would insist that this part of the analysis is essential for our later discussion of rationality and citizenship. If we are to understand the relationship between the moral requirements of individualism and the economics of competitive advantage in decision making, we must have a theory of how moral standards are produced and behaviour is regulated. Our analysis traces these processes to the interactional order. Since our data consist of interview interaction, we must rely on this evidence to develop the theory of moral regulation in decision making.

In the following section, we will delineate the interactional order and demonstrate its relevance for the study of decision making. Drawing on the work of Goffman,[5] we will show how the interviewees' attempts to mobilize their socially approved attributes and sustain a creditable "face" throughout the interview allow them both to produce selves, and to communicate meaning, within an order that is created ("out of nothing", as it were) in the interview setting.

This order is so taken for granted that it can seldom be noticed, except when it is disturbed. In the next section, we look at some interviews in which the respondents use unorthodox interactional ploys (jokes, exaggeration, apparent irrelevancies) to produce themselves, or seem unwilling to sustain interaction (giving very brief, unelaborated answers). These provide important clues about the nature of the interactional order and the self it sustains.

Another kind of breach in this order is analyzed in the next section. Despite the co-operative efforts of interviewer and interviewee to sustain the "normal appearances" of their encounter (by "giving and saving face"), these aspects of the exchange can be temporarily disturbed by interviewees themselves. Two such examples will be examined in detail: a couple whose son has been expelled from school review their decisions over his education, and an accountant, threatened with redundancy, reconstructs with his wife their reactions to the dread of this threat. We show how their intensified efforts to improvise an account of these events give rise to changes in the interviewees' "faces" and the interactional order of the interview.

This leads to an exploration of the relationship of the interactional order with the institutional structures of society, which forms the final section of the chapter. Here we draw on Durkheim's theory of anomie to argue that the "external realities" of the wider world are sustained by interactional practices that refer to the institutional order. Thus the things members do to sustain a sense of stable relations are essential for the maintenance of "objective reality". This has important implications for our analysis of moral regulation in the following chapter. Interactional improvisation is the stuff of decision making, and allows us to understand how the morality of individualism is used to regulate actions taken in line with decisions.

Interaction, order, selves

Selves depend on each other for their successful production; but this interdependence allows the communication of meaning and the creation of order. The work of Goffman and Garfinkel has recently been developed, notably by Rawls and Hilbert, into an analysis of the interactional order that links with the classical sociology of Durkheim and Weber.

A research interview is a particular kind of interactive theatre – a "set piece" in which the parties have certain conventional rôles and rights to do with the setting and answering of questions. However, although there are publicly available and culturally sanctioned expectations about what a research interview is, these encounters were (like all others in which we are required to produce and maintain accountable selves) fraught with alarming possibilities, for interviewees and interviewer alike. They took place in respondents' homes, and hence provided visible evidence of what they had made of themselves materially, of the couple's informal co-operation (e.g. over the minor hospitalities of receiving a visitor), of their children's behaviour, and so on. The researcher might cause offence by mistake (touching on a sensitive issue) or by pressing a point too far, or he might fail to sustain the interview interaction.

Goffman examines the way in which the parties manage such hazards of their encounters in terms of "face work". "Face" is, in his analysis, the social value that is claimed by an individual during a particular social interaction, based on "approved social attributes".[6] Since each self in interaction is emotionally committed to maintaining its own face, they are mutually dependent on establishing a "working acceptance" of each others' faces to accomplish their interaction. This gives rise to a certain *order* within the interaction, which Goffman calls "the expressive order". He uses the term "ritual" to describe face work, because the symbolic components of it are worth and respect: interaction ritual is about respect for each other's faces as "sacred objects" that can be exalted or debased, depending on their symbolic treatment.[7] Face work is co-operative, participants saving their own faces and giving face to each other, for instance by ignoring lapses or incoherences, avoiding awkward topics, paraphrasing politely, or feigning comprehension.

Within an interaction such as an interview, each self, playing a ritual game of face work, takes a "line" according to the amount and kind of social value being claimed, and tries to sustain it in a way appropriate to this encounter. In these interviews, the respondents' line is established through the account of what they have made of themselves and of putting the family first (moral adequacy). However, this must also be made consistent with the contingencies of the interview, i.e. with incidents and impressions "whose effective symbolic implications threaten face".[8] Even when the individual's face is not in immediate jeopardy, its successful maintenance depends on sustaining coherent links between the interactional order of the interview and the narrative reconstruction of past events, by hooking the account into the contingent fabric of these incidents and impressions.

Q: Can you tell me what sort of decisions you've been making recently
    [. . .]?

Mrs Teak: Well, I can just think of one practical one really. Above where we're sitting here, there's a flat roof which needs to be resurfaced because it's very bad and we had to make the decision of what material to put up there . . .   (Mrs Teak, 8)

The interactional skills of participation are most at a premium in informal settings – friendly encounters, pub meetings, coffee breaks – and particularly where familiar participants are doing the face work of their membership group. By contrast, the research interview is somewhat formal and staid, with an established procedure for taking turns, question and answer, and polite listening. Whereas a member of a tea-break gathering has to establish an appropriate context for an autobiographical anecdote ("a funny thing happened to me . . . ", or "that reminds me of . . . "), interviewees are invited to tell their stories, and are guaranteed a high degree of ritual respect, which in informal gatherings depends on their skills as storytellers.

Conversely, there are certain requirements of the research interview that impose constraints. Respondents are supposed to confine themselves to relevant answers and to reply in ways that contribute to the research inquiry (as well as to "give face" to the interviewer as a serious social scientist). All this helps explain why many of the accounts seem "bland" in transcript and the overall tone is one of earnestness in the quest for moral adequacy. The interviewees' versions are orderly, organized, reasonable, and rather like each other.

One way in which the ritual element in the interaction becomes visible is when interviewees give accounts of surprising themselves by what they have made of themselves, laying claims to value and respect that were not implicit in their social rôles, and which demonstrate that they have developed their potential further than they themselves anticipated. Mrs Willow was not a very successful nursing student, and did not feel that she achieved much in her early employment as a nurse, but recently she has come to be recognized as a writer and lecturer on her specialism.

Mrs Willow: . . . I suddenly realized that people had tremendous faith in me, and that I could do it, and I went on and did other training, and when I was asked to go and start lecturing and teaching, and by going and doing other courses, I suddenly found out that, certainly in the world of practice nursing, most people know who I am, because I teach a lot and write articles. And it just was like a light switching on, somebody had valued what I was doing in a way, and I suppose it just snowballed, and it's difficult to stop doing it.

(Mrs Willow, 39)

Similarly Mr Linden, who left school without taking "A" levels and worked in the civil service and a clerical post in an insurance company, describes his excitement at finding himself in a dynamic division of a major London insurer.

Mr Linden: . . . here I was on committees, rubbing shoulders with people like . . . the Queen's solicitor was on a committee that I was on.

They were very, very powerful and influential men. Those that were in the industry were keen to be seen around [company], and I was rubbing shoulders with them, and I got to be known by a variety of people [. . .] And I don't mean that as an ego trip . . .

(Mr Linden, 24)

Heretics and fundamentalists

What Goffman's analysis postulates is an unseen, unnoticed, taken-for-granted order within the interview (or any other such encounter) in which the interaction ritual of mobilizing socially creditable "faces" and negotiating ritual respect not only allows selves to be produced, but also enables meaning to be communicated. So far we have given a few brief examples of how the accountability adopted by the interviewees to claim social value (what they have made of themselves and how they have put the family first) is linked into everyday contingency and local circumstances, and how claims to special respect – not obviously due to their current rôle and status – are made.

In this section, we look at those moments in which this interactional order of exchanges of ritual respect were disrupted because the interviewees produced selves that did not do "face work" in quite this way.[9] Instead of claiming respect by sober and reasonable accounts of what they had made of themselves and how they had put the family first, a few male interviewees intermittently replied in jokey, irreverent and occasionally apparently irrelevant ways. They sometimes reinforced this by their posture and manner. Other men gave replies that were so brief and attenuated that the momentum of the interview was almost impossible to sustain; they did not display the interactional competence required to maintain the informal order of the exchange. (Paradoxically, because these men did not produce standard "interview selves", they seemed more "individuals" than those who did, by virtue of their unorthodoxy.)

The first group occasionally subverted the interview (and hence their presentation of a morally adequate self) by not giving a coherent, serious account of how what they have made of themselves constituted an instance of putting family first. Hence the self they achieved in the interview account was *heretical* in terms of the requirements of individualism and partnership, and risked *offending* the interviewer and breaching the expectations of the research project. Hence we refer to them as "heretics".

57

One of the clearest examples of "heresy" is Mr Larch's account of how he came to be supporting Ms Plum (his cohabitee) in her art business. Ms Plum is his fourth partner, after two marriages and a long cohabitation.

Mr Larch: She [former cohabitee] had two children and my children used to come at weekends or whenever they wanted to, and she had a rather rebellious daughter and I think in the end the wedge split us up, because basically the daughter should have been put to sleep when she was born, I think. And that split us up, and I met Melissa in someone else's house down the road here, about six years ago – I met the dog first, I think, she had a collie dog. She was an [art worker] and I liked [art], I have always done [art] at evening classes and things – and I upped and went.

Q: Upped and went?

Mr Larch: I moved in with M. C. Plum like any sensible person would.

(Mr Larch, 20)

Mr Larch makes no attempt to give a morally adequate account of the breakup, perhaps aware that any such will sound partisan, unconvincing and incoherent. Instead he relies on interactional skills – jokey, male-orientated, defying conventional morality and designed to portray himself as a "character" or an "original". In rather the same way, Mr Hazel, a university lecturer whose wife is a university research assistant, speaks of the National Curriculum.

Mr Hazel: . . . it's just a complete cock-up, where they've actually spatched together a Frankenstein's monster, which seems to have satisfied various interest groups, and you suddenly realize the wretched thing is literally Frankenstein, because this thing just ain't got no . . . nothing at all to recommend it . . . it just won't work, it's an idiot's charter, it's just non-viable. But that's within the political debate. It's all very peculiar . . . I do sound . . . when you play this back it'll sound quite odd. All I suggest is you go away and read the National Curriculum (subject) document and what they've put down [. . .] and then you'll suddenly realize, it just won't work, it's got no coherence to it, it's got no logical pattern to it, it's got no pedagogy to it, it's just an ungodly mess. Never mind.

(Mr Hazel, 19)

Earlier, he uses exaggerated language to describe his motives and his family's situation, and subverts the rôles and rights of the interview situation by asking the interviewer, when describing the advantages of living in this city:

Mr Hazel: . . . I mean, would you go and work in the middle of Sheffield or somewhere?

Q: I've actually got an application in for Sheffield!

Mr Hazel: Why are you going to Sheffield, because it's there I suppose?

Q: Because it's a job.

Mr Hazel: Because it's a job, absolutely, change your job . . . and if you're young it might be quite a nice and exciting thing, but in terms of people settled with families, the South West is extremely attractive . . .   (Mr Hazel, 7)

Such heretical interaction helps to establish a "face" that is more flexible and incorporates rights and rôles from other interactions (the pub perhaps, or the staff club) into the interview situation. Being a "heretic" (i.e. being *continually* heretical, as opposed to producing a few heretical *moments*, as most interviewees do) is an artful interactional practice for presenting a self that transcends the "bland" rôle of interviewee giving "good data". Mr Lime (see p. 173) is another who does this (e.g. by teasing his wife). "Heretics" tend also to adopt informal (near horizontal) postures, to welcome interruptions and to revel in apparently irrelevant details. But, by creating an interactional order that is different from the standard interview one, they also make visible the characteristics of the informal order produced by orthodox selves.

By contrast, those who give attenuated, minimalist responses risk falling short of the accomplishment of convincing stories or the maintenance of interview interaction by their withholding of facts, reasons and motives. While not attempting to display selves that are original, creative or innovatory, they also refuse to employ the extended version of the conventional repertoire of individualistic or family-orientated legitimations of choices, or rather they refuse to do so in the manner prescribed for "good data". Without being unorthodox, offensive or frivolous in their answers, they do not seem to feel obliged to accomplish (or are unable to accomplish) the full form of the conventional self of these accounts, to "make face" in the usual ways. In this sense, the self is withheld, absent without explanation. We call such responses *fundamentalist*.

Fundamentalists are not unorthodox in the way that heretics are; indeed, they are hyper-orthodox. They are fundamentalist in their strict and literal adherence to the requirements of moral adequacy – making something of themselves and putting the family first – but they appear to make no effort at the elaborations required for interactional competence. Mr Poplar, a local authority civil engineer, is asked about his reasons for not moving away:

Q: Are there any particular reasons why you stayed in [city]?

Mr Poplar: Family basically.

Q: In what sort of sense?

Mr Poplar: I came out [of university] in 1972 and there weren't all that many jobs around until the eighties, by which time I was fairly settled. (Mr Poplar, 1)

Such fundamentalist *moments* are common in interviews, as when respondents give brief answers, which seem to indicate that the topic should not be pursued much further or that their reasoning or decision is "just natural". However, consistently fundamentalist respondents sustain this mode virtually throughout their interviews, treating all questions like unexploded bombs. Hence the interview lacks any momentum, other than that which the interviewer can generate. Mr Poplar never elaborates, and the whole interview continues in this mode. Similarly, Mr Silverbirch's answers are all brief and minimalist, though strictly orthodox.

Q: Are you currently employed at the moment?

Mr Silverbirch: Yes I am, chartered surveying.

Q: Are you a partner in a practice, or . . . ?

Mr Silverbirch: I am in a practice, yes.

Q: And that's in [city] is it?

Mr Silverbirch: Yes.

Q: And how many partners are there?

Mr Silverbirch: In fact I'm the sole principal.

Q: Right, so what prompted you setting up on your own then?

Mr Silverbirch: I inherited the business.

Q: From?

Mr Silverbirch: My father.   (Mr Silverbirch, 1)

Soon after this, it emerges that he has another employment.

Q: So how are these two jobs worked together?

Mr Silverbirch: It just means I have to work long hours [. . .]

Q: So what prompted you to take that on?

Mr Silverbirch: Because of lack of business in the residential property market.

Q: So how long have you been doing it then?

Mr Silverbirch: Two years.

Q: And that's when . . . ?

Mr Silverbirch: . . . that's when the market went.

Q: So what sort of decision-making process did you go through in order to make that decision?

Mr Silverbirch: Purely on monetary market terms.
                                                 (Mr Silverbirch, 2–3)

Fundamentalism is thus a form of interactional minimalism, by which interviewees "save face" through strict adherence to the canons of moral adequacy, but at the expense of interactional competence. The interviewer is left speculating about issues that cannot be discussed, but also with his rôle and rights subverted – he cannot sustain the interview or get the "good data" he needs. Where a fundamentalist mode of accounting is adopted, alarm at the interview process seems to have become pervasive.

Alarm and "strangeness"

"Doing" an interview is (for both interviewer and interviewee) a process of routinizing a potentially alarming situation – in this case the almost Pinteresque scenario of a stranger (sometimes wet and dishevelled, as Marcus Redley travelled by bicycle) arriving at a house to ask open-ended questions. The "normal appearances" of the encounter are sustained – and hence alarm contained – by co-operative face work, which creates the impression of order and stability and manages the threats posed by this intervention in interviewees' lives, interruptions by third parties, the failure of the tape recorder, and so on. Heresy and fundamentalism are identifiable because the ways the respondents manage alarm, and the kinds of interactional order this creates, are noticeably different from the standard interview exchange.

If interviewer and interviewee, in co-operating to give and save face during most of these interviews, produce an interactional order of "normal appearances", what is the status of this order? How does the attempt at moral adequacy in the accounts, incorporated into the interaction as claims of social value by each "face", relate to society's structures? We start to address these issues by examining in detail some moments in the interviews when the respondents recognize – and comment on – situations in which the routine realities of "normal appearances" do not apply. Because these are necessarily reconstructions of such moments, they do not always convey the feeling of alarm or dread; however, two of these, which will be more closely analyzed, do have this special quality.

Within the interview transcripts, respondents signal their awareness that some new, unexpected and dreaded situation has emerged (or is threatening) by saying that it is "strange", or that their reaction is "daft" or "cockeyed". They indicate difficulties in incorporating this into coherent accounts, or sustaining the interview interaction when confronted with these new circumstances and their reactions to them. They are required to improvise within the interview, to make a new sense of this element in their situation, in order to restore the stability and normality of the interactional order, which has been breached by a moment of heightened intensity. "Strangeness" thus signals the threat of a breakdown in normal appearances and the improvised (and hence original) efforts made by the interviewees to manage alarm and restore routine order.

A brief instance of this – Mr Box's comment on the "strangeness" of suddenly having his mother living nearby – has already been given (see p. 41). A more prolonged moment occurs when Mr and Mrs Laburnum are asked about their elder son's education at a private school.

Q: I was wondering whether you both thought that was a success?

Mr and Mrs Laburnum: [laugh].

Mr Laburnum: That's a very sort of meaningful question at the moment. I'm struck dumb really.

Mrs Laburnum: It was an unmitigated disaster really.

Mr Laburnum: I think it was disastrous, yes. I think it probably was on most levels really, certainly academically. [. . .] He didn't fall in with any sort of norm of private/public boarding school at all, did he? [. . .]

Mrs Laburnum: It did teach him a few things, but I mean, he was thrown out actually in the end, but we put him somewhere else because he was in the middle of exams, and that's been even worse. [. . .] Academically none of them have worked, but then nowhere would have worked really.

Mr Laburnum: I don't think that would have worked anyway. Just not that way inclined, I'm afraid [. . .]

Mrs Laburnum: When he left we should have sent him to a tutorial college in [city] and kept him at home really, because the last little effort has been even worse really.

Mr Laburnum: Yes, what we shouldn't have done was continue in the boarding school situation.

Mrs Laburnum: But we were trying to provide him with the things he wouldn't have got, like sport, which he was good at [. . .] but it was a mistake.

(Mr and Mrs Laburnum, 30–2)

At this point, the interviewer changes the subject, by asking them about their other son's reactions. The account is left without a conclusion, incomplete, and it is the researcher who restores normal appearances and routine realities. The breach in these – signalled by Mr Laburnum saying that he is "struck dumb" – is not repaired by their account up to this point, but they have persisted in trying to repair it. Despite their repeated acknowledgement that "nothing would have worked", they attempt to reconstruct "what we should have done", and to identify their "mistakes". Their son "didn't fall in with any sort of norm" of boarding school education, yet they require themselves – in the face of this "unmitigated disaster" – to give an account of what a responsible parent should have done when his state dayschool career went awry, and again when he was expelled. It is clear that they are caught between their conviction that "nowhere would have worked" and their efforts to give a proper, morally adequate account. Even *in extremis*, such an account is required, and not just any account will do.

Because these events are current and unresolved, it is the "meaningful question" that provokes alarm in Mr and Mrs Laburnum. In the second instance, the threat to routine realities is of longer duration.

Mr and Mrs Rowan (a manager in an accountancy firm and a school meals and classroom assistant) are talking, towards the end of their joint interview, about the insecurity of his well paid job (see also p. 193). They have a daughter at a private school, and they are planning to have their son privately educated too. Mr and Mrs Rowan are "serious" interviewees, who sit up at a table and give careful, reasoned answers. He is asked whether he is worried about the recession.

Mr Rowan: Economic-wise, the only worries I had were regarding re-dundancies because it was happening in the accountancy practices throughout the UK. There were more and more redundancies. It was even happening in the firm I work for, but not in [city], it was other offices throughout the UK [. . .] I suppose I did worry about it but now I'm not worrying about it – if I start worrying about it then my job will suffer, and I could be the number one candidate to go if I start worrying about it. I suppose we did start thinking, two months back, if I lose my job what the hell will we do, how will we cope, what will we sell first? I think it came down to keeping the caravan and sell-ing the house . . .

Mrs Rowan: Yes, we'd live in the caravan . . . lovely.

Mr Rowan: Because if it's based on that, yes we could still keep Emma at school.

Mrs Rowan: We'd really want to do that, that would be our one main concern.

Mr Rowan: It's daft, because regardless of what we think of money, the main priority as far as we're concerned is the children's education. We wouldn't care where we lived as long as we could give the kids the right education. I think that's fair enough to say.

(Mr and Mrs Rowan, 27–8)

Here the interview interaction has a different quality about it. Mr Rowan starts by outlining the *anxious* nature of their deliberations over what would happen if he lost his job, an anxiety heightened by knowing that worrying will itself make him more vulnerable to redundancy. The more intense na-ture of the dilemma facing them, and their discussion of it, is signalled by the question "what the hell will we do?" – an uncharacteristically emphatic use of words. Their decision is first expressed tentatively ("I think it came down to"), as if Mr Rowan is checking with his wife that it is alright to tell the interviewer; but she endorses it, again uncharacteristically emotively ("lovely"). Finally he acknowledges that this choice, made in the face of a conflict between the advantages of home ownership and private education, is "daft", and concludes that "regardless of what we think of money" (he is an *accountant*) the children's educational needs have priority.

Like Mr and Mrs Laburnum in the previous instance, Mr and Mrs Rowan are unable to sustain their "faces", as cautious economic actors and sober interviewees, in describing their threatening circumstances. The normal appearances of the interview interaction are replaced by a moment of alarm, which has the following characteristics:

(a) *Strangeness.* Despite their previously consistent presentation of them-selves in orthodox terms as serious interviewees, giving good data, Mr and Mrs Rowan at this point, right at the end of their joint interview, briefly become "strange". Their routine performance of the interview requirements is disturbed by this recollection; this in turn disturbs their routine selves. In Travers' phrase, they become, during this passage, "strangers to themselves",[10] both in the story (the successful account-ant and his respectable wife sell their house and live in a caravan like gypsies) but also in the interaction (they use "swear words" and emo-tive language).

(b) *Heightened intensity*: In this example the intensity of the interview in-teraction is heightened, along with the emphatic and emotive use of language. This is signalled in the change in style in Mr Rowan's speech, from the almost impersonal accountant's analysis of the first sentence ("Economic-wise, the only worries I had were regarding redundancies") to the short, sharp questions at the end of this speech episode ("what the hell will we do, how will we cope, what will we sell first?"). Mrs Rowan, whose last speech episode is a modest statement of intent ("Ac-tually I wouldn't mind bringing more into the family, I'd feel I was doing a little bit more towards it"), states categorically and intensely, "We'd really want to do that, that would be our one main concern".

(c) *Uncertainty*: In contrast with the reasoned decisions, made on reflec-tion and by discussion and planning, that characterize the rest of the account, Mr and Mrs Rowan at this point evoke an ambience of uncer-tainty, doubt and fear, which enters the current interaction. In his account of the risk of redundancy, he starts worrying, his work suffers, and he becomes "the number one candidate to go". Doubts creep into his account of their discussion together: "I suppose we did start thinking"; "I think it came down to". The strangeness of their choice strikes him as "daft", and he concludes, "I think that's fair enough to say", as if he is struggling to convey an accurate account at this point.

Travers' analysis of such moments of "strangeness" uses concepts derived from Goffman, though he deploys them to somewhat different effect.[11] Travers sees the ritual dimension of interaction as managing "a diffuse state of constant alarm" that is a "necessary potential of the routine grounds that are kept routine because of some continuous – though unformulated and abeyant – reference to what might be alarming".[12] For Travers, normal appearances are interactional realities, routine realities, containing no alarming signals. Interaction moves between "frames" (reciprocal organizations of reality), always grounded in uncertainty, but trying to stave off the threat of a withdrawal of reality. Frames and routine grounds are produced by interactants "like reassuring familiarities", to keep awe and dread at bay.[13]

Sure enough, Mr and Mrs Rowan quickly restore routine normal appearances, and revert to their orthodox selves at the conclusion of the interview. They reconstruct the order of their lives, and remake something of themselves in the familiar, routine sensible ways that characterize the rest of their account. They transform themselves from gypsies with a wild emotional commitment to private education, back into an accountant and a school assistant, seeking advantages for their children and economizing on luxuries. The transcript continues:

Mrs Rowan: Yes. Because without a good backing in education nowadays, I'm afraid I don't think they'll get very far. They need the pieces of paper to prove that they can do something.

Mr Rowan: I suppose we have cut back a bit on the expense, we haven't had the central heating on as much, we've not had the lights on as early in the night as possible. It's the usual things you just try and cut down a bit, so that your money going out isn't as much as it was the last quarter . . .

Mrs Rowan: Although they always seem to be a bit more . . .

Mr Rowan: Yes, you can't win.

(Mr and Mrs Rowan, 28)

Thus the sensible, routine frame is restored, and Mr and Mrs Rowan reorganize themselves hastily back from the caravan and into the everyday routine realities of sensible domestic interaction. Yet the intense pitch of their previous exchange – in which they briefly disturbed their frames, and became strangers to their prudent, economising selves – made this section of the interview much more vivid, less bland, and in this sense *more real* than the normal appearances that they hastily repair. As Travers remarks, "The enhanced rituality of the stranger to its self makes it feel . . . as if it is a truer self than the one it was before."[14] Furthermore, through the experience of becoming engrossed in ritual reality, interactants can transform themselves, innovate and change. Order is not a stable condition of routine normal appearances, but is permanently under construction through accounting. Evolution and social change require selves that produce appearances that are both abnormal and acceptable, such as innovators and critical thinkers.

The "moment of strangeness" in the Rowans' joint interview occupies less than a page of transcript: it is a vivid passage of originality in an otherwise strictly orthodox account of making something of oneself and putting the family first. Mr and Mrs Rowan would not, we suspect, count themselves, or expect to be counted, as innovators or critical social thinkers. Yet – faced with the dread prospect of redundancy and the collapse of the fragile pyramid of credit on which their everyday world of house and garden, school and office, precariously balances – they construct an alternative in which they emerge as creative pioneers of the new era, the frontiers-folk of Majorism. Hence we need to understand how structure and constraint enter interaction, and how interaction in turn reconstructs the realities that lurk beyond the household.

Constraint, reality, structure

Something about the urgency with which Mr and Mrs Laburnum and Mr and Mrs Rowan strive to give accounts of these events alerts us to issues beyond the interview's interactional order. It is as if much more than their "face" in this encounter is at stake: giving an acceptable account of the unpredictable, the dreaded and the "unmitigated disaster" seems to be more fundamental to their sense of order and reality than the requirements of the research interview would warrant. In this section we consider recent claims by social theorists that the interactional order of such encounters is fundamental to the experience of a stable society and reality. This implies that, when confronted with such threatening events, actors feel compelled to improvise an adequate account, on pain of losing the sense of external order and stability in their lives.

What is communicated by the intensity of these passages is a very strong sense of exterior moral constraint. Both couples seem to experience the obligation to account for their situation within the framework of responsibility for self and family (outlined in the last chapter) with special force. Yet the standards and requirements of their accountability do not prescribe what they should do under these new and dreadful circumstances. Hence, while taking personal responsibility for what happens next, they ask "What the hell will we do?" in a situation where "nothing works".

Durkheim's analysis of morality and society argued that members mobilize the "collective consciousness" (in this case the moral accountability of individualism) to *produce* such exterior constraint, albeit in an "individualized" version of their own. Society and morality are experienced as external, real and obligatory: when individuals confront moral reality, they are confronting society. Therefore, "even while they are being individualised – and thus becoming elements of our personalities – collective ideals preserve their characteristic property: the prestige with which they are clothed. Although they are our own, they speak to us with a tone and an accent that are entirely different from those of our other states of consciousness. They command us; they impose respect: . . . We realise that they represent something within us that is superior to us".[15]

This implies that individuals are obliged to experience the world in certain ways, which seem to arise from external reality ("social facts"). Hilbert argues that it entails that society and reality are identical.[16] While the independence of reality from subjective experience seems essential for anyone to experience objective reality, it is society that provides the terms of experience, and thus makes experience possible.

Hence, whatever members do to sustain a sense of a stable moral order is also the activity that sustains the impression of stable and objective reality.[17] These interviewees must account for their new circumstances within the requirements of individualism, or lose this sense of a reliable external order: how they improvise to do so constitutes both social order and objective reality. "Wherever artful practices fail or promise to fail to reproduce membership and social order, there is also an imminent collapse of objective reality and subjective experience."[18]

Hilbert argues that moments such as the ones we analyzed in the last section must be understood in terms of Durkheim's concept of *anomie*. Where members of society have trouble in using cultural resources to account for their circumstances (in developing "artful practices" for accounting for their situation) this is experienced as a disturbance of external reality. Anomie occurs when individuals cannot use cultural resources to provide an account – when there seems no way to use them correctly or incorrectly ("nothing works").[19] Thus, in the face of incipient anomie at such moments of "strangeness", respondents like these struggle to improvise an account in order to preserve their ability to construct order and reality.

Under "normal" conditions, they could draw on cultural resources (what "everyone knows" about the educational system and the labour market) to give an account of their decisions within the standard repertoires of individualism and family responsibility. What others know and do about schooling and job security would both constrain their account and validate it as realistic and acceptable. Under conditions of rapid and unpredictable change, such a version is not available to them, and they must try to mobilize these resources in new ways, to avoid the terrifying "unreal" feeling that any account or no account would do. Where many individuals lack readily accessible cultural resources for standard accounts, there develops a sense of moral groundlessness and an absence of social accountability.

The cultural resources used by the interviewees include references to institutional structures and formal systems. Mr and Mrs Laburnum refer to state and private education, tutorial colleges, day and boarding schools, examinations and sporting events. Analyses that explain social order in terms of these institutional structures miss the processes by which these become meaningful and morally relevant at the level of decision making and action. Institutions become part of everyday reality, and enter the accountability framework of people like these interviewees, through their discourses of choice under constraint. Mr Rowan's account employs concepts (the recession, employment trends, redundancy) in ways that are not personal or arbitrary, but subject to social sanctions. The language he uses is shared with other accountants, newsreaders and politicians; his handling of these concepts must display his competence in organizing descriptions of his own decisions that correspond with what members "know" about global market forces and corporate strategies. Yet he must also demonstrate that economic forecasts cannot predict what will happen in his case, that he is aware that he is accountable for his decisions, and that not just any account will do.

Goffman's interactional order is constrained through the mutual commitment of participants to each other's "face" and to reciprocity in communication that allows selves, meaning and order to be produced. These are interactional achievements, which are not derived from institutional structures. Anne Warfield Rawls points out that Goffman's work recognizes that the constraints imposed on interaction by the achievement of mutual understanding are different from those imposed by social institutions, and that these interactional constraints are the sources of the social selves of the interactional order.[20] But interactions such as research interviews deal in accounts, through which participants make themselves accountable to the formal institutional structures of society. Although the self-organizing interactional order is responsive to the needs of self and discourse, it has an institutional context, whose constraints are introduced through accounts: actions must be accountable retrospectively in institutional terms. "Meaning . . . is not institutionally defined, but is in fact a constant interactional achievement which is nevertheless responsive to an institutional accountability framework."[21]

Rawls' theory of a *sui generis* interactional order, which is still accountable to the formal institutional order of social structures, implies that we should analyze these interviews so as to demonstrate how social selves, interactionally produced, account for decisions in the formal spheres of economy and polity. She argues that meaning, self *and institutional order* are all interactional achievements, locally produced.[22] Our research study offers evidence on how actors' accounts, by their use of institutional frameworks, introduce the constraints of the formal order into the informally achieved order of their interactions.

The examples given in the second half of this chapter show interviewees having trouble in accounting for their situations in terms of the institutional structure, yet insisting that such a version is not only possible but necessary. The accountability framework of individualism, which provides the cultural resources for such descriptions, requires them to demonstrate awareness of impersonal institutional constraint, yet take personal responsibility for their decisions within it. Their artful practices of improvisation expand the repertoire of cultural resources, as they discover new and creative ways of giving meaningful accounts. Under threat of redundancy, Mr and Mrs Rowan's hitherto prosaic version springs to life as they explore the frontiers of the property-owning democracy.

Conclusions

This chapter started with an analysis of interview interaction – how the participants produce selves and communicate meaning in such encounters. Goffman's work on interaction ritual allowed us to examine how the interviewees' mobilization of their socially valued attributes, and the interviewers' of their social scientific credentials, contributed to the production of a local order, and how retrospective reconstructions were related to the contingencies of these exchanges. Such processes were more visible when interviewees produced unorthodox selves, using "heretical" interactive ploys or relying on minimal, "fundamentalist" responses.

The "normal appearances" and "routine realities" of the interactional order were thus shown to allow the potential alarm in such encounters to be co-operatively managed by the exchange of reciprocal ritual respect. Heretical selves – like Mr Larch and Mr Hazel – sought to establish a different kind of order by their irreverent replies, which borrowed from the repertoires of jovial male sociability, perhaps to deflect attention from difficulties in sustaining morally adequate accounts. Fundamentalist selves – like Mr Poplar and Mr Silverbirch – gave such brief replies (perhaps because of alarm over accounting) that the interactional order could barely be sustained.

In the study of decision making, the agent's construction of the moral parameters of choice and the structural constraints in which it is made are of key importance. We have argued that interview moments when respondents signal alarm and describe "strangeness" in their own reactions, provide significant evidence of the processes through which they experience moral and social realities, in the form of obligations, responsibilities and constraints. Within the interviews, this was shown by an intense requirement to give a coherent account of unpredictable and alarming events. They strove to deploy cultural resources, including versions of the institutional order and their own responsibility for finding solutions to their circumstances within its constraints, to repair the disruptions to the interactional order of "normal appearances" caused by these moments of alarm.

If – as Hilbert, following Durkheim, suggests – such repair work is necessary for respondents' sense not only of stability and order, but of external reality itself, we might expect to find evidence of attempts to "normalize" non-standard situations in many other accounts. In particular, our study might provide an understanding of the processes postulated by Rawls, the interactional order of the encounter producing the institutional order through its accountability framework for retrospective reconstructions. This will be the subject of the next chapter.

References

1. H. Garfinkel, *Studies in ethnomethodology* (Englewood Cliffs, NJ: Prentice-Hall, 1967).
2. M. Redley, "Interview moments: how is it that some respondents appear to have more personality than others?", paper given to 13th Discourse Analysis Workshop, Exeter University, September 1991.
3. See, for instance, A. Warfield Rawls, "The interaction order *sui generis*: Goffman's contribution to social theory", *Sociological Theory* **5** (2) (1987), 136–49; and in *The interaction order: new directions in the study of social order*, D. T. Helm et al (eds) (New York: Irvington, 1989).
4. R. A. Hilbert, *The classical roots of ethnomethodology: Durkheim, Weber and Garfinkel* (Chapel Hill, NC: University of North Carolina Press, 1992).
5. Especially E. Goffman, *Interaction ritual* (New York: Doubleday Anchor, 1969).
6. E. Goffman, "On face-work: an analysis of ritual elements in social interaction", *Psychiatry* **18** (3) (1955), 213–31.
7. Ibid., p. 221.
8. Ibid., p. 227.
9. M. Redley, "Interview moments".
10. A. Travers, "Strangers to themselves: how interactants are other than they are", *British Journal of Sociology* **43** (4) (1992), 601–37.
11. Ibid., pp. 611–13, 617–18.
12. Ibid., p. 609.
13. Ibid.
14. Ibid., p. 632.
15. E. Durkheim, *The rules of sociological method* (1895; New York: Free Press, 1938), pp. lvi-lvii (footnote).
16. Hilbert, *The classical roots of ethnomethodology*, Ch. 4.
17. Ibid., p. 83.
18. Ibid.
19. Ibid., p. 91.
20. A. Warfield Rawls, "Language, self and social order: a reformulation of Goffman and Sacks", *Human Studies* **12** (1989), 148.
21. Rawls, "An ethnomethodological perspective on social theory", in *The interaction order*, D. T. Helm et al. (eds) (New York: Irvington, 1989), p. 16.
22. Rawls, "Language, self and social order", pp. 148–9 and 166.

CHAPTER 4

Double Jeopardy and the
Moral Regulation of the Self

What we have been trying to do in this part of the book is show how individualist (accounting) selves become social (interacting) selves; and conversely how the moral standards of individualism come to be part of the accomplishment of interactional competence. So far we have argued that both are achieved when interviewees attempt morally adequate reconstructions of their decisions, using cultural resources and skilfully mobilizing them within the ritual exchanges that produce the local order of the interview interaction.

We have made the link between the act of reporting decisions and what is reported in terms of individualism, a way of being in the world and organizing their experiences that was adopted by the interviewees for giving their accounts. Thus our analysis seeks to contribute to theory on how agents make choices, by showing how the production of a meaningful self-identity is linked with the construction of external realities. They explain their "lifestyles" by telling what they have made of themselves and how they have put the family first.

In this chapter, we aim to develop this analysis by examining more closely how the moral requirements of individualism influenced the decisions made. The cultural resources available to these interviewees consisted of known "facts" about the world and "norms" about how to live in it. What did their retrospective reconstructions reveal about how they organized their experience so as to make choices between options? How did they apply the moral standards of individualism to changing social and economic circumstances?

Within the mainstream traditions of the social sciences, the method for attempting an answer to these questions would be to try to identify the *rules* of individualistic morality, and how these respondents aligned their accounts with these rules. The idea that morality and order can be understood in terms of rule-following has long been fundamental to most philosophical and sociological theorizing: it analyzes moral regulation in terms of a set of principles (preferably coherent, consistent and comprehensive) governing individuals' relations with others. With a few dissenting voices,[1] philosophers have conducted ethical enquiries in these terms. In the functionalist theory that dominated sociological thought until the 1970s, social order can be explained in terms of norms and values that are analytically distinct from factual social relations: people behave as they do because they respect a "body of rules" or "normative system".[2]

This view has been radically challenged by the ethnomethodology of Garfinkel and his followers.[3] They analyzed social order in terms of the social practices of members rather than the prescriptions of rules; hence they saw moral and factual order as self-contained and self-sufficient. Following Wittgenstein's critique of ethics as rule-following,[4] they insisted that rules can never unambiguously prescribe behaviour; the norms that are supposed to stabilize behaviour are themselves imprecise and have to be interpreted. Their empirical studies showed that practitioners (such as clinicians[5] or police personnel[6]) identified and upheld "good standards" in their fields without being able to specify the rules governing such standards. Indeed, good practice often consisted in departing from the literal prescriptions of laws and procedures, and acting in ways indicated by the particular context of the decision – the contingencies of personality and circumstance.[7] Thus the order and stability of their relations depended on their "artful practices" and skilful improvisation. This did not imply that they were free to improvise or "bend" rules in any way they pleased. On the contrary, the orderly and normative nature of their practices consisted in the interpretation and adaptation of rules within particular contexts and their ability to recognize instances of, and regulate themselves and each other according to, such contextualized standards of "good practice".

This seems to imply that morality is somehow "internal" to individuals (as artful practitioners) or groups (as upholders of their own standards). Yet people's own accounts of their actions reconstruct these in terms of a structure and pattern, according to an order that they experience as transcending everyday contingency. In managing inherent ambiguity and instability, they *produce* order and predictability, which they then talk about as factual and taken for granted.[8] Thus members' accounts display themselves living within and taking for granted the products of their own artful practices, which provide stability for all the practical purposes of their daily lives. As Hilbert points out, this can be understood in terms of

Durkheim's analysis of morality as "external and constraining",[9] as transcendent and even "sacred",[10] and yet as produced by people themselves (the "collective conscience"). Moral regulation is provided through the *sui generis* social order: society and morality are equivalent.[11]

Following this theoretical line, we turn in this chapter to a more detailed analysis of the *interpretative repertoires* displayed in these accounts.[12] Interviewees' interpretations of the moral requirements of individualism are variable;[13] there are major inconsistencies between and within accounts over the way in which key terms are employed. Indeed, the same terms are often used to legitimate apparently incompatibly different choices. Although some of this variability can be attributed to the interactional manoeuvring that was analyzed in the previous chapter (for instance, the use of ploys to distract from problems of moral adequacy in the account), it is clear that most of the respondents are making serious attempts to locate their decisions within the moral parameters of the individualist ethic for most of their accounts. Yet they use these standards to justify a wide variety of choices.

Hence we focus first on the repertoires characteristic of individualism – the terms employed to describe choices, how they are combined, and the way key metaphors are used – as a starting point for studying the moral regulation of decision making. In the next section we look at the concept of "career" in the accounts. Although there is great variation over what is claimed (or disclaimed) in using (or avoiding) this term for framing the narrative reconstruction of a set of decisions, it is clearly central to interviewees' repertoires of what they have made of themselves.

This leads to an analysis of where respondents have trouble in accounting for decisions in these transcripts. In the following section, we look at the accounts of the small group of women who opt to give versions of their labour-market choices in terms of a "career". The hard rhetorical work that they are required to do to reconcile accounts of "career" decisions with their versions of their responsibility for child care and domestic organization gives indications of why most women adopt a "non-career" framework to describe their choices. The repertoires of individualistic accountability that provide the cultural resources for better-off British women's narratives of their employment decisions do allow "careerist" accounts, but women are required to demonstrate awareness that careers are in tension with family responsibilities. Hence the key metaphors of being "torn" between "career" and family, or "balancing" conflicting demands, are prominent in such accounts.

The "troubles" encountered by these interviewees in giving their accounts are by no means as acute as the moments of alarm experienced by Mr and Mrs Laburnum and Mr and Mrs Rowan in the previous chapter. However, they do feel required to give more elaborate, complex and multi-stranded versions of their reasons for decisions than others, and simultaneously to do more "face work" for sustaining moral adequacy and to engage more intensely with the interviewer to ensure meaningful communication. We use the term "double jeopardy" to describe the dual threats to moral adequacy and interactional competence in such versions. Their accountability for both "career" and "family" requires the respondents to employ more rhetorical effort and improvisational skill to show what they have made of themselves and how they put the family first, and their accounts are more vulnerable to interactional subversion within the contingencies of the interview (including contradiction by their partners).

However, such accounts do provide important evidence on the relationship between the norms of individualism and the choices made by agents. In the next section, we examine how another key term, "family", is used to "normalize" the circumstances of "non-standard households". Only one of the households in our sample contains three generations, and this couple are also jointly responsible for a nephew and niece who live with them. Their account of how they came to be in this situation shows how the term "family" is used to legitimate these unique decisions, and thus the prioritization of wider kinship ties. Yet in other accounts, the same term is used to disclaim responsibility for kin outside the nuclear unit.

This illustrates what Garfinkel calls the "indexical" character of many of the key terms in the repertoires of individualism. [14] In this final section of the chapter, we analyze the processes of moral regulation in two non-standard households (a recently reconstituted family and two couples living together), to show how these employ the repertoires of individualism to legitimate decisions that are quite different from the ones that are accounted for by others adopting the same accountability framework. These versions both demonstrate the experience of moral obligation (they describe a strong sense of moral commitment and constraint) and show how interviewees regulate their own and each others' behaviour by the use of these repertoires.

We draw the conclusion that these agents do not derive their decisions from prescriptive norms or a body of rules, but exercise judgement in interpreting moral requirements. In their narratives of responsibility for self and family, they interpret the terms of the individualistic repertoire in context, and subsequently regulate their own and others' behaviour in line with this shared *practical* interpretation. In this sense, these agents act like the skilled practitioners of ethnomethodological studies, artfully defining their own standards in particular contexts, and monitoring them within the practices of their micro-communities of mutual commitment.

"Careers"

In their narratives of what they have made of themselves, interviewees interpret their labour-market decisions, accounting for how their moves enhanced their capacities. This interpretation involves selection of those features of the work that they did in a succession of posts that fulfilled the moral requirements of the individualist ethic. Conversely, their reasons for leaving jobs are given in terms of those features that were incompatible with their responsibilities to make something of themselves and put the family first.

As is familiar from the survey[15] literature (and will be further analyzed in Part II) most of the men were in full-time work, and they were concentrated in senior or managerial posts, whereas most of the women were doing part-time work and were disproportionately – given that their educational qualifications were the same as the men's – in manual or clerical posts. Most couples accounted for their relative positions (a full-time working man with a partner earning on average about one-third of his salary) in terms of the man's "career" and the woman's "non-career". (For details of the jobs and earnings of the 36 couples, see Appendix A, p. 240.)

This notion of a "career" is a key element in the interpretative repertoires of decision making they deploy: both men and women orientate their accounts to this concept. However, their accountability in terms of "career" is strongly gendered, since men are required to show how they have made something of themselves in a way consistent with being the primary provider of family income, whereas women have to show that they have taken primary responsibility for organizing the household. Hence men who do not construct their labour-market decisions in terms of "career" are accountable to show that they earn sufficient notwithstanding this, and women who avow "careerism" must demonstrate how they reconcile this with household responsibility.

There are major inconsistencies in the way the term "career" is used, both within and between accounts. Although most men claim to be following "careers" and most women claim not to be, the implications of the term vary according to whether it is used in the context of male or female accounts. The meaning adopted in the standard repertoire of men's accounts (implicitly in most cases) is well captured by Mr Hawthorn.

Mr Hawthorn: . . . the normal professional thing where people go for jobs with perks, you know, with fringe benefits like having a car, [. . .] seeking advancement . . . (Mr Hawthorn, 17, 24)

The pathway of "seeking advancement" thus includes both incremental increases in earnings and the accumulation of perks; but men who move out of regular employment into self-employment or become directors of their own companies have the option of constructing this decision in terms of "non-career" (Mr Hawthorn himself, Mr Larch) or "career" (Mr Birch, Mr Alder, Mr Lime, etc.). Conversely, some men in regular employment (e.g. Mr Pear, Mr Teak) give versions of their employment decisions that reject "career".

Women whose accounts of their decisions disclaim "career" reject "advancement" and incremental accumulation as a motive, and adopt a more self-developmental agenda. Here Mr Hawthorn's partner, Ms Whitebeam, is asked why she has opted for part-time work.

Ms Whitebeam: Because I am also involved in a lot of other things, and I didn't want to take a full-time job and then have to drop everything else. [. . .] I'm involved in a counselling organization called [name] which takes up a lot of time too [. . .] maybe about three hours a week, and then there's often weekends. The other thing is that I'm also involved with the Women's Centre and pregnancy testing, which again is on a rota system. (Ms Whitebeam, 3)

This diverse portfolio of activities, some of which are unpaid, and with no incremental accumulation (e.g. of pension rights) is also characteristic of the few men (six in all) who give non-career accounts of their decisions.

Mr Teak: I've never got the satisfaction out of teaching that I thought I might. On the other hand, I don't hate it, I feel fairly neutral about it. I just thought it would be nice to do a little bit less of it, and that made me feel a bit more positive about the time I now do, doing three days a week rather than five, and I wanted a bit more time to myself for a variety of reasons. I've got one or two little things I wanted to pursue, and just to have a more relaxing life, and do domestic things. (Mr Teak, 16)

Mr Larch: I have never done a 9 to 5 in my life – I've done a 3 o'clock
in the morning till half past 8 or 9 in the morning [. . .] So I've
always had time to go to sale rooms and speculate or buy things.

(Mr Larch and Ms Plum, 30)

Mr Hawthorn: I'd rather have the flexibility now, so that enables me
to do other things with my time [. . .] I've spent a total of about
seven months over there [France] working on [holiday home], doing
it up. That's something I've been enabled to do by being freelance
[. . .] I've also used some of the breaks from employment to do this
[charity's name] thing [. . .] I haven't had a career, like most of my
contemporaries have. I mean a lot of people who are contemporaries of mine are now directors of public companies and that sort of
thing. Whereas I haven't sought advancement on that level, so in
many ways . . . job-wise I've always run with a lot of slack.

(Mr Hawthorn, 13–24)

Mr Pear, a senior technician in a college, explains that he will not be
applying for further promotion because he does not want "the additional
responsibility which will then make me more of an integral part of the college mechanism [. . .] The more responsibility you have, then I think that
pulls you away – you know, there's a greater commitment to the work than
there is to the home base" (p. 16). The job, however, provides "tremendous
resources which we can utilise to fulfil various projects that we get up to
within our own family and social aspect". It gives him time for these too.

Mr Pear: Then there are a whole range of things that I can get up to
which involves things with Frances [partner], things with the kids,
or things that I get up to on my own accord – doing this, doing that,
playing around with this – dilettante is my middle name.

(Mr Pear, 22–3)

Thus the men who give "non-career" accounts of their decisions emphasize both their autonomy and the aspects of their working life that
allow them to "put the family first" – to help out more or spend more
"quality time" with partners and children. Women who account for their
decisions in terms of "careers" are conversely required – as we shall show
in the next section – to do hard rhetorical work to reconcile this with the
needs of children.

The trajectories of the self[16] that are characteristic of these gendered
accounts – men's pursuit of promotion, perks and pensions; women's rejec-

tion of "careerism" after childbearing, and subsequent self-developmental pathway – sound as if they are strongly determined by the hierarchical structures of employment and the conventions of the traditional division of domestic labour. However, the interviewees reconstruct the decisions that gave them their direction as individual *choices*: they relate them to the projects of a life plan,[17] rather than progress down a track that has been laid down by institutional rules or gendered norms. Women insist that they prefer the options that are consistent with their child care responsibilities.

Ms Whitebeam: I feel like life is more than just a full-time job, and that
I still want to be able to grow my new vegetables. I want to be able
to have time to decorate. I want to do these other activities and that
for me is what getting a balanced life is about . . .

(Ms Whitebeam, 5)

Most men's account of their "careers" emphasize the diversity of their employment rôles, and the opportunities for an autonomous self to make something of itself while gaining salary increments and fringe benefits.

. . . I think the length of service not only relates to promotion but
also interesting opportunities, if you like, and after five years the
opportunity arose to go and work in Nigeria for six months, so that
provided an interesting break.

(Mr Box, architect, explaining why he has
been 17 years with his firm (14))

So it was rather lucky in fact, the job itself. What's interesting is that
it turned out professionally [. . .] I had exponential horizons as far
as work was concerned. It turned out to be very interesting because
it gave me a wider variety of work. [. . .] The work was simply more
varied here, so there was a kind of serendipity there – I didn't know
it was going to be advantageous but it turned out to be very good.

(Mr Oak, teacher, explaining advantages
of move to present post (17))

. . . there was a desire to be insatiably curious about things, which
has stayed, I suppose, academic in that sense, but a small amount
of utilitarianism as well, so I've always written for schools and things.
I've been a very fluent scribbler, I'm not a natural writer, but I'm a
fluent scribbler.

(Mr Hazel, university lecturer,
explaining his academic career, (4–5)

Double jeopardy – "career" women

Only a small minority of the women interviewees (8 out of 36) give an account of how they reached their current labour-market position in terms of a "career". Those who do are not all in full-time employment or self-employment; some who deploy "career" repertoires describe their progress as "on hold" because of their child care and domestic responsibilities. Conversely, several women in full-time work give "non-career" accounts, disclaiming any pursuit of advancement or fringe benefits. Thus we would stress that "careerism" is *a kind of autobiographical narrative*, a particular mode of accounting for labour-market decisions, rather than a distinctive, coherent relationship between posts held over time. Women who give "career" accounts do more rhetorical work to justify this, and their involvement in the interview interaction is more intense. Our analysis aims to show that this was because they experienced a sense of threat, both to the moral adequacy of their accounts and to their interactional accomplishment of them – double jeopardy.

In this section we will argue that most women opt for a "non-career" version of themselves because in a "career" account it is much more difficult to demonstrate that they prioritize the needs of children and partnership. Since all but one (Mrs Palm) of the women in our sample take primary responsibility for child care and household organization in their accounts, they require themselves to give discursive justifications of how they reconcile their "career" with these obligations. Furthermore, speaking as such accountable custodians of the household, they are more open to interactional subversion within the contingencies of a home-based interview – accountability for anything that goes wrong or looks wrong. Finally, the fact that both interviewers are men reinforces their vulnerability, given this accounting framework.

The difference between "career" and "non-career" versions is nicely captured by Mrs Maple, one of the women who opts for the latter kind of account. She is a craft worker and is currently the main earner in her household (her husband is a trained teacher but at present is doing only part-time sessional work). Mrs Maple was successful, and her business was expanding, before she had a child; she still employs an accountant. However, in speaking about how she gets work, she says:

Mrs Maple: I've been doing it for nearly 20 years now and I don't think I've got as big a network as I should have, but I think since I had Felicity [daughter] I haven't pursued it as a career ambition, I've just let it happen. If I was really serious about this job that I do, as a career, I'd be living in London, I wouldn't be living in [city]. And if I was really serious, I'd be going to the right tea parties on Sunday afternoons. I mean it happens in every job I suppose, but I don't bother.

(Mrs Maple, 3)

Mrs Maple's account can be contrasted with that of Ms Plum, an art worker, who produces for "the one-off, high price, individual market – retailing to galleries".

Ms Plum: Very few people are picked up and given a lot of publicity and acclaim, but behind those very few people there are people who have exhibitions, are collected, etc., and I suppose I will aim to be one of those – and I am becoming one of those, but I've still got a long way to go. So the money I get from my work will hinge on my reputation, which hinges on exposure through galleries and exhibitions. So, I've made headway but there's a way to go yet.

(Ms Plum, 1–2)

Unlike Mrs Maple, Ms Plum constructs her future path as upwards and onwards – hers is a programme for extending her fame and fortune. In this sense she is, like the businessmen among the male careerists, "seeking advancement". However, like all the women who give "career" accounts, she has many reservations about this pathway. These are not simply anxieties and doubts (which enter the men's accounts also), but conflicts between advancement-orientated actions and decisions and responsibilities for children. Despite the acceptance of moral accountability in terms of making something of themselves (which is superficially the same accountability framework as the men's), these women also regarded themselves as accountable for the day-to-day care of children. The nature of this accountability for children was not that of oversight and monitoring of their progress towards autonomy and readiness for self-reliance in a world of competitive individualists (as it is for the men as fathers). As qualitative research such as Yeandle's,[18] Brannen and Moss's[19] and Boulton's[20] shows, it is detailed executive responsibility for what happens to them from hour to hour, and for the quality of care that is given to them, that actually accomplishes their nurturance and socialization. When women speak about concerns over their children, these are not of the overall, developmental and educational nature – as in the men's accounts. They are about the practicalities of finding suitable child-minders, of transporting them to school or to after-school activities, of arranging holidays to suit their needs, and so on.

These women construct their accounts of their "careers" as accommodating this kind of executive responsibility. For them, "putting family first" is not simply, as it is for men, a matter of prioritizing the expenditure of resources in favour of advantages for children (although several women did, they said, spend their earnings on school fees). Rather, it is a matter of building their accountability for child care into the fabric of a morally adequate version of making something of themselves, through seeking advancement.

This feature of "career" women's versions is well captured in Ms Plum's account, following straight after the advancement-orientated passage previously quoted.

Q: So other than actually producing the pieces of [art work], what else do you do in order to stake your claim?

Ms Plum: [. . .] At the moment I'm not pushing, because I can't cope with it. I can't cope with producing work, looking after small children, and trying to seek publicity and further work obligations. I just can't do it, so I'm stalling. At the moment I'm only doing what people ask me to do, and what I reckon is that if I can just keep ticking over on that level until the children are bigger, then I will be able to start pushing and looking to get bigger articles in magazines and stuff like that. But I don't do any of that at the moment. I don't do anything at all. I'm lying low. (Ms Plum, 2)

A similar line is developed in the account of Mrs Lime, one of only three women in this sample with a "career" in commerce. When she had her daughter (now aged nearly 2) she was able to return after maternity leave to her previous job, as a personnel manager with a large retail chain, on a part-time basis. She describes her position in the company at the moment, and her plans for the future.

Mrs Lime: It's part time at the moment. Yes, I was full time but now I'm part time.

Q: And you went part time because?

Mrs Lime: Because I had the baby, and I didn't want to go back full time. In fact I wrote and told them that I wasn't going to come back unless they would consider me for part-time work, which I didn't think they would – and they did. [. . .]

Q: I see. So, do you intend to return full time?

Mrs Lime: I would like to at some stage, but I intend to have another child sometime, so I'd like to continue part time at the moment and then, hopefully, if I have another child and he or she gets off to school, then I would like to go back to full time. I just have to hope there's an opportunity there for me with the same company.

Q: So, in any sense of the word, are you developing your career through working part time?

Mrs Lime: I don't know about developing, but I'm keeping in touch, and something like personnel – I mean employment law changes, company policy changes, even the few months I was away on maternity leave there were loads of changes. So I'm keeping in touch with what's going on. [. . .] and so if I was to go back full time, I'd have full knowledge of the job. Whereas, if I wasn't part time at all, i.e. didn't do any work, it would be like going to a new job and learning it all over again.   (Mrs Lime, 17–18)

At one point, later in the interview, Mrs Lime is asked, "So would a 'career woman' be the right sort of adjective to describe your movements [between jobs and locations, up to present post]?" and she answers, "Yes. With [chain's name] it was very much a case of if you wanted to get on you had to be prepared to move to the relevant jobs" (p. 25). But, within the construction of herself as a "career woman", she takes for granted her accountability for the details of providing care for her daughter.

Several women who give "career" accounts of their decisions describe circumstances in which they gave up jobs that enhanced their earning potential because their demands conflicted with the requirements of family responsibility.

Mrs Sycamore: . . . it was quite normal at that time for me to work between 50, 60 hours a week, and that is not fair on my husband and my children who are first. And when it comes to between a job, my health, my family, the job doesn't stand a chance, I owe my health to my children and my husband [. . .] The time that I was there I enjoyed very much indeed; I'd made a great deal of friends, with some very nice people, but I was in the wrong place at the wrong time . . .   (Mrs Sycamore, 10)

Ms Blackthorn: I returned to work from years ago after a nine year gap, through necessity, and started where I could with a part-time job and

84

then built up. I did full-time for a bit, which I found too much, went
back to part time   (Ms Blackthorn, 20)

Ms Blackthorn explains her moves as a "balancing act" between the
conflicting demands of "career" and family.

Ms Blackthorn: I think managing one's time, work vis-à-vis family, is
very, very hard, and the needs of the children and the needs of me.
And there's always the guilt feelings, that if I don't get on the ladder now and start working up, the later I leave it the older I become,
and that the children are still very young. So it's a balancing act, and
I certainly never feel I get it quite right.   (Ms Blackthorn, 33)

In this passage, Ms Blackthorn reconstructs a range of emotions and
psychological needs, the structural requirements of a "career" and their
conflict with family life. Unlike "career" accounts by men, who try to show
what they have made of themselves through seeking advancement and how
this has enabled them to gain advantages for their families, these women
interviewees convey making something of themselves and putting the family first as in considerable tension, and engage more intensely in the interview to describe this "balancing act", declaring each decision to be an ad-
justment that is provisional and fallible, and "never getting it quite right".

Mrs Dogwood says that she returned to teaching four-and-a-half months
after the birth of her son Harry largely for financial reasons, but with doubts
about whether she would "cope".

Mrs Dogwood: Psychologically me leaving the baby, just to see how it
went, because you can imagine it was a big change in life. It was quite
late – I was 37 when I had Harry, and I'd been working for a long
time – and physically and emotionally it sort of knocked me up for
a while, and so four-and-a-half months isn't very old to go back into
work . . . and I suffered during that time a complete lack of confidence too, which I'd not actually had before.   (Mrs Dogwood, 3–4)

Significantly, only Mrs Palm – who has negotiated a "rôle swap" with
her partner – gives an account of her teaching "career" that does not include reference to these conflicts and tensions. Because Mr Palm left his
"career" to take primary responsibility for child care and the household
work, her version can focus on the development of her capacities without
this undermining its moral adequacy in terms of putting the family first.

This contrasts with Mrs Pine's account. Her husband has recently accepted a prestigious academic post in a city in the Midlands, and she is

staying on in their house until their daughters have completed their examinations, when she will join him there. After she moves, she does not expect to be able to pursue her "career" in teaching.

Mrs Pine: When we move to [city's name] and I give up my teaching job here, I will probably find it difficult to get another teaching job, because in this experience of local school management I would be an expensive teacher to employ [. . .] Because I'm at the top of the scale, and previously that didn't matter. [. . .] So there will be problems about getting a job.   (Mrs Pine, 16–17)

She might have strengthened her claims to a post by improving her qualifications, but gave up this attempt; she describes this in terms of the conflicting pull of her obligations.

Mrs Pine: Again, I think that would be difficult because I haven't got any higher qualifications, and last year I did attempt – I did start an M.Ed. – but I just found the work load of organizing a class of very little children and trying to do an M.Ed. and running a house, a family by myself just too much. I couldn't do it.   (Mrs Pine, 17–18)

Mrs Pine's version of her "career" uses few of the elements in the male discourse of advancement. Like other women's accounts, it describes an attempt to balance the demands of job and family, demonstrating the capacity to reason about these feelings and achieve a provisional equilibrium. Not only does she justify giving up her higher degree course in these terms; she constructs the decision to follow her partner to the Midlands as a positive one – because of its implications for his "career" – despite the probability that she will have to take up a different kind of work (for further discussion, see Ch.5, pp. 106–109).

In these women's accounts, therefore, the discourses of "career" are adapted to fit the gendered accountability of their domestic rôles. This requires a good deal of rhetorical work and an intensity of interactional involvement, whereas "non-career" accounts appear often to be quite easily accomplished. In the next section, we will develop our analysis of how key terms like "career" are combined with others (like "family") as elements in the interpretative repertoires of individualism.

Moral regulation

So far we have shown that the variability of the accounts (inconsistencies over how terms are used, and between the decisions that they are employed to justify) can be traced to the nature of interpretative repertoires. "Career" is a key concept in orientating narratives of labour-market decisions, yet its meaning is defined in context. It is an "indexical" term in Garfinkel's sense, whose meaning becomes determinate only through its use in an account. When women (or self-employed men) employ it in the context of their choices, it has quite different implications from those of incremental advancement and fringe benefits in men's accounts.

The "double jeopardy" experienced by women giving "career" accounts seems to indicate that decisions are not to be analyzed in terms of prescriptions for choices derived from the rules and norms provided by moral principles. The requirements of the individualistic ethic must be interpreted within their particular circumstances. Where these involve unpredictable changes and unanticipated contingencies, interpretations must create the sense of order and stability by improvising accounts of their situation, using cultural resources. As we saw in the previous chapter, it is members' own artful practices that construct this order through their everyday interactions. In this final section, we examine how the term "family" is used by interviewees to provide moral regulation of important decisions, made in unusual and stressful circumstances.

The "indexical" nature of the term "family" has been explored by qualitative researchers, who have drawn attention to the variable way it is employed to regulate a wide variety of contrasting moral issues.[21] The interviews we draw on in this section are accounts by people living in "non-standard" household units – an extended family, a recently reconstituted family, and two couples living together. In very different ways, the couples seek to "normalize" their situations. They try to show how their living arrangements have been arrived at by responding to a set of unique or very unusual contingencies, in which the accepted moral requirements of self-identity and "family" are reinterpreted and developed. Because their situations are unusual, they become aware of the taken-for-granted order of an external and constraining morality as they do the discursive work of improvising an account in terms of the standards of moral adequacy that apply to people like themselves.

There are several sections of these interviews in which respondents describe their efforts to do the right thing under special circumstances. In order to provide evidence of the processes of moral regulation in practical action, we focus on those contexts in which interviewees recognize the force of moral constraint (they *feel* an obligation to act in a certain way), and analyze how they account for what they actually did. In other words, we observe them "doing morality" in their accounts – regulating their own and each other's behaviour – to understand how the regulatory order of individualism and prioritizing family commitments is produced. There are interesting differences between, as well as similarities in, the way the term "family" is used to regulate decisions and normalize situations.

Mrs Elder is a part-time typesetter for a country town weekly newspaper: her salary is a small fraction of her husband's as a manager in an accountancy firm. They have a daughter aged 10. When Mr and Mrs Elder moved to Devon 10 years previously, her parents moved with them (they had recently retired) and they bought a large house, which was divided between them. Mrs Elder's family originated from the town where they settled, and her brother was already living there, as a lone parent with two children. Six years later, Mrs Elder's father died, and almost immediately after this her brother died, leaving his two children (who were teenagers) as orphans. They are asked whether they discussed the question of whether the three of them (the couple and Mrs Elder's recently widowed mother) would take in her brother's children.

Mrs Elder: No.

Mr Elder: Well, you don't have any choice in these things really. Well, you do have a choice: either you do or you don't. And if you say, "Yes, we've got no choice, it's family", you have to do something. So they just had to come here.

Mrs Elder: Well there was just no question about that. My brother died very quickly, and it just so happens Jane (his daughter) was coming here that night for her tea and we had to tell her that her father had died. Well, what do you say? "We'll see about getting you somewhere?" You just don't do that.

(Mr and Mrs Elder, 25)

This situation is considerably more threatening and disturbing than the one faced by Mr and Mrs Rowan (see Ch.3, pp. 64–7). Mrs Elder's brother's death, following so quickly on her father's, confronts them with an immediate decision. Their reconstruction of it is the reverse side of Mr and Mrs Rowan's account of "strangeness" (incipient anomie). In Mr Elder's account, as soon as they recognize that their nephew and niece are "family" they have no choice – "they just had to come here". The moral compulsion to take them into their household (they are in fact cared for by Mrs Elder's mother) is experienced as external, constraining and overwhelmingly obligatory. Mrs Elder reinforces the point very strongly when she adds that "there was just no question about that" and that the alternative was unthinkable: "You just don't do that".

The interesting thing about this version of those very dramatic events is that the reasoning for their decision (if it can be called that) is so brief and pithy. Although the image of the girl coming to the house to be told of her father's death is vivid, the account of how they came to "do the right thing" takes two or three short sentences. This is the obverse of the hard rhetorical work of the previous two sections: it condenses a moral code, with strongly binding obligations (which do not even need to be discussed) into less than 100 words. Yet, as we have seen in Chapter 2, Mr and Mrs Elder's conception of "family" – the concept that triggers their duty to take in their nephew and niece – is shared by only a small minority of the couples. It was because they were involved on a daily basis with their kin, already sharing the house with her mother and interacting with her brother's family, that the obligation was experienced as unquestionable. Their definition of the "family" that must be put first is extensive: it includes the kin with whom they share membership and mutual assistance.

This way of "doing morality" – reconstructing the decision to do the right thing under the threat of a totally unpredictable contingency that undermined all their assumptions about the family's future life-course – has about it some of the characteristics of Durkheim's "mechanical solidarity".[22] Mr and Mrs Elder know at once, without reflection, what they have to do. The obligation to take their nephew and niece into their household is as "real and factual" to them as her brother's death – there was no question about it. It is part of the taken-for-granted structure of reality, the reality of an extended family of which they are members, with a determined place in the organization of the kinship group and clear duties that attend it. This is all the more striking because of the very different interpretation of the rule "always put the family first" adopted by the majority of the interviewees, who prioritize the needs of nuclear family members over other kin. Indeed, Mrs Laburnum would "leave the country" if faced with her parents' need for care.

Yet Mr and Mrs Elder "normalize" their exceptional situation (as the only extended-family household in the sample) by reference to "family", as if this term had the same meaning to them as to all others. The experience of the "externality and constraint" of morality – in this case the overwhelming force of their obligations to kin – is described by the use of a term that can serve their rhetorical purposes because of its "indexical" qualities; its meaning is very indeterminate out of context. Thus, when Mr and Mrs Elder experience their kinship duty as emanating from outside themselves (in society or a moral sphere), they are able to interpret their responsibilities, using a discourse of "family" as a cultural resource to account for their decision, even though it flouts the moral priorities of the majority of the couples, who have no local kin.

By contrast, Mr Spruce and Ms Blackthorn, who have recently started to live together, account for the consequences of this decision for their children in terms of the rights and needs of the individual. Until recently, Mr Spruce has been living alone, having separated from his wife and (teenage) children, while Ms Blackthorn has for several years been a lone parent of two younger children, following divorce. Here they describe the aftermath of their decision that he should move into Ms Blackthorn's household.

Ms Blackthorn: The children obviously take longer, because you're not the natural father, whom they do see, and because I was on my own with them for four years. So that takes longer. There's no resentment, but it takes longer to establish the position in the household, if you like, or how things are going to work.

Mr Spruce: We did talk.

Ms Blackthorn: We've talked a lot about that, haven't we.

Mr Spruce: Well it's very important both for my children, as well as Emma's, that they accept that we have requirements and desires as well, but also that we are considering them within the plan of things. So, we took Alex [her son] out . . .

Ms Blackthorn: . . . When you were going to move [in], and talked to him about it, and told him what we were going to do and why. Or to a degree, as far as we knew. It was actually conscious to tell him and to include him in at the beginning. And likewise you did with yours.

Q: Was there a difference in the way different ones reacted or did it work out the same?

Ms Blackthorn: I wasn't there when you told yours, it took longer.

Mr Spruce: Well, you can see reactions. They all react differently, I think, it is very difficult to define exactly the way they do react, but they react differently. I don't think there's any resentment or any feeling from my children, and indeed they all get on very well.

Ms Blackthorn: I think also the fact that it's a different set of circumstances for my children, because they were used to Tom coming over in the evenings and it built up gradually [. . .] Whereas Tom's children obviously, certainly initially, you told them about it before we met in fact, didn't you?

Mr Spruce: Mm [. . .]

Q: If you had to give a kind of mini-advice [manual] to step-parents, as it was, what would it be? What would the first principle be, do you think?

Ms Blackthorn: Honesty. I think you have to be honest about what's going on. And I don't know about yours so much but I think with Alex living in it the whole time, it was important for him to know where he stood in it all, and that we were very aware of the fact that it's his home, he has the right to comment and the right to say he doesn't like something.

Mr Spruce: In my direction, it's very much an encroachment on territory and relationships, that for my children it's not so much . . . you know, they've come here. It's more, as you said, once they get to teenagers, it's like taking them away from something, like friends or something, when they come over, and there's that whole issue.

Q: But what about Alex, you've invited him to comment and to say if there's anything he didn't like. Has he?

Ms Blackthorn: He's made odd comments. They came out initially when we talked to him.

Mr Spruce: Yes, we did say that certainly I wasn't attempting to replace his father, and indeed I don't like the word step-parent. He calls me Tom and we have a relationship, which is fine. It's not a parental relationship, albeit that we talk about things that fathers and sons talk about. But I can never be Alex's father, and I never seek to be. I think that was our initial approach to Alex.

Ms Blackthorn: And he needed to understand that. He needed to put

91

in place his father, and you, I think. His father's remarried and has
a new family, so there was that to consider. Because he has a step-
mother and a new family there. So that was all tying in as well.

(Mr Spruce and Ms Blackthorn, 48–50)

Compared with Mr and Mrs Elder's account of their family crisis, this
is a long, careful and reflective version of how Mr Spruce and Ms Blackthorn
have handled their new situation. Focusing on the different needs of the
individuals in the situation, they use a discourse of rights and needs to
show how these were taken into account in the reconstitution of the household. Far from working within a taken-for-granted definition of the "family", they demonstrate their concern to renegotiate "family" rôles and
norms, redefining their mutual obligations and commitments and the
implications of their special circumstances. They "do morality" by a form
of empathic discussion of feelings: individuals are constructed in terms of
their "requirements and desires" (Mr Spruce), and "the right to comment
and the right to say he doesn"t like something" (Ms Blackthorn).

Although quite different from the form of moral regulation practised by
the Elders, the morality seems equally powerful. Mr Spruce and Ms
Blackthorn's account is impressive because of its scrupulous concern about
the individual feelings of all involved (cf. Mr Larch's jokey irreverence in his
version of reconstituting a household, p. 58). Their respect for the dignity
(even sanctity) of the individual child or adult seems as powerfully felt and
as obligatory as the Elders' sense of "family" solidarity. The requirements,
desires and rights attributed to the individuals in their situation are as
factual and real to them as their kinship responsibilities are to Mr and Mrs
Elder. Reality and morality are one and the same.

What we seem to be seeing here is something stronger and more morally compelling than a description of the personal choices of two adults
and how they then squared these with their children. It is the *moral commitment to choice*, and hence to the morality of individualism as a collective system, collectively enforced. This form of moral regulation presup-
poses a "moral something",[23] whose force is reflected in this passage – a
strongly felt commitment to the individual as "sacred" and entitled to the
consideration, support, empathy and consultation described in this account, which is the "other side" of personal choice and "making something
of oneself". It is because the circumstances are so unusual that these aspects of the morality of individualism become quite explicit.

The final instance of a "non-standard" household is that of the Oaks and
Teaks, two couples who share a house. Friends for many years (Mr Oak and

Mr Teak went to school together), they decided to buy a house jointly and merge their households when they were living as close neighbours in another town.

Mr Oak: It's just the people we happened to be closest to at the time, and loved, and it just got a bit ridiculous. We were seeing them a lot, doing a lot of things with them, sharing two allotments, in and out of each other's houses, taking [children's] bedding from house to house, which I think was a kind of image which got a bit stupid – we thought this is crazy, carrying beds between houses, why don't we actually [live together]?   (Mr and Mrs Oak, 29)

The two couples account for their decision, and their present lifestyle in a large house in the city, in terms of a discourse of practical advantages and advantages in terms of relationships. The choice of sharing with another couple is reconstructed as making the "richer" experiences available for adults and children through the multiplicity of others.

Mr Teak: I was keen on the richness that may come from living in close proximity with another family who I was very fond of, and had a lot in common with. There was quite a lot of buzz about our relationships and about ideas we have in common – ideas on how you brought up children, ideas on how you wanted to live your life in terms of work.

Q: Could you perhaps say what these ideas are? [. . .]

Mr Teak: Well I think one of the big things that attracted me to living together was that although we were both happy in our nuclear families, one of the weaknesses of the nuclear family is that it isn't in any wider setting. It's the little boxes, as the song goes. And your next-door neighbour, sometimes, I mean emotionally in terms of your own day-to-day life can be a million miles away. One of the great things about living with another couple, especially if they like yourself are happy to bring the feelings out in the front, is that you get a different perspective on yourself. [. . .] I think that's very important, the same for children as they grow up – being able to have perspectives from other adults or our own children. And sometimes that can be quite refreshing – I'm not saying it can't sometimes be a bit painful, it can – but I think it can be refreshing as well.

(Mr and Mrs Teak, 31–2)

They are asked about how they make household decisions – is it different from the way a couple living on their own decide things?

Mr Oak: . . . It's just that it may take longer; there's more negotiation but the same care, consideration, love, affection. The same things come in, the same respect for self and individuality, but the same sense of having to respond to the fact that you're not an island.

Mrs Oak: There's that sort of level of consultation, isn't there? I mean you and I in our marriage consult about what either of us wants to do individually, and we consult collectively.

(Mr and Mrs Oak, 33)

Mr Teak: I don't think that a lot of the time we actually proceed with our decision making in any different way from when there was just you and I. It's more complicated with four, and there's more viewpoints and feelings.

Mrs Teak: This would probably frustrate a lot of people, because basically we do all have more sort of . . . I don't know how to express it . . . but we're not always thinking of number one, I mean your own needs, and you are more aware of other people around and how you fit in with them before you act.

(Mr and Mrs Teak, 36)

Here we can recognize the same moral commitments as in Mr Spruce and Ms Blackthorn's accounts – to "care, consideration, love, affection", "self and individuality" (Mr Oak) and "your own needs, and [being] aware of other people" (Mrs Teak) – but deployed to describe the enhanced possibilities of the dual-couple household. They use the cultural resources of individualism – the discourses of a developmental self that respects the feelings and desires of others – to account for their choice of an unusual living unit. The moral force of these commitments seems to be experienced as equally binding, but these same elements are woven into a description of how they can find better expression in a dual-couple household. Mr and Mrs Oak insist that their mutual moral obligations are stronger than would be the case in a "commune".

Mrs Oak: I always think of communes as being bigger too, a few more people . . .

Mr Oak: And coming and going, and the flexibility to move out and move in. I think we'd made a fairly clear decision – that doesn't mean

94

we were inflexible. We always said that if we have to move apart, we'll do that, but we'll make sure we do it well, and that there's nothing left hanging over. There wasn't the freedom to come and go, it was quite a powerful commitment.

(Mr and Mrs Oak, 31)

This passage makes explicit the discursive moral regulation of this "non-standard" household. Within their membership, they have developed a shared practice, within which it is possible to say that things are done "well", and the members experience a strong (external) constraint arising from their "powerful commitment" to each other. Yet they reject the "ideology connected to communes" (Mr Oak), and instead equate their household with a "family".

Mrs Oak: It's a bit like families living together [. . .]

Mr Oak: It's more like a family, I think.

Mrs Oak: Because we know someone else who's done it with brothers and sisters, haven't we, and the other generations, and that feels more like what we're doing.

(Mr and Mrs Oak, 30)

Drawing on the cultural resources of wider society, they assimilate their account of their household to the standard ones of "family": it is like a family, only *better*, *richer*, and more *refreshing* – it provides a "buzz" for relationships, and a mirror for selves, that is lacking in nuclear family households. Hence the rhetoric of individualism and the family is deployed in an original way and transformed so as to provide a new and wider "setting" (Mr Teak) for these relationships.

Conclusions

In this chapter we have analyzed the way in which these interviewees interpret the moral requirements of individualism in their practical decisions. By examining how terms like "career" and "family" are used in the accounts, we conclude that interpretative repertoires made up of indexical expressions allow stability and moral regulation to be maintained in ambiguous, fluid and unpredictable contexts. The moral accountability adopted by the interviewees provides a sense of real and binding obligation, though their versions are cobbled together out of these plastic cultural artefacts. People in situations of great potential stress and disruption are able to make artful use of these repertoires to make their lives orderly and "normal". They use concepts like "career" and "family" to describe the elements of their projects and commitments – to self-development and to others. Having thus ordered and regulated themselves and each other, they give accounts from within these constraints, experienced as real and obligatory. This applies to "career" women's versions of the tension between their jobs and their children's needs (the demands of two rival imperatives of work and family), as well as to the moral force of commitments to the "sacred" rights of beloved others, experienced by members of "non-standard" households.

What does this tell us about social order? Surely not that interviewees achieve stability in their relationships by aligning themselves with moral rules and norms. If this were so, it would be hard to understand how Mr and Mrs Elder are able to provide an apparently supportive and enabling home for their nephew (now at university) and niece by such radically different interpretations of "family" obligations from the apparently equally successful parenting of Mr Spruce and Ms Blackthorn. Nor would it be easy to understand how the heretical Mr Larch has managed to remain on such good terms with his six children by three different partnerships, and why he gives daily care to his elderly mother. Above all, it would not explain how all these respondents are able to give accounts from within a common framework of moral individualism, telling us what they had made of themselves and how they had put the family first.

Rather, it suggests that the kind of order produced by these interviewees is the *sui generis* order of Durkheim's moral reality and of the ethnomethodologists' artful practices. In most of the accounts, this is largely the unnoticed, taken-for-granted order of normal appearances, never questioned because it is as "real and factual" as familiar everyday objects. Yet for these interviewees in non-standard situations, the double jeopardy of the interview or the manifestly unusual nature of their household arrangements call forth an account of how their particular relationships are regulated. In producing their versions of this, they reveal the practices of moral regulation that also sustain "standard" relations.

In the next part of the book, we will look at how agents like these – selves produced in interactional ritual, accomplishing morally adequate narratives of their decisions through artful practices that order and stabilize their experiences of external reality – co-ordinate these choices. In what sense can such decisions be described as *rational* or *strategic*? What is their relevance for the economic theory of decision making?

References

1. For instance, L. Wittgenstein, *Philosophical investigations* (London: Macmillan, 1953).
2. For instance, T. Parsons, *The structure of social action* (1937; New York: Free Press, 1968), especially pp. 312–20.
3. H. Garfinkel, *Studies in ethnomethodology* (Englewood Cliffs, NJ: Prentice-Hall, 1967).
4. Wittgenstein, *Philosophical investigations*.
5. D. Sudnow, *Passing on: the social organisation of dying* (Englewood Cliffs, NJ: Prentice-Hall, 1967).
6. E. Bittner, "The police on skid row: a study in peace keeping", *American Sociological Review* **32** (1965), 699–715.
7. Ibid.
8. R. A. Hilbert, *The classical roots of ethnomethodology: Durkheim, Weber and Garfinkel* (Chapel Hill, NC: University of North Carolina Press, 1992), pp. 56–7.
9. Ibid., Ch. 2. See E. Durkheim, *The rules of sociological method* (1895; New York: Free Press, 1938), pp. 14–46.
10. E. Durkheim, *The division of labour in society* (1893; New York: Free Press, 1933).
11. Ibid., p. 228.
12. M. Wetherell & J. Potter, "Discourse analysis and the identification of interpretative repertoires", in *Analysing everyday explanation*, C. Antaki (ed.), 168–83 (London: Sage, 1988).
13. Ibid., pp. 171–2.
14. Garfinkel, *Studies in ethnomethodology*, pp. 4–7.
15. J. Martin & C. Roberts, *Women and employment: a lifetime perspective* (London: Department of Employment, 1984); C. Marsh, *Hours of work of women and men in Britain* (London: Equal Opportunities Commission, HMSO, 1991).
16. A. Giddens, *Modernity and self-identity: self and society in the late modern age* (Oxford: Polity, 1991), Ch. 3.
17. Ibid., pp. 85–8.
18. S. Yeandle, *Women's working lives: patterns and strategies* (London: Tavistock, 1984).
19. J. Brannen & P. Moss, *Managing mothers: dual earner households after maternity leave* (London: Unwin Hyman, 1991).
20. M. G. Boulton, *On being a mother: a study of women with pre-school children* (London: Tavistock, 1982).
21. J. F. Gubrium, "The family as project"; J. Bernardes, "'Family ideology': identification and exploration", *Sociological Review* **33** (4) (1985), 679–702.
22. Durkheim, *The division of labour in society*.
23. Ibid., pp. 200–29. See also R. Collins, "On the microfoundations of macrosociology", *American Journal of Sociology* **86** (1981), 984–1014; A. Giddens, *Capitalism and modern social theory* (Cambridge: Cambridge University Press, 1971), pp. 88–9.

PART II: DECISIONS

CHAPTER 5

Co-ordination, Co-operation
and Bargaining

In the second part of the book, we shift the focus from the agents giving these accounts to the decisions they describe. How are couples' decisions co-ordinated? In what sense can these be said to be *rational* choices? How important is what agents *say* about how they decided, when survey evidence can tell us what they *do*? How do they combine calculative and normative reasoning? How do power and resistance to it influence decisions?

The new dimension for this part of our analysis is provided by economic theory. Microeconomics has forged one of the most powerful tools of present-day social science – rational choice theory. By viewing social actors as economizing agents, all seeking to maximize utility under constraint, theorists of this school have invaded the territory of family sociology, social policy, political science and international relations, supplying elegant and persuasive models to explain decisions. Becker's hypothesis that "a person decides to marry when the utility expected from marriage exceeds that expected from staying single or for an additional search for a more suitable mate"[1] encapsulates this hard-nosed and rigorous approach to the analysis of human relations. Rational choice theory postulates an ideal-type situation in which each individual has fully ordered preferences, complete information and perfect skill in computing as the limiting case of rational social action, defined by Weber as that which "takes account of the behaviour of others and is thereby orientated in its course".[2] What can such an approach tell us about the decision making of the couples we interviewed?

The key theoretical issue for this chapter is the status of this form of explanation in relation to the sociological analysis of agents, accounts and moral regulation that was developed in Part I. Clearly rational choice theory is an abstraction[3] from that rather cobbled-together, do-it-yourself order of

100

everyday interaction; yet equally clearly the interviewees aspired to portray themselves as some kind of rational economic agents, even (as we shall see) in their relationships with their partners. On the one hand, the assumptions that allow theorists to model social life as games played by bargain-hunting individuals with common knowledge are overtly unrealistic; yet on the other hand flesh-and-blood interviewees seemed at some points to be lining up their decisions with this austere model.

The ideal-type world of rational choice might be compared to a decoy duck:[4] it doesn't look much like a duck, and certainly doesn't behave like a duck (except that it floats) yet despite its artificial features, real ducks "adopt" it as if it were a duck. In a similar way, interviewees seemed attract-ed to economic discourse and to use it to legitimate their decisions, albeit somewhat selectively. Perhaps, then, its assumptions about human agents are more descriptively accurate than they at first appear, since the whole model has impressive success in prediction and explanatory power. Our aim in this part of the book is to identify its strengths and where it needs to be supplemented by other theoretical analyses, which rely on evidence such as our research study.

In this chapter we will introduce rational choice and game theory by analyzing how couples co-ordinated their decisions. First of all, we will see whether it is possible to provide a game-theoretical explanation of how they formed households and arrived at their particular configurations over working hours, the domestic division of labour, housing arrangements, the number and spacing of children, the timing of retirement and so on, given their different preference schedules in these matters. In view of the fact that all, as good individualists, took responsibility for what they made of themselves in the public and domestic spheres, and described their deci-sions as *choices*, how did they take account of each others' actions, and steer their own accordingly?

Starting from abstract theoretical models of such problems in the form of games, we go on in the next section to look at examples of interviewees describing these problems of co-ordination as they arise in their lives and how they "solve" them. We show that their versions of decisions refer to "bargaining" and "pay-offs" in terms that sound like those of the theory, but that these are considerably modified by other discourses, which do much to transform the apparent adoption of the model.

Games and decisions

A central puzzle for our research was how couples decided on their shared, joint lifestyles, particularly in relation to living together and getting married, hours of paid and unpaid work, responsibility for domestic chores, when to have children (and how many), where to live, when to retire, and so on. The research invited them to account for their situations in all these matters, both as individuals and as couples (through the joint interviews); we wanted to see how what they said about their decisions in the individual interviews translated into a "joint" account of them. We were particularly interested in whether they identified "strategies"[5] for co-operation and co-ordination as a couple, and how they reached agreement over what to do and who should do it.

All these questions are crucial for the social scientific study of rationality and decision making, an area strongly contested between economics and the other major disciplines. Survey evidence repeatedly shows patterns that require explanation – the predominance of couple households, of full-time employment for men and part-time for women, smaller families, the rise in owner-occupation, the shorter working life. Although there are well known demand-side, structural, policy and other factors (such as employers' preferences for married women part-time labour to increase "flexibility" and reduce non-wage costs,[6] tax incentives for owner-occupation, early retirement schemes,[7] and so on), there are still important questions about why individuals and households behave as they do in response to the opportunities and constraints these present.

Two-thirds of our sample of households contained a man in full-time employment or self-employment and a woman in part-time work, a reflection of the British population in this income group at this stage of the life cycle.[8] All were owner-occupiers. The average number of children in their households was 2.1. How can we explain the predominance of these patterns, yet go on to understand the individual variations, such as the couple who had done a "rôle swap" (Mr and Mrs Palm), the two couples who shared a house and pooled their resources (Mr and Mrs Oak and Mr and Mrs Teak), or those who had large families (Mr Larch was the father of six children by three of his four relationships)?

In recent years, both game-theoretical[9] and strategic[10] explanations of these phenomena have been developed. One way to evaluate the explanatory power of these models is to set out the decisions facing the interviewees during their life course in the form of games. We will then go on to look at interviewees' accounts of how they co-ordinate decisions and plan for the future, to compare them with the model's explanations.

Jack and Jill are both intelligent young people, with some education and job-relevant training (among the 28 couples who indicated their level of educational attainment, 17 men and 16 women had degrees or equivalent, 2 men and 3 women had "A" levels, and 5 men and 6 women had 2 or more "O" levels). Let us suppose that they meet at college or during professional training, just when they are deciding what employment path to follow, what kind of accommodation to take, whether to live alone or with others, and whether (and when) to have children. Both know that marriage has a one in three chance of ending in divorce in its first 20 years, according to recent British statistics.[11] Both must make these long-term decisions under conditions of great uncertainty: they cannot reliably know in advance about their own future health or that of their partner, the market value of their abilities, future overall or specific demand for labour, and so on. How can we represent their options on all these issues as a game, so as to capture the essential decisions to be made and the possible bargains to be struck between them as they consider whether or not to form a partnership?

For the purposes of the kind of game to be explored here, we must assume that Jack and Jill already have well formed and consistently ordered preferences over employment, income at various stages of the life cycle, housing arrangements, age of retirement, and so on. Let us imagine that Jack's first preference is to be a solicitor, to live in a modern, labour-saving house by the sea, to have one child, to reach a peak of household income of £35,000 at age 35 and then maintain this, and to retire at 55. Jill would most like to be an accountant, to live in an old house in town, to have three children, to have incremental increases in household income till the age of 60, and to retire at 65. Jack and Jill have other preferences on all these issues, and each has attached to it a "pay-off" – the gain or loss in terms of utility that they would accrue from each outcome, represented as a score.

One way of representing each of the particular decisions – over employment, income, housing, children, etc. – is as a Prisoner's Dilemma game. In this kind of game, the "co-operative" outcome is hard to reach, because individuals stand to gain a higher pay-off from their first ("selfish") preference. For illustration, Figure 5.1 shows such a game over accommodation: Jack likes living in his flat in a modern house by the sea (pay-off 3) and hates the idea of moving into Jill's flat in an old house in the city (pay-off 0); Jill has exactly the opposite preferences. Because Jill cannot rely on

Jack to give in his notice on his flat if she does so first (and vice versa), they seem destined to continue to live separately (even though this is their worst option – each will get a pay-off of 1 if they stay put). They cannot move together into a new flat in neutral territory (pay-off 2 for each), which is the best overall solution in terms of total utility, because if either decided to move it would pay the other not to move. Hence the Nash equilibrium in the game (the point at which neither can improve on his or her pay-off by choosing otherwise) is that they stay bleakly apart (pay-off 1,1).

	Jill Move	Stay
Jack Move	2, 2	0, 3
Stay	3, 0	1, 1

Figure 5.1 A Prisoner's Dilemma.
In each quarter read the first figure as Jack's payoff, and the second as Jill's.

There is some evidence from the interviews of situations like this occurring within partnerships. Mr and Mrs Ash (who happen to be a solicitor and an accountant respectively) do not find it easy to agree over household tasks, child care and do-it-yourself:

Mr Ash: We have two opposing views of how we should approach unpaid work. Megan's view is, where Megan enjoys gardening and DIY [. . .] and [. . .] my view [. . .] is the complete opposite, where I don't like DIY, don't like gardening, all the other chores, and therefore you might as well get some one in to do it.

Q: Oh, now that's interesting.

Mrs Ash: Yes, I think Mark would like to spend minimal time at home maintaining the house, let alone improving it, maintaining it.

Mr Ash: I see my time outside work as leisure time, rather than having to do things I'd rather not do.

Mrs Ash: Whereas I certainly see gardening, I enjoy it, but it's still hard work, so I prefer to share some of it, but Mark then says "Oh, you're enjoying yourself", which I find hard work if I'm digging away or whatever. So yes, we do tend to agree less on this than anything else.
(Mr and Mrs Ash, 15–16)

Mrs Ash here indicates her willingness to find a co-operative solution to the problem of the chores (sharing them), but Mr Ash will quickly exploit her willingness to do any of it, turning the outcome from a small pay-off for both (2, 2) to a big one for him and a negative one for her – in the form of "hard work" and tiredness (3, 0). However, she has indicated earlier that she does not find his proposed compromise – "getting someone in to do it" – acceptable, because such tasks can (in moderation) be "quite fun". So the likely outcome is that the house will remain undecorated and the garden uncultivated (1, 1). Because they are both after the big pay-off (Mr Ash's "leisure", Mrs Ash's "fun"), the outcome is the worst for both – a mess.

Prisoner's Dilemmas are notoriously a feature of any game-theoretical analysis of social relations. They are a good way to state the fundamental issue about any form of co-operation – how does it get started? In the case of a partnership, given different preferences over such fundamental issues, the question posed by the Prisoner's Dilemma is how single people form households.

So Jack and Jill would have difficulty in getting started as a couple if all these decisions were best represented as Prisoner's Dilemmas. But a more likely configuration of preferences and outcomes (given their mutual attraction) is the aptly-named "Battle of the Sexes". Here Jack and Jill enjoy each other's company so much that their original preferences are modified because of the high value they put on living together. Jack would now rather move to an old house (pay-off 1) with Jill than a new one alone (pay-off −1), because (*pace* Mr Ash) he prefers sharing the do-it-yourself to a life of lonely leisure – even though his first choice would be that they both move to a new house (pay-off 2). Conversely, Jill would rather move to a new house with Jack (pay-off 1) than to an old one on her own (pay-off −1), even if it means some interesting interior design projects (which she could undertake if they both moved to an old house – pay-off 2) have to be sacrificed. The issue is which of the two simultaneous moves to choose, and again the result may be stalemate.

		Jill	
		Move to old house	Move to new house
Jack	Move to old house	1, 2	−1, −1
	Move to new house	−1, −1	2, 1

Figure 5.2 A "Battle of the Sexes".

The options and pay-offs could thus be represented as in Figure 5.2

Here the difficulty is over which of two possible Nash equilibria, each giving the same overall utility (but each favouring one over the other), they are to choose. There are many more examples of this kind of situation in the interviews (see, for instance, Mr and Mrs Hemlock, pp. 27–8). Dr and Mrs Conifer were living happily in Scotland when he applied unsuccessfully for promotion in his department. He then faced a dilemma: he very much wanted the promotion, but Mrs Conifer did not want to leave her job, their house, or the group of friends she had. As he put it in his interview, "the chances of another one [job] coming up were remote, and I couldn't see any more in Scotland either, so [. . .] I applied . . . for several posts in England" (p. 11). Mrs Conifer was at the time "having a very good spell [. . .] working half time and a small baby who still slept a lot" (p. 45). When Dr Conifer was offered his senior post in this city, she was quite clear about her reaction.

Mrs Conifer: Well, I didn't want . . . well there's no doubt about the fact that I didn't want to move to [city]. I can remember when he 'phoned me to tell me he had the job I really felt quite sick because I didn't . . . it certainly was not something I wanted to do [. . .].

Dr Conifer: I think you have to put yourself into the position of professional people who had been in a place for eight years. There was nowhere forward for us there. We could have stayed there but we would have become the same as . . . there were people in the department who had been there too long.

Mrs Conifer: This is true.

Dr Conifer: And we knew what we felt about them, and we didn't want to become that way.   (Dr and Mrs Conifer, 65–6)

Later, Mrs Conifer adds, "Personally I didn't want to move, but the logic was inescapable I suppose really" (p. 68) and "I think that surely all through a partnership you make decisions [. . .] you don't particularly go along with" (p. 70). This sounds like saying that, even though she "lost" this Battle of the Sexes (her husband's first preference for promotion got priority over her preference for their house and lifestyle in Scotland), being together in partnership was the most important thing for them. Hence it is an example of a pay-off of 2, 1 in the man's favour.

The important question, of course, is then to consider how often this kind of decision works out to the advantage to the man. Game theory has difficulties in showing how *power* is exercised in such situations. Dr Conifer had a *career*; Mrs Conifer did not. She describes herself as having been in "a weak bargaining position" (p. 68). Furthermore, she was taking account of potential long-term *negative* pay-offs in their partnership when she added, "you don't want [. . .] to live with somebody who can throw it back at you and say, 'You stopped me doing that'"(p. 70).

This draws attention to the long-term nature of partnership: it is a *lifetime* strategy, not merely a child-rearing one. Mrs Conifer's weak position may be temporary, during the children's dependence. If she can put up with the move to England, whatever the short-term losses for herself, not only will he be happier and more congenial, but also his eventual pension will be larger, and they may be able to move back to Scotland for their retirement. The success of the strategy can be finally judged only at the postretirement stage. Strategies will be discussed in the next section.

Finally, there may be other situations – notably over tiresome household work – that can best be represented as a "Chicken Game". Take the example of cleaning: Jack and Jill both have full-time jobs and neither enjoys chores. Hence they would each prefer that the other did all the cleaning. The worst outcome for both would be that the house became so dirty as to be unhygienic. However, each has enough to gain from the other doing the cleaning to try to put off the evil hour (when it *must* be done) to the last possible moment, in the hope that the other will crack first, and do it. The danger is that both leave it till too late. This can be represented as in Figure 5.3.

	Jill	
	Clean	Don't clean
Jack Clean	1, 1	0, 3
Don't clean	3, 0	−3, −3

Figure 5.3 A "Chicken Game".

Exactly such a situation was reported by several of the interviewees over issues of cleaning and washing up. Here Mr and Mrs Linden describe how she came to do most of the cleaning when they were first married.

Mrs Linden: Leo [. . .] says, "Oh it doesn't matter."

Mr Linden: Yes, it's not that I wouldn't do it . . .

Mrs Linden: "Oh don't worry, it doesn't matter, it doesn't matter whether people notice it's a tip". But I say, "Ahhh . . . !"

Mr Linden: Yes, but it's a perception of a tip, isn't it? I wouldn't not do it out of malice, I just wouldn't do it this week, or today, or whatever way you want to . . .

(Mr and Mrs Linden, 74–5)

However, this was not the end of the story. Eventually, Mr and Mrs Linden made what they described as a "bargain" or "contract" under which she had children (which was not his first preference), gave up her job and did *all* the housework, while he worked longer hours. In the long term the game was about *rôles* rather than *tasks*.

Bargaining strategies

Thus both Battle of the Sexes and Chicken games capture some elements in the decisions that shape the day-to-day lives of the couples we interviewed, but they omit other crucial ones, particularly the processes of *bargaining* mentioned by both Mrs Conifer and Mrs Linden. Game theory tries to represent this aspect of social relations though the notion of a "supergame" – a series of repeated games between the same two players.

Here the Nash equilibrium solution is the one in which each player's *strategy* (pattern of choices over a long sequence of moves) is the best possible reply to the other's. Each can achieve the highest overall pay-off if the players can find dependable ways of responding to each other's choices and minimizing mutually frustrating defections ("bargains") within the rules of the rational choice game (no communication except through the moves themselves).

Thus for instance a Chicken supergame can be "solved" if, by signalling willingness to co-operate in sharing tasks (by opening with a "clean" move in the series), Jack and Jill can establish a reliable pattern of non-defection; and Battle of the Sexes supergame players can establish a stable co-operation by "taking turns" on alternate plays to allow each other's first preferences. Even Prisoner's Dilemma, the hardest game to "solve", has been shown by the political scientist Robert Axelrod to be capable of producing systematic supergame co-operation by a strategy of "Tit for Tat", where any defection from the initial co-operative move is immediately and minimally "punished" by a single retaliatory defection, before resuming co-operation.[12] This has been claimed to demonstrate how people (and animals) establish stable social relations over time, since Tit for Tat is the most "successful" strategy in such a supergame, even when played against a whole range of cunningly exploitative or sneakily unreliable rivals.

However, we have already seen some of the reasons why these "solutions" may not be so readily achievable. Both Battle of the Sexes and Chicken supergame co-operative equilibria can be sabotaged by "precommitment" on the part of one player. In the case of Dr Conifer, his (or perhaps *their*) commitment to his career meant that he *had* to move to England: Mrs Conifer commented that "the logic was inescapable, I suppose" and hence that she was in "a weak bargaining position". If having a "career" gives men a precommitment in many of these partnership decisions that can be represented as Battles of the Sexes, then taking turns is ruled out. This indeed was a feature of the relations between partners among our interviewees: once a man established a career, and a woman left hers to have a baby, then his preferences (especially relating to employment) seemed to take priority.

Indeed, when women define "being supportive" in partnership, it is usually in terms of their partner's career. As with Mrs Conifer, Mrs Hemlock and Mrs Pine (see p. 86), this involves the subordination of women's employment choices, and willingness to move to new areas for the sake of the man's career and also to take domestic pressures off their partners. Mrs Ash explains her reaction when her husband's career advancement was made conditional on a move to this city from where they were living and she was working previously.

Mrs Ash: I can remember you [husband] saying, "Oh well, shall I throw him back the partnership [in solicitors' firm] if we don't want to move then?" and I obviously said, "Don't be so silly!"

Q: Why did you say that? [. . .]

Mrs Ash: Well, because it's far more important for Mark to get on [. . .] it was never serious that we'd do anything else but move. It was just a bit aggravating, having to adjust to moving again . . .

(Mr and Mrs Ash, 10)

However, choice of a house and schools for children could give women a counter precommitment on certain other decisions (see Mr and Mrs Hazel, pp. 134–5). The overall pattern of relationships suggests that men's careers gave male-orientated decisions a dominant status. "Taking turns" was used as a strategy only in one household, Mr and Mrs Palm, who alternated over career moves and over household tasks and child care; in the others where men had anything like successful careers, women accommodated their decisions to them.

Nearly all the women interviewees say they chose the *rôle* of mother out of preference rather than convention or subservience. Mrs Linden is a good example of this: she claims that the solution that she and her husband have adopted to the Chicken supergame over chores and child care is one in which both achieve a 2, 2 solution. This is because the division of labour (his career, her rôle as full-time mother) is in fact a co-operative compromise: each gets a reasonable deal.

Mrs Linden: Yes, I don't begrudge you a career.

Mr Linden: Yes, I'm saying it in the sense of you don't begrudge being at home [. . .] You made it clear that you wanted children, and I made it . . . I was honest, I think, and said, well children weren't on my list of things to do in life, but I didn't feel, given the opportunity, given the option of having Rachel and children as opposed to being on my own, or going for someone else, then I took the view of, it's have Rachel, and if you have children you have children. Because when you get married you don't know that you're definitely both fertile and so forth, so that's a gamble.

Mrs Linden: I agreed you wouldn't have to change smelly nappies.

(Mr and Mrs Linden, 68–9)

The rôle division of career man and home-based woman is thus represented as a contractual solution to the supergame, with both parties precommitted to their separate spheres, at least until the children are at school. Mr and Mrs Linden are unusual in spelling out that this was a "deal" or "bargain" between them from the start of their partnership and in doing so in somewhat game-theoretical terms. But some other couples talked – slightly jokingly – about why they would not be willing to "take turns" over careers and domesticity, in terms of a similar precommitment. Mr Beech is a full-time solicitor; his wife works part time, also as a solicitor. They are asked about the idea of a rôle swap, which he had mentioned in his interview; at first he claims he is keen.

Mr Beech: Well, I reckon I would have a serious go at it.

Mrs Beech: No chance [. . .]

Q: Why wouldn't you give him the chance?

Mrs Beech: What, to sit at home while I went out to work? Well, because I'm probably onto a winner, you know. Basically because society accepts the fact that women stay at home, the man goes out to work, and as long as that traditional rôle is established, I would like to sit around [. . .]

Q: Would you consider moving to another job?

Mr Beech: Yes, I would consider it; I haven't really thought about it at the moment, but I think that long-term wise I find it difficult to imagine for the next 25 years or so, I remain a solicitor in private practice [. . .]

Q: That would mean leaving the profession? [. . .] Would you go out looking for it?

Mr Beech: Not at the moment because the children are very young, and the business . . . I can't afford to sort of dabble with everyone else's lives . . .

(Mr and Mrs Beech, 7)

Here Mr and Mrs Beech give very different reasons for precommitment – hers love of leisure, his concern for his family's welfare – but from the point of view of game theory this is irrelevant. Although he talks of a rôle swap (i.e. taking turns), he then makes it clear that he is precommitted to a rôle of main family earner, just as she is to one of main provider of child care.

But Mrs Redwood, a trained teacher, did not choose the rôle of mother and care-giver; she says it was thrust upon her, because her husband (also a solicitor) moved to this city, where she had no employment opportunity.

Mrs Redwood: I felt really fed up when I just didn't get a job. Yes, I was frustrated and I think basically that's why I had my first child when I did.

Q: You didn't not go into teaching because the first child was on the way?

Mrs Redwood: Oh no, no. I had my child because I couldn't get a job basically. And I felt fairly fed up about the whole thing because we were newly married and we had a mortgage, and [. . .] I mean, this is what I've struggled to get through college, etc., all for nothing.

(Mrs Redwood, 4)

Here we have Mrs Redwood apparently saying that her husband's precommitment to his career means that she cannot ever get her first preference in a Battle of the Sexes supergame, and that this was why she adopted the rôle of mother at this early stage of their marriage. However, in the joint interview she makes it clear that she has much invested in his career – she says that she is "in a blind panic" at the fall in his firm's profits that year (see pp. 162–3).

If we are to explain the co-ordination of choices between these couples in terms of bargaining strategies, this must be seen in a *life-time* perspective. Perhaps partnership can be analyzed as a Battle of the Sexes supergame, with each partner's strategy the best reply to the other's; but this only works if we recognize that the pay-offs change at different stages of the life cycle. The woman may settle for lower pay-offs during the children's dependence, so long as she can rely on higher pay-offs at the retirement stage – in other words, the couple "take turns" between the two Nash equilibria in the supergame, not between plays but between *series of plays at different life cycle periods*. This would then explain their rôles within the domestic division of labour, as well as particular decisions at points along the way, as best replies to each other's strategies in terms of overall household utility.

Explaining and understanding

Game theory seems to be offering us an elegant and persuasive way of formulating the kinds of decisions being described in the interviews with these couples. If we take them to be *rational agents*, with the abilities to order any set of options and to predict the probability of any outcome, and perfect knowledge of each other's preferences, then they are able to absorb such issues as love, sympathy, parental duty and ambition into their calculations as part of their pay-offs, and simply act so as to maximize their "utils". This fits Mr and Mrs Linden's account quite neatly: his knowledge of her liking for children and domesticity and her knowledge of his career aspirations and aversion to nappies were the basis of their contract, involving a rational "gamble" (in his words) that they would be fertile, he would make career progress, and so on. The idea of a supergame allows us to see them both making strategic decisions in relation to each other's preferences over the life cycle; later in the interview they can discuss and predict future moves of jobs and homes, and even retirement, on something like this basis.

However, doubts at once creep in. If their relationship is really to be analyzed in terms of such calculative factors, does it have built into it an allowance for the probability of divorce – a one in three chance in actuarial terms? In giving up her very successful career (she was a teacher and then a manager in industry) in favour of full-time motherhood, has Mrs Linden included a prediction of her husband's fidelity and reliability, and does she have a strategy of what to do if he leaves her in the lurch? Above all, does the perception of each other as rational agents make it easier or harder for them to agree their "contract", to adopt precommitting rôles, and to reach day-to-day decisions?[13]

These are troubling and fundamental questions, and Mr and Mrs Linden occasionally indicate an awareness of how the last, in particular, is crucial. Mr Linden explains that, shortly after they were married, she actually applied for a very lucrative and responsible job (a big improvement on his current one) on his behalf. After some discussion of this, the following exchange occurs:

Mr Linden: . . . one might suggest that it was in her interest to get me a good job.

Mrs Linden: That's true (laughs).

Mr Linden: Because the better the job, the better the income; the better the income, the more one can provide . . . if you're going to look at it on a very basic . . .

Mrs Linden: I didn't think of it from that point of view.

Mr Linden: I don't say that you did, but one could say that there was an ulterior motive for you to get me a better job.

(Mr and Mrs Linden, 71–2)

Here they seem to be equivocal about accounting for their actions, decisions and rôles in purely calculative terms; Mrs Linden denies having considered the issue in these terms, and Mr Linden demotes such calculation to the status of an "ulterior motive". If so, from what point of view *did* Mrs Linden think about it, and what was her "interior motive"? The answer (given slightly earlier in the interview) is quite revealing:

Mrs Linden: Well, he had a lot of potential there. No . . . you needed to settle down – wasting things a bit, you must admit. You were fairly fed up with [previous employment] by then. You weren't being stretched.

Mr Linden: Oh yes.

Mrs Linden: You wanted something else. I'm not sure you actually had . . . I don't know why you didn't do a bit more . . . lack of confidence maybe [. . .] I think I felt that Leo was capable of possibly more than he felt he was capable of at that time. I thought he'd be happier if he actually realized it.   (Mr and Mrs Linden, 65–6)

This seems like a very different kind of game in which, far from assuming that Mr Linden is a rational agent and simply taking his preferences into account in making her choices, she instead believes that he is only partly aware of his potential and tries to make things happen that will allow him to develop it. This involves her in trying to guess how he might react under certain conditions, including a hypothetical pathway that might follow if one difficult step is taken. It also means that their interaction is a matter not simply of calculating the consequences of each other's preferences, but of trying to influence them in a sensitive way. This transforms not only the game but the very nature of the players. Instead of being some kind of all-purpose, neutral Jack and Jill, playing a generic contest (which can serve as well to explain international relations or electoral behaviour), they emerge as partners in a very context-dependent encounter, "reached by a trajectory, and fraught with expectations".[14] The trajectory is the integration between the context (partnership) and the moves (decisions): what can be decided is governed by the "rules" of partnership, which is a very specific kind of relationship, with rules that are quite different from the rules of other "games". Hence game theory, while providing a challenging formulation of the abstract issues of co-operation between rational agents, misses the specifics of decision making within forms of life such as politics, community and the household.

For these couples, their expectations of each other are not simply predictions, based on knowledge about preferences and probabilities. They are *normative*, in the sense that each feels entitled to an interactive response because of their previous interaction, their mutual commitments and their joint plans for the future. Mrs Linden does not assume that her husband will stay with her only for as long as their relationship works to his advantage; she thinks that she has a right to expect his support, for her and the children. Equally, although he can speculate about her "ulterior" motive for applying on his behalf for the job, he believes that her "interior" motive – what she thought and felt at the time – was based on concern for his good and for the good of the family.

However, we should not get carried away by the uplifting moral character of the relationship between these partners. A satisfactory understanding of partnership must also account for Mrs Conifer's dilemma (her "weak bargaining position") and for Mrs Redwood's frustration ("I felt really fed up"). Both Mrs Conifer and Mrs Redwood were encountering unexpected consequences of their decisions within partnerships – in Mrs Conifer's case, some 10 years down the road from marriage, and in Mrs Redwood's case, almost immediately. The trajectory of their relationships turned out to require them to move backwards, so to speak, up a rather steep slope. Because of their husbands' precommitments to careers, both were faced with giving up what they valued (interesting employment and other aspects of a good life) for the sake of sustaining their partnerships, and to honour promises they had made whose implications they had not fully grasped.

Hence a fuller understanding of decision making must include the possibility, not only of normative expectations and moral commitments, but also of structural and systematic changes within the relationship itself. As the game of partnership proceeds, the "rules" may subtly change, not necessarily by the power-greedy machinations of one party, but perhaps by the interaction between the partners' strategies and choices. Thus we need a way of analyzing specific, partnership-contextual strategies, and the interaction between *rôles* over a long period, as well as the influences on particular decisions.

Our data provide us with a way of looking for these strategies and interactive patterns – for example, between career men and non-career women, or between two partners who are non-careerists – over a longish period, and at how responsibilities for children are handled in such relationships. Some couples, like Mr and Mrs Ash and Mr and Mrs Beech, are still at quite an early stage of their employment and family life cycles. Others, like Mr and Mrs Birch, are further down the road, and are already dealing with the secondary effects of each others' decisions, rôles and strategies. Mr Birch has used his redundancy money from his previous managerial post to start a small brewery. Mrs Birch is unimpressed by the results of this so far (Mr Birch has recently awarded himself a pay cut) and is protecting her career (as a teacher), her share in the house and her pension.

Mr Birch: That money [redundancy payment] has actually been invested in shares, so that's one commitment, and the other one is the guarantee of the overdraft. But that's the area of insecurity [. . .]

Mrs Birch: I also made a decision, though, that I wouldn't actually be involved as a director or anything like this, so that in fact I wasn't going to be liable for the monies when it came to it. Only try to keep a portion anyway of our finances separate from the business, so we don't collapse completely.

Mr Birch: Oh yes, you mean your share of the house is not involved. At the same time, you have the option, in the way that the business is set up originally, to take up shares if you wish, or transfer some of mine to you, if it proves financially advantageous. We haven't got to that situation yet.

Mrs Birch: Definitely not.   (Mr and Mrs Birch, 17)

Here the trajectory of their partnership has changed, and Mrs Birch's expectations, as the wife of a man whose background was a research scientist, have had to be adapted. Up to now he has been the primary earner, but she now finds herself in this rôle, with its attendant responsibilities. Econometric research suggests that men and women respond differently to incentives (like promotion)[15] and constraints (like taxation),[16] but this is because men are usually in the primary earning rôle. In this situation, Mrs Birch's behaviour changes.

Mr Birch presents the progress of his career, from research into management and on to self-employment, as coherent and rational; she questions this. She does not oppose her husband's new venture, but nor does she support it. Instead she relies on her own career, which she says is now the main source of household income, which is not what she expected. She indicates that she does not regard his new enterprise as in line with the trajectory of their relationship by saying "We're not managers or business people at all"(p. 20); then the following exchange occurs:

Mr Birch: Sorry for interrupting. I was going to say that, as far as finances go, we have a shared bank account [. . .]

Mrs Birch: [indistinct]

Mr Birch: Some people do, some people run their accounts separately.

Mrs Birch: Good idea, why haven't we discussed this earlier? [laughs]

Mr Birch: We don't work like that.   (Mr and Mrs Birch, 20)

In these passages, Mr and Mrs Birch's actions are heavily meaningful for themselves and each other: they are being interpreted by each other, and each takes account of the other's action in choosing his or her course. However, the interpretation and the account taken seem far closer to Weber's *verstehen*[17] than to game-theoretical bargaining; if there is a game going on here, then the intersubjective meanings need to be understood if we are to unravel the strategies and follow the moves. Mr Birch presents his version of his actions in terms of the instrumental rationality of economics – as if speaking to an auditor or potential investor. Mrs Birch explicitly rejects this kind of account (and hence implicitly questions Mr Birch's actions) in saying, "We're not managers or business people at all": the "we" in question is their partnership, whose normative expectations have been disturbed by his venture. When she says that she is holding on to "a portion anyway of our finances separate from the business, so we don't collapse completely", she is not just giving instrumental reasons for her actions, she is appealing to goals and values that are intrinsic to their partnership and their rôles as parents. Although she uses the language of prudence in this passage, it is framed in terms of a value-rational prioritization of the family over his business. She is implicitly "putting the family first" and questioning whether his entrepreneurial actions are in line with the values of partnership and parenthood.

This understanding of the joint interview with Mr and Mrs Birch is derived not from a game-theoretical reconstruction of their options and pay-offs, but from a *reading* of the text. In Weber's terms, it is *sociological* understanding, because we are able to identify common patterns in partnerships and the meanings that partners give them. "Putting the family first" is, we shall argue, a fundamental element in the moral code through which these couples regulate their partnerships, and interviewees constantly give accounts of their actions in terms of the value-rationality of this goal. Part of this is that partners should be "supportive" of each other: for the women in this study, this usually means being proactive in protecting their career-orientated partners from the stresses and the burdens of bringing up children (see pp. 47–8). However, we also identify a group of partnerships in which the woman has begun to see her partner's career as a "shaky investment", and seeks to protect "the family" by developing her own career (if she already has one, as in the case of Mrs Birch) or by embarking on a career. The phenomenon of "shaky investment relations" between partners is based on a reading of the joint interviews in which women implicitly or explicitly do not accept their partners' instrumentally rational accounts of their employment or self-employment actions.

How do we, as researchers, recognize a "shaky investment relationship"? First, we start from an analysis of the accountability frameworks adopted by men and women in partnerships where the man has a career – particularly the accounts of "supportiveness" given by non-careerist women with careerist partners. In the case of self-employed men this usually consists of the woman being employed by the business for at least part of her working time, a practice that is partly justified in terms of its tax advantages. Taking this as the "ideal-typical" case of a woman being "supportive" of her self-employed partner, the interviewer asks Mrs Birch:

Q: But there's no sense in which you could possibly give up your job and help [in your husband's business]?

Mrs Birch: Not until it actually makes money. I have to keep the job to bring in the money, to keep the household going. We simply couldn't do it without my salary at the moment, but there again I don't know if I'd want to. It's not my line of interest at all; as Adrian said, he's not interested in going into teaching, or different jobs that don't hold particular interest for him. I feel the same as well. My area of interest is not in [brewing] or manufacturing industry generally. So we have to keep our separate employment.

(Mr and Mrs Birch, 20)

Mrs Birch is able to show that she is not failing to be "supportive" by appealing to the priority of the household's income: she is "putting the family first" by protecting her career as a teacher. But if our reading of the data is convincing, it raises a number of other theoretical puzzles about the "forms of life" constituted by partnerships. In Chapter 4 we have already criticized the idea that the moral regulation of these partnerships can be understood in terms of rules that prescribe decisions, and have rejected an analysis of the accounts in terms of a search for such rules. In the case of partnerships – relationships based on intimacy and the sharing of personal vulnerability – we have traced the "code"[18] of partners' obligations to each other – the normative standards of partnership – to the informal order of their everyday interactions. Can partnership be understood as a "game", in the sense of being a "form of life" constructed through the intersubjective exchange of meaningful actions between the couple? And if social actions and social relations have to be understood, as it were, from within, by interpretation of their text, is there no "external" world of actions and relations, no "objective" context in which these interpretations can be located other than the one created by the retrospective reconstructions in their accounts? These puzzles will be addressed in Chapter 6.

Talking about economics

What we have seen so far is that the game-theoretical analysis of co-ordination between partners (represented as ideally rational agents with consistently ordered preferences, complete information and the ability to calculate probabilities, including those of each other's choices) can explain the problems of co-ordination in partnership and indicate possible solutions. We have also seen that actual agents (the interviewees) do adopt the instrumental rationality of economic analysis, including a version of bargaining games, in their accounts of how they co-ordinate their decisions. They also introduce into their versions a description of the institutional economic constraints on actions, locating their accounts in a world of markets, firms and public sector borrowing requirements. But co-ordination in partnership is also described in terms of a process of moral regulation, including frequent references to the requirements of family priority. Thus economic factors are incorporated into the accountability of agents who must reason, not only about the probabilities of events (including each other's choices) but also about the moral and emotional implications of their actions, a rationality of values. There is some kind of code, interpreted through talking about decisions, that regulates partnership decisions.

In introducing the idea of such a code, we have already strayed some way from the abstract model of rational decision making put forward by game theorists. In that ideal-type world of economizing agents, talk is of little significance, because individuals reveal their preferences in their behaviour. Outcomes are explained in terms of the ordering of these preferences and the mutual gains to the players. Since there is no gap between desires and actions to be filled, *post hoc* accounts of decisions are either redundant or misleading.

But this is not the whole story. Oddly enough, economics itself has returned to the issue of human communication's rôle in exchange, production and property ownership.[19] Animals, like humans, live in conditions of scarcity and have well ordered preferences. But animals do not have *property* (as opposed to *territory*), and they do not trade or produce (beavers, for instance, conserve a territory and do ecological work, but they do not produce goods or exchange them).[20] Individual animals competing for food and shelter face a version of the game with which we started this chapter, which might be called the Rat's Dilemma.[21] Even if their preferences are such that mutual advantage could be gained from exchange, they cannot achieve this because each individual stands to gain more from grabbing what is offered than from offering something in return. Trade cannot get started until a system of restraint allows individuals to have their claims to ownership respected, to negotiate a price and to rely on payment in exchange. If communication were not a necessary condition for such institutions and transactions, we might wonder why human beings learned to talk, and particularly why they learned to talk about economics.

David Hume, Adam Smith and their Scottish Enlightenment followers regarded these issues as central to the understanding of human nature, morality and economic behaviour. Smith, for instance, conjectured that language was necessary for trade to get started;[22] Hume, following Aristotle,[23] pointed out that choice was always deliberative, and not merely voluntary. Commercial relations require a language community and a code of conduct; talking about economics serves not merely to reconstruct the translation of desire into action, but to affirm the practices of ownership, production and exchange, to reach bargains, to uphold contracts, and to sustain the morality of investments. Ordinary people's economic ideas and practices are what maintains and regulates economic relations. If language is a necessary condition for the economic order, we may safely assume that other relationships (which lack the convenience of price tags, trolleys, cash registers and other retailing technology for easing the journey between wants and their satisfaction) also rely on talking for their processes of co-ordinating individuals' decisions.

Of course, it may be that these practices and codes can in turn be explained by game theories. Indeed David Levy, who has re-emphasized the significance of communication and morality for economic relations, has also produced rather elegant rational choice analyses of the very behaviours and norms on which he argues that exchange and property rest.[24] Thus it may be possible to use game-theoretical models to explain the content of the partnership code – why its normative constraints take the particular forms they do. In other words, economic theory may be able to specify why moral regulation through talking about decisions results in the configurations of rôles that we have seen in our sample, and how the elements in the code of partnership contribute to these outcomes.

Conclusions

In this chapter, we have outlined rational choice and game theory, and indicated how some interviewees introduce elements of their analysis into their accounts of co-ordinating their decisions. But we have gone on to argue that moral regulation, through a partnership code, is central to their accounts of co-operative decision making. Economists are becoming aware of the deliberative aspects of choice and the importance of communication in exchange and production. Yet they claim that rational choice theory can explain the content of a prudent morality of restraint and co-operation.

So we have the paradox that the agents who appear in rational choice and games theory cannot start trading without language and morality, but that their enabling codes and practices can be "explained" by those theories. It may be that we need a sociological insider's understanding to read the "code" of partnership, but that this can in turn be explained by setting it out as a bargaining game with pay-offs. From the inside, as it were, the interviewees talked about being influenced both by the laws of economics and by the norms of their partnership, and sometimes described their decisions in terms of a bargaining game, but they could not specify these decisions in terms of a set of consistent rules or principles. We are left with a continuing puzzle about how to theorize rationality and decision making in everyday life.

In this second part of this book, we want to use rational choice theory to analyze some of the configurations of rôles and actions that have been investigated in this chapter. So far we have introduced, but not really explored the substance of, a possible economic rationality in the patterns of behaviour identified. In Chapter 7 we will return to this theme and to the use of this methodology. However, in Chapter 6 we will focus on the interviewees' accounts of their decision making and how it is regulated through the partnership code. In particular, we will consider how they use both economic and moral reasons for decisions in their accounts.

References

1. G. S. Becker, *The economic approach to human behavior* (Chicago: University of Chicago Press, 1976), p. 10.
2. M. Weber, *Economy and society* (1922; ed. G. Roth and C. Wittich, New York: Bedminster Press, 1968), p. 5.
3. M. Hollis, "Moves and motives in the games we play", *Analysis* **50** (2) (1990), 49–63.
4. We are indebted for this analogy to W. Van Trier of de Studiecentrum voor

Economisch en Sociaal Onderzoek, University of St Ignatius, Antwerp.

5. See for instance G. Crow, "The use of the concept of 'strategy' in recent sociologi-cal literature", *Sociology* **23** (1) (1989), 1–24.

6. S. Horrell, J. Rubery, B. Burchell, *Working time patterns: constraints and preferences*, Department of Economics, Cambridge University, 1989; C. Marsh, *Hours of work of women and men in Britain* (London: Equal Opportunities Commission, HMSO, 1991); P. Hewitt, *About time: the revolution in work and family life* (London: IPPR/Rivers Oram Press, 1993), pp. 98 and 129; C. Hakim, "Workforce restructuring, social insur-ance coverage and the black economy", *Journal of Social Policy* **18** (4) (1989), 471–503.

7. About half of men in the age group 60–64 were still in employment in the late 1980s in Britain, many of these part time. See T. Schuller & A. Walker, *The time of our life* (London: IPPR, 1990), Table 4. The same trend towards earlier retirement is evident in most European countries (*Financial Times*, 22 July 1992, reporting an OECD survey).

8. Marsh, *Hours of work of women and men in Britain*. The majority of women in all age groups above 35 were in part-time work by the 1990s (Office for Population Censuses and Surveys, *Labour Force Survey, 1988 and 1989*, HMSO, 1991, Table 5.9).

9. A. Carling, *Social division* (London: Verso, 1991).

10. R. E. Pahl, *Divisions of labour* (Oxford: Blackwell, 1984), pp. 20 and 133.

11. J. Haskey, "Current prospects for the proportion of marriages ending in divorce", *Population Trends* **44** (1989), 9–16. The median length of marriage in Britain is about 9 years.

12. R. Axelrod, *The evolution of co-operation* (New York: Basic Books, 1984).

13. J. Elster, *Ulysses and the sirens* (Cambridge: Cambridge University Press, 1979).

14. Hollis, "Moves and motives", p. 56.

15. J. A. Hausman, "Labour supply", in *How taxes affect economic behaviour*, H. J. Aaron & J. A. Pechman (eds), pp. 27–84 (Washington DC: Brookings Institution, 1981).

16. S. James & C. Nobes, *The economics of taxation*, 4th edition (London: Prentice Hall, 1992).

17. M. Weber, "Verification in sociological analysis", in *The interpretation of social real-ity*, J. E. T. Eldridge (ed.) (New York: Joseph, 1971), pp. 92–102.

18. For the notion of a "code" see D. Lawrence Wieder, *Language and social reality: the case of telling the convict code* (The Hague: Mouton, 1970).

19. D. Levy, *The economic ideas of ordinary people: from preferences to trade* (London: Routledge, 1992).

20. Ibid., Ch. 2.

21. Ibid., Ch. 3.

22. A. Smith, *An inquiry into the nature and causes of the wealth of nations* (1776; ed. W. B. Todd, Oxford: Clarendon Press, 1976), p. 25.

23. Aristotle, *Nicomachean ethics*, translated W. D. Barnes, revised J. O. Urmson, in *The Complete Works of Aristotle*, ed. J. Barnes (Princeton, NJ: Princeton University Press, 1984), 111167–10.

24. Levy, *The economic ideas of ordinary people*, Ch. 8.

CHAPTER 6

"Rationality" and Partnership

If the way that couples reasoned about decisions was different from the way
rational agents chose bargaining strategies in game-theoretical models, in
what sense were their decisions *rational*? In this chapter, we look in more
detail at the sort of reasoning couples did, especially in the joint interviews,
to see how their partnership code regulated their decisions.

We analyze the way in which interviewees reason about their decisions,
and describe how they "agree" upon them. We argue that the partnership
code is not a set of principles for prescribing choices or resolving disputes,
but rather a set of "cultural resources" for regulating economic and inter-
personal behaviour in households. The terms of the code are "indexical"
in Garfinkel's sense – their meaning varies with the context in which they
are used and is ultimately determined by the context of actions and relations in which they are employed. But they are not arbitrary – members
do not let each other use them in a way that violates their standards of
stability and order in partnership. Thus Mrs Birch will not endorse her
husband's account of his business "success" (see p. 116) while she is providing most of the family's income; nor will Ms Plum let Mr Larch get away
with calling her business a "success" while his assets are guaranteeing her
overdraft.

The partnership code is thus indeterminate until it is elaborated in their
talk, when it takes on an external and constraining form, which gives
everyday life an orderly and predictable pattern that is sufficient for practical purposes. This moral reality allows them to co-ordinate their decisions
so long as the partners' elaborating interpretations are reciprocal. Cryptic
and oblique allusions to the code allow the interviewers to make sense of
these reciprocities in exchanges between the couples.

In the first section of the chapter, we examine the way in which interviewees deploy cultural resources to reason about economics and family

life in answer to our questions, and what it takes in turn for us as interviewers to be "satisfied" or "convinced" by their answers. What we are looking at here is not a set of principles for reconciling the apparent inconsistencies between instrumental and moral reasoning, but how interviewees use cryptic and indexical expressions to organize actions that are ambiguous (or possibly meaningless) in such a way as to produce for themselves (and us) a stable social order. Their use of these resources creates "structured, recognizable, repetitive, patterned behaviour",[1] and provides the context in which their indexical concepts become precise enough to be practically meaningful. In reasoning about their decisions in terms of economic advantage and "quality of family life", they display how their descriptions of the social order become part of the social order they describe.

In the second and third sections, we look at how couples use a self-elaborating code[2] to regulate everyday life and reach "joint decisions". They tell us that they "discuss" or "negotiate" issues over major expenditures, shares of housework and bringing up the children, but they are unable to specify the way in which agreement is reached, or even what an agreement would look like. Thus not only is the partnership code indexical (it provides an index of what kinds of actions are going on in the household), it is also "reflexive" – it shows how members stand in relation to each other, for instance how decisions about men's careers are to be related to family leisure activities. Using examples of how interviewees can interpret what is "agreed" or "understood" in widely divergent ways, we show how the continual indeterminacy allowed by the code is functional for the stability of the family's organization for everyday purposes, because it enables flexibility and autonomy for the partners.

The final section takes the couples' accounts of their children's needs as a topic for analyzing the moral regulation of the household through these discursive practices. One of the most debated decisions for these couples concerned their children's education – the rival merits of state and private schooling. They deploy discourses of long-term economic advantage and of psychological and social need to construct quite elaborate justifications for their choices of one system or the other. Since this is seen as an important decision and as an index of responsible parenting, a range of cultural resources are employed in lengthy descriptions of decision making. Yet even here – the context in which couples spelt out the rule of "putting the family first" – there was evidence of the provisional nature of such reasoning and of scope for reinterpretation of the reasons for decisions.

124

"Quantity" and "quality" reasoning

Part of what couples meant by "putting the family first" was that decisions about employment and expenditure should be evaluated in terms of the quality of family life. The idea of "quality time" with the children was part of the self-elaborating partnership code, and referred to by so many of the interviewees that we as interviewers came to use the expression in asking about leisure activities. Here Mr Cedar, a highly paid regional manager of a car parts sales network, shows how the term is used in relation to such decisions.

Mr Cedar: . . . I'm very conscious of the fact that, with the children, I won't see much of them during the week, and so, come the weekends, I'm always around on a weekend, very rarely would I ever work then [. . .] That's part of the other thing, why we bought the caravan which you probably saw outside the house [indistinct] and I was concerned that we'd [indistinct] enough of their time, and that the problem there with having a house like we've got, we spend a fair bit of time doing work on the house or in the garden, that you tend to lose quality time then with the children, so we bought the caravan to make sure that as many weekends as we can we just go off on a Friday night and come back on a Sunday, load it up and off we go.   (Mr Cedar, 9)

This kind of reasoning was very important for our investigation of rationality in decision making. Max Weber's analysis of rational social action defined it as meaningful, publicly recognizable activity, orientated to such activity by others, and linking means to ends.[3] But he distinguished between *zweckrational* (instrumental) rationality, which uses calculated expectations of the behaviour of people and things to achieve the actor's purposes, and *wertrational* (value) rationality, which involves the pursuit of ethical, aesthetic or religious ends, regardless of the consequences.[4] These are ideal types in Weber's theory, and he specifically indicates that "in the great majority of cases actual action goes on in the state of inarticulate half-consciousness or actual unconsciousness of its subjective meaning".[5] However this distinction has been widely used to analyze social action, by economists and philosophers as well as by sociologists (as we saw in the previous chapter, in Levy's account of "the economic ideas of ordinary people"). Furthermore, just as there are many passages in the interviews that attempt to justify decisions in line with their economic consequences, so there are

125

some (like the one just quoted from Mr Cedar) that identify and value particular ends as good in themselves. Often these focus on the quality of family
life and the needs of children, as when Mr Rowan (see p. 64) says that he
would continue to pay for his daughter's education even if he were made
redundant – "regardless of what we think of money, the main priority as
far as we're concerned is the children's education". Hence value rationality seems to provide the core of the partnership code, in which giving children "quality time" is an explicit feature, along with supportiveness.

Although it was clear from our data that the interviewees were combining these two kinds of reasoning in certain patterns, we found it extremely difficult to plot and theorise these in our analysis. This was partly
because we were treating the two types of rationality in the Weberian way,
seeing value rationality as a distinctively moral category regulating certain
kinds of decisions, providing a formal normative structure, charged with
emotion, that "governed" the family sphere.[6] At a later stage of the analysis, we wondered whether what we were seeing was a kind of "two-tier
moral psychology, whose lower tier is broadly Humean and whose upper
tier is firmly not".[7] Men like Mr Cedar and Mr Rowan have lower-tier
precommitments to their careers that are instrumentally rational for purposes of security and material comfort; but the couples' upper-tier
precommitments (to quality of family life and their children's futures) are
bound up in the normative nexus of family relations, and hence are morally binding. Moral rationality, on this analysis, involves internalizing some
features of the context and choosing from the universal, impartial, impersonal standpoint, in the manner of Kant. It seemed possibly to provide a
kind of ethical supreme court, to which one of the partners (usually the
woman) could refer decisions for the application of rules of conduct that
are different from those governing the everyday practicalities of domestic
or economic life. Hence the partnership code might "constitute the form
of life which a moral agent embodies".[8]

However, after trying out this way of analyzing the accounts, we aban-
doned it. The main objection was that it turned the interviewees into "cultural dopes", at least in relation to partnership: they became so embedded in their form of life that they lost their capacity to assess their choices
and actions by standards other than those intrinsic to it. Although there
are times in the interviews when they lapse into the caring, sharing talk
in which their interests seem almost inseparable from each other's in partnership, they always retain the capacity to make instrumental judgements
about partnership itself – to evaluate what is in it for them. This is par-

ticularly obvious in the "shaky investment" partnerships analyzed in the last chapter, in the rare cases (such as Mrs Fieldmaple, see p. 36) where they explicitly anticipate the possible breakdown of marriages, and when they describe past marriages that have failed. No-one expresses this more robustly than Mr Larch when he says that, in response to the difficulties in his previous relationship, "I did what any sensible person would do: I went to live with M. C. Plum" (his present partner).

Instead, we began to analyze the kinds of reasoning about decisions that characterized their accounts and that seemed to "satisfy" us as interviewers, to the extent that we responded by closing this topic and turning to another. This involves addressing rationality as a situated interactional *accomplishment* of an intersubjectively meaningful activity, the research interview. This way of looking at versions of decisions is in line with recent sociological theory on rationality: it analyzes the conceptual tools used by social actors, how they make links between different discourses of choosing, and the surrounding conditions for accounting for decisions as rational.[9] Thus choice and decision making are studied as techniques for connecting beliefs, desires and actions, and accounts of how this is done well enough to "convince" the hearer are of particular significance for the understanding of rationality.

The interviews consist of sustained pieces of "publicly displayed and continually updated" intersubjective understanding,[10] in which meaning is achieved by the interactants. This is possible partly because certain organizational features of the talk enable one person to display their interpretation of the other's utterances,[11] and allow reciprocal understanding to be communicated. Talk is *designed* to maintain intersubjectivity, and it is to the "design features" of a meaningfully rational account that our attention turned – features that were artfully accomplished but largely unnoticed aspects of the accounts of making a decision.

When we looked at the sequences of questions and answers in the interviews within this frame, we noticed that there was a design feature of accounts of decisions (as rational and meaningful choices) that seemed to lead us to signal our acceptance of the respondent's version (by a positive interpretation or a different question, rather than further "probing" or seeking further clarification). This was a combination of "quantity" (calculative or economic) and "quality" (value-orientated) reasoning.[12] A neat example is the following answer from Mrs Alder, a craft worker who also does the books for her husband's building business:

Q: Why have you decided to be self-employed rather than just staying at home, or having a full-time paid job?

Mrs Alder: I chose self-employment because it's convenient. I've got three children and if I'm working here from home then I'm available if they're sick or whatever, and I enjoy the freedom of it. [My craft] is something you either do self-employed or you don't do at all because otherwise the commercial equipment means sitting in a factory making [artefacts] and that doesn't appeal to me at all. I like the variety and I like being able to organize my own timetable.

(Mrs Alder, 2)

This answer has both elements – the explanation in terms of the economics of commercial (factory) production or home-based craft work, and the appeal to the values of family responsibility, freedom and variety, i.e. quality of life – that are design features of the answers that we as interviewers seemed to signal as "acceptable" (meaningfully rational). The interviewer immediately asks another question, "So have you ever had a full-time paid job?", referring to her employment history, a different topic. What Mrs Alder has done is to provide a non-contradictory version of her choice of employment in terms of two accountability criteria, economic rationality and value rationality, quantity and quality factors. Often the "reasoning", especially in relation to values and the family, is so brief and pithy as to be cryptic (Mrs Alder is unusually clear), but even in the face of apparently incomplete accounts (for instance, a sentence tailing off unfinished, or the mere mention of "family reasons") we as interviewers seemed predisposed to "accept" answers with this design feature.

This does not imply that there is an identifiable relationship of "rationality" between the economic reasoning and the quality of life value-orientation of the accounts, or that the interviewees were consciously lining up their versions of decisions in this way. The design feature is one we have identified in our analysis (we were not aware of it at the time) as a way of understanding the interviews as accomplishments of intersubjectively meaningful interaction. Nor does this design feature require the interviewees as social actors to produce particular kinds of reasoning to outcomes that are prescribed by the norms of accountability they adopt. But they do have to be artful in managing the non-contradictory dual reasoning in their versions of decisions, since, once given, this takes on the character of an external and obligatory "social fact" against which the rationality (or otherwise) of the decision is to be assessed.

Here Mr Pear explains why he has applied for one promotion (to senior technician) in his job, but will not apply for another (he does not see his employment as a "career").

Mr Pear: I did apply, reluctantly, for the post of senior technician – in fact the post came up for the principal technician, or it will when this fellow, the chief technician, retires soon – but I doubt whether I will apply for it; (a) because the financial incentive isn't very great, and (b) which is more important to me, I don't [want] the additional responsibility which would then make me an integral part of the college mechanism. Senior technician gives me the responsibility to work on my own initiative and yet a flexibility to mould the college round my social life. The more responsibility you have, then I think that pulls you away – you know, there's a greater commitment to the work place than there is to the home base.   (Mr Pear, 17)

Mr Pear's prioritization of "home base" over "work place" is the opposite of the decision made by those (the majority of men) who construct "career" accounts of the pursuit of incremental advantage, but it has the design features required for acceptance of rationality. So too does Mrs Dogwood's account of her return to full-time teaching after having her only child, Harry.

Mrs Dogwood: I don't think I could have stayed at home, I think realistically I have to work. After all that time, knowing that I've got the skills and the experience to be working and earning – because if I'd stayed at home it wouldn't have been an enriching experience because we'd have had no money – I would have been with Harry but not able to do anything. So I think psychologically I couldn't be out of work.   (Mrs Dogwood, 3–4)

As with Mr Pear's cryptic references to "social life" and "home base" (expanded elsewhere in his account), Mrs Dogwood uses a shorthand of "enriching experience . . . not able to do anything" to refer to the "quality" dimensions in her decision. But in each case the interviewer does not ask for further clarification; he accepts this version as having accomplished a meaningful account of a decision over employment. The interviewer is able to "make sense" of the account as rational, despite the lack of any overt *reasoning* of these qualitative factors, apparently because of a cultural preference for a version of decisions with these design features.

This is more obvious in the following extract from the interview with

Mr Mahogany, who owns and works a large farm, which he has built up. He gives a highly reasoned and economistic account of the expansion of his business, but the interviewer does not seem "satisfied" with this impressive accomplishment. Towards the end of the interview, he asks Mr Mahogany whether he would consider a business in computer software, if it could be proved to be more profitable.

Mr Mahogany: No, I wouldn't be interested in that.

Q: Because?

Mr Mahogany: I just think that some things that look as if they're more profitable in the short term don't always turn out to be that way.

Q: Say I could convince you that it would be, suppose I could produce a hard and fast case, to take you right out of the farming way of life, and give you a completely different life, then what?

Mr Mahogany: It would obviously depend very much on the circumstances. I don't think I'd be very keen to do that to be honest. My goal has always been to have lots of acres I can look out over and I'm here on the job every day, and sometimes it can get over-burdening, but I think I'd still put up with a lower income in farming than . . .

Q: But it's a lifestyle thing as well?

Mr Mahogany: It is a bit as well, yes. You certainly wouldn't do it just for the money [laughs].

(Mr Mahogany, 15–16)

Here the interviewer pursues the topic, even paraphrasing what Mr Mahogany says, to put it into an "acceptable" quality-of-life reason, which Mr Mahogany finally adopts. It is only after the respondent confirms that he has both quantity and quality reasons for his decision that the topic is dropped and the interview ends.

Of course, not all the interviewees are able to give non-contradictory dual-accountability versions of all their decisions. When they have trouble in doing so (they cannot make economic and quality-of-life factors non-contradictory), they then reconstruct their choices as "irrational" and seek psychological reasons for this in themselves and their situation. One example will suffice at this point. Here Mr Alder, a builder, is trying to explain why he does not train his son, who wants to join him in the family building business, even though it would be economically advantageous to do so.

Failing to give non-contradictory quantity and quality reasons, he blames his irrational feelings.

Mr Alder: Yes, he starts next year. So he's looking elsewhere for some-body because I say I will not train him. He gets his training elsewhere and then when he's trained he can come in with me.

Q: The reason for that being?

Mr Alder: Well I think, when I actually analyze my attitude towards him I'm very hard on him, I'm very analytical of his every move, and you probably have the correct word for it, but I think I'm going through a stage with him where I actually resent him becoming a man. It's strange, I hate myself for it. I can feel myself bubbling and yet because he's actually developing and getting bigger, I tend to shout at him but I don't really want to. It's something I'm really struggling with at the moment. I find him really annoying and yet with my apprentice, who's the same age, I'm far more tolerant of the kid and it really baffles me . . .   (Mr Alder, 30)

Mr Alder goes on struggling with this, and criticizing himself, and then eventually changes the subject. The psychological "explanation" attempts to rationalize what he himself describes as an irrational ("really weird" later in the same passage) reaction, but he ends up by trying to restate the situation in a form that has the "rational" design features just before raising the next topic. He says, "So that is why, coming back [to the decision] I want [outside] training for him ['quantity' economic reason], because I feel I should be too hard on him and he wouldn't survive ['quality-of-life' reasoning]", and then pauses before changing the subject, as if looking for confirmation that he has accomplished his task.

All this seems to indicate a preference for these design features of accounts of decisions, shared by interviewees and the interviewers and constituting intersubjectively meaningful versions of rationality. The rationality of the accounts is established "in and through" the doing of the interview, as an interactional achievement, and not by reference to a logical relation with formal ("institutional" or "structural") standards of rationality or a particular relationship between calculative motives and ethical standards. The orderly and purposeful "normal appearances" of everyday domestic decision making are sustained by these accounts of non-contradictory quantity and quality reasons for choices, which then become part of what is experienced as external and constraining in partnership.

"Joint decisions", "discussion" and "agreement"

So far we have looked at the accounts of decisions given by the respondents to the interviewers, and how both sides seemed to prefer (and see as rational) versions with this design feature. In this section we will look at how the self-elaborating partnership code allows couples to reach "joint decisions" or "agreements", and how this quantity and quality reasoning features in their accounts of these.

Although they do not use the same words in every case, couples insist that being supportive in partnership and putting the family first involves "discussion" or "negotiation" over reaching decisions, which are therefore joint decisions, and "co-operation" or "teamwork" in carrying them through. These expressions are clearly indexical in the sense defined at the start of the chapter – they allow partnership to be regulated and ordered, and the partners to experience obligation and constraint in their everyday relations (they are bound by what they have agreed to do) – but we will argue that the code itself and the decisions to which it gives rise are so indeterminate as to allow a wide variety of meanings in different contexts. Thus partners' actions are not prescribed in advance, and partnership retains the flexibility that is required by the unpredictability of domestic life. Within their different rôles, men and women have the autonomy to interpret the code and their agreements in divergent ways.

Our aim in the joint interviews was to focus on decisions that the couples had described as important (or at least significant) in their individual accounts, and to invite them to talk about them; in effect we were inviting them to provide a joint reconstruction of their reasoning. This often felt difficult and sometimes embarrassing (especially where there were obvious discrepancies in their individual accounts). Although they frequently mentioned their expectation that decisions should be discussed or negotiated and agreement reached, the number of decisions where they could give a coherent version of such a process, or what had been agreed, was very small. This covered the whole range of choices, from having children, through moving house, budgeting and expenditure, whether to hire paid help, to employment decisions and their implications. Furthermore, in the few examples where they could reconstruct a decision as an agreement, when they were asked about how this was implemented they told of more apparent breaches than observances of what had been decided.

There are some examples of undiscussed, unnegotiated decisions, somewhat shamefacedly acknowledged, in the interviews, but these are usually claimed to be exceptional. Far more common is a lack of any coherence in giving a joint account. These passages make up the bulk of the material in the joint interviews, and are very difficult to reproduce because they tend to be lengthy and rambling. A few examples will give the flavour of hundreds of pages of text, in which couples attempt to convey what they have "agreed" and "decided", and why.

Mr and Mrs Fieldmaple are asked how they decided to stay in this area when his department at the university was being closed down, rather than move elsewhere.

Mrs Fieldmaple: I don't think Jonathan ever, ever thought that he'd move from here.

Mr Fieldmaple: Not from [city].

Mrs Fieldmaple: No, I think he thought he might work for himself as a consultant or do something like that, didn't you?

Mr Fieldmaple: Mm.

Mrs Fieldmaple: . . . but I don't think you ever . . .

Mr Fieldmaple: We did talk about it, we talked about it in terms of why I was fed up with what I was doing . . .

Mrs Fieldmaple: Well we did, yes, I mean we did go to America and live in America for a year, didn't we, 'cause you did a year there, so that was one change, um, I'm trying to think what else. No I can't think, I mean you just didn't want to move away from [city] so that was a . . . (Mr and Mrs Fieldmaple, 5)

Mr and Mrs Chestnut are asked about how they've decided that she will not work full time until the children leave school, and perhaps not even then.

Q: So is this not something that you've both discussed together?

Mrs Chestnut: I don't think we've really discussed it, it just seemed to come natural . . .

Mr Chestnut: Well, we must have discussed it, it's just something we've not really gone into in a big discussion because we probably agreed on it right away so there's no need for a discussion.

Mrs Chestnut: But it's got to be the circumstances you see, it must be

133

that we can manage as we are . . .

(Mr and Mrs Chestnut, 31)

A little later, they say that they very nearly emigrated to Australia and even had a cage made for the dog, to transport it with them, but the sale of their house fell through and in the two or three months it took to rearrange the sale they changed their minds: "If the sale had gone through we would have gone."

Mr and Mrs Dogwood (both teachers) are particularly insistent that their decisions are all taken jointly, but in answer to the first question that they are asked about a significant one – their choice to live in this city – they do not describe any discussion:

Mr Dogwood: Well, that was a joint decision.

Mrs Dogwood: Because when we got together I was in London and John was here . . . Who to move? . . . Because you had interviews in London, hadn't you, first?

Mr Dogwood: . . . Reluctantly.

Mrs Dogwood: But I hadn't wanted to leave London.

Q: So how did you actually negotiate?

Mrs Dogwood: Well first of all John applied for jobs in London, and I think if the jobs had been a bit more appealing . . .

Mr Dogwood: . . . If I'd been successful in an appealing job . . .

Mrs Dogwood: You had intended to do that, hadn't you?

Mr Dogwood: Yes.

Mrs Dogwood: [. . .] So in the end I decided I'd do it . . . I'd come down without a job.

(Mr and Mrs Dogwood, 26–7)

Mr and Mrs Hazel have recently moved from a large, four-storey Georgian house to one that is more modern. They are asked what reasons led to the move.

Mr Hazel: Well I didn't want to move . . .

Mrs Hazel: To create a better environment for bringing up children. In all honesty it was extremely difficult, the house, to keep an eye

134

on them, and a very exhausting house, and this is just a much more family-orientated house [. . .]

Q: So how did you mutually resolve this difference?

Mrs Hazel: Go on, you give your version [laughs].

Mr Hazel: I am very bad at making these . . . I don't want to be . . . I mean let me just say she gives the impression . . . I do [indistinct]. I can be very forceful, but there is this issue that she does tend to articulate the decision in a way in which it becomes a great burden, a declaration of intent, in the sense of a policy which is carried through. So I always say, "Well, if you want [indistinct] . . . ", so I've said this for years, and this time she did, and we have.

(Mr and Mrs Hazel, 39)

We would emphasize that these are chosen from a large number of similar examples. In the light of our analysis of quantity and quality reasoning in the previous section, this is perhaps not so surprising. If these couples have a design preference for such answers to questions about decision making, what is required of them is an account that fuses two sets of dual-accountability, non-contradictory versions. Given the fact that partnership involves different rôles and different kinds of "supportiveness" for almost all the couples, to construct such an answer is very demanding.

However, some couples do pull off joint accounts of some decisions that do accomplish this combination of quantity and quality reasoning by both partners in a non-contradictory way. The interesting thing for us was to see that, having succeeded in identifying a decision and the reasoning that led them (after discussion) to agree on it, they then did not stick to it, or interpreted it in different ways. The clearest example of this is Mr and Mrs Elm's version of their reasons for deciding that he should give up his employment as an accountant and set up his own business, working from their home. Although this was his third change of work in a period of five years, they are both able to give economic and quality of life reasons for it that are non-contradictory. The drop in his earnings is agreed to be "slight"; his income is still adequate. He says he was working long hours in his previous employment, was away from the family, and couldn't sleep at night, thus giving "quality of life" as well as economic reasons for changing. Mrs Elm, who is also a graduate and does some nursery teaching to a small occasional group of young children, is asked whether she worries about his changes of work.

DECISIONS

Mrs Elm: I can see why he's done it. Sometimes I worry it might become a permanent pattern, but I do see the reasons he's done it, and I think if I'd been in a similar position I'd have done exactly the same thing.

Q: So, you would say that you've been supportive?

Mrs Elm: I hope so. Ask him.

Mr Elm: All of those decisions have been joint decisions, we've discussed them and agreed that it's right to do what we did do.

(Mr and Mrs Elm, 19)

Mr Elm goes on to say that he is unlikely to change again because of the need for continuity with clients, employing staff of his own, and concentrating on specialized work. Then he is asked:

Q: One of the reasons for you setting out to be self-employed was to be closer to your family. Would you see yourself always having an office that was here in the home?

Mr Elm: No. I should think it's quite likely that I will move out. Especially employing staff. The benefits of working from home are outweighed by the disadvantages, especially for Iris having staff wandering round the house periodically, making cups of coffee.

Q: Do you feel it's a potential disadvantage having people wandering around making cups of coffee?

Mrs Elm: Yes. When it was just Rory, it was like he was working from home. Now it's become that the office is alongside the house. So the home bit of it has decreased and the office bit has increased and it's not the same thing really.

Q: And you think that's a change that's not for the good.

Mrs Elm: In terms of the family, no. The quality of life of the children and of myself is diminished because of that.

(Mr and Mrs Elm, 19–20)

Here the decision is changed, and some of the reasoning behind it is undermined, but Mr and Mrs Elm maintain their non-contradictory dual accounting. Not only do they agree, they also both use economic reasoning (the expansion of his business) and quality-of-life reasoning to justify

136

the move to office premises elsewhere. But later in the interview Mr Elm is asked:

Q: One of the reasons you went into self-employment was to spend more time with your family. Has that occurred or not?

Mr Elm: I haven't spent more time with the family, but what time I do spend with them is of high quality. When I was working for a big firm, towards the end I was extremely tired. [. . .] So it's better than it was, and it will increasingly get better provided we get over the next couple of months.

Mrs Elm: The thing was we weren't just looking at the present, we were looking at the future, and looking at what was happening to the men who were further up the scale than Rory. They had less and less time. The set-up was such that the next promotion meant overtime was unpaid, and you were expected to do that as part of the job. So the whole way of looking at life was: this man's the company staff, and the family is second. So that was what was going to happen in future.

Mr Elm: And just as I didn't want to be a company man, you didn't want to be married to one.

(Mr and Mrs Elm, 24)

Here the reasoning gets a little shakier and more provisional (it all depends on the next couple of months), but Mr and Mrs Elm continue valiantly to provide designed-to-convince explanations and to support each other in such a way that these reinforce the appearance of joint decisions. The difficulty, of course, is that things do not work out as planned, so their account is of why what was given as the reason for a decision has not happened, and why they hope it will in future (by which time Mr Elm will probably not be working at home, which was the original decision).

This should not be taken as a criticism of their account. Indeed, it is remarkable that they (unlike most other couples most of the time) are able to keep up the appearance of both "jointness" and "rationality" in their choices, despite the constant need to adapt to unpredictable circumstances. Especially in the fluid world of self-employment and working from home, *flexibility* is an essential aspect of partnership, and to tie themselves to rules and principles that would prevent them from adapting and changing in these ways would be to lose much of the potential benefit of this form of social organization. Autonomy is also vital, since both must take decisions for themselves. In the next section we will show how, in the everyday running of households and decisions about expenditure, this kind of flexibility is preserved, either by having no identifiable rules or by reinterpreting them rather spectacularly.

Good housekeeping

The running of the household itself seemed to provide another possible focus for discussion or negotiation – over how to spend the household income. Here again, however, we found few couples gave a coherent account of how they organized their work or family expenditure, and those who were able to do so then went on to give examples that showed they often "bent" their own "rules".

In the course of interviewing these couples, we were initially surprised by how many told us that they did not have any system for organizing their household expenditure. After all, one of the most potent images of British politics in the 1980s was Mrs Thatcher's prudent housekeeper: she proclaimed herself unashamed of preaching "the homilies of housekeeping, the parables of the parlour . . . [which] would have saved many a financier from failure and many a country from crisis".[13] In our study of low-income couples, we did indeed hear many accounts of very careful budgeting.[14] But among better-off couples the following were typical of the great majority:

Mrs Hemlock: We don't actually do budgeting. It all goes into the same pot, and I don't think we're aware of whose money is whose – we don't have separate [accounts] [. . .] because we don't budget, we spend without thinking . . .   (Mrs Hemlock, 15)

Mrs Alder: We're a bit lazy about it, we don't really budget very much. We have a tendency, because some things are on the business, so things like the telephone and the car come straight out of the business. The rest of it, we really do live how we want to and pay the bills and find the money rather than strictly budgeting.   (Mrs Alder, 10)

Mr Redwood: . . . What I'm really saying is that I've never been desperately worried if for a few months the expenditure exceeded the income, because at the end of the day it's all going to roughly come out in the wash. I just never see very much fun in actually having a strict budget for housekeeping and a strict budget for clothes and all the rest of it, because there's no point in having money if it's just sort of money sitting there in the bank . . .

(Mr and Mrs Redwood, 49–50)

Dr Pine: In fact, I'm totally ignorant about anything to do with money or anything of that kind [. . .] I mean on Saturday mornings I go through my bills that need to be paid and pay those out, like the gas bill this morning and boring things like that. But otherwise we just let the world run on.   (Dr Pine, 13)

However, a few couples did give us detailed accounts of how they budgeted. Mr and Mrs Rowan (accountant and school meals assistant) are one such – Mrs Rowan keeps a detailed record of all expenditure, and they plan together exactly what to spend on large items. However, this is their account of going to buy a caravan.

Mr Rowan: . . . And we then went out with the intention of trying to get a caravan.

Mrs Rowan: They changed it, didn't they?

Mr Rowan: Well they changed it. We'd done our budgeting, we'd taken everything into account, based on the prices last year and allowing for an increase in prices, hadn't we?

Mrs Rowan: Mm.

Mr Rowan: We had gone through the whole budget that we had, and worked out that yes, we could afford to buy a caravan as long as we didn't go over a certain sum. When we actually went to the place, they'd changed the style of the ones we'd seen the year before and we didn't like it as much. And then we saw this one. We were up there for a whole afternoon umming and ahhing as to whether we could afford it.

Mrs Rowan: Because this one was dearer. A lot better.

Mr Rowan: It's a lot better but it was dearer. [. . .] It was outside of what we'd call our budget for buying a caravan.

Mrs Rowan: It meant stretching it a bit.

139

Mr Rowan: And we decided in the end that with stretching it we could afford it, and it was worthwhile getting it because it had everything we wanted . . .

(Mr and Mrs Rowan, 19–21)

Having constructed such a strict rule of prudence, Mr and Mrs Rowan finally opt for flexibility ("stretching it") and end up behaving more as the other couples describe themselves doing. This shows clearly how "rules" have the function of providing order – something clearly important in financial matters for the Rowans – but that their terms are indexical enough not to prescribe choices in specific instances.

It might be argued, of course, that better-off couples are being "rational" in not budgeting, since this takes time, and – as Mr Redwood says in a passage only part of which was quoted, and which has the design features of a "rational" account – "the only purpose of having money is so you can use it and enjoy it". Mr and Mrs Rowan are (as we have already seen, pp. 64–6) in a state of some anxiety about his job, so they may be an exception. However, Mr Cedar is one of the highest earners among the interviewees, and he and his wife also budget strictly, because he has never had any job security and they want to save, "to have some money behind them". They too saw a caravan they liked.

Q: Was there a conflict between, shall we buy a caravan or shall we put this money behind us? Did you sort of . . .

Mrs Cedar: No, because we do have these flashes of things, don't we?

Mr Cedar: Yes, we have a brainstorm. There wasn't really, because we [. . .] were talking about the lack of quality time with them [the children], and that took priority really, and we sort of said, "Yes, let's do it", because we do want to spend more time with them [. . .] Originally we went to look at second-hand ones, didn't we, but that's not the same [. . .]

Mrs Cedar: It was just really a brainstorm thing really, wasn't it? We didn't think about it in depth, we just thought, well, we think this is a good thing to do.

(Mr and Mrs Cedar, 34–5)

While both partners acknowledge the "irrational" (hasty) nature of their joint decision to break (or rather reinterpret) their rule of frugality and saving (the "brainstorm"), they do try to rationalize it in terms of "quality time", "the children taking priority" and new caravans being "better" (perhaps value for money). Their budgeting regime breaks down, yet they preserve the sense of order and security, of having enough "money behind them", and of themselves as rational economic agents who put the family first.

In this section we have seen that, despite the partnership code of jointness in decisions, discussion and family responsibility, most couples give haphazard accounts of their housekeeping: men leave domestic organization to women, and both disclaim any organization of the household budget. Those who do plan, negotiate and agree budgets seem to break their own rules in important ways – they reinterpret them in context, stretching their limits to allow new possibilities. The partnership code therefore provides an indexical order within which partners operate with more autonomy and flexibility than would be possible under a more precisely stipulated code, or one that was more strictly policed by the partners.

Children's schooling

Despite the rather casual and improvised nature of much of the everyday order of partnership, and the couples' difficulties in giving joint accounts of "discussions" and "agreements", there was one topic over which decision making was taken very seriously. On the subject of children's education, the couples gave carefully reasoned versions of their decisions, whether to use the state system or the private one; they had clearly discussed this issue, and spoke at length on the factors that influenced their choices. This decision was one over which the priority of children's needs was crucially at stake, and the couple's moral adequacy as responsible parents was on the line in their accounts.

Indeed, it was in this context that the concept of "putting the family first" was most explicitly deployed – and in a way that indicated that family members' needs should be prioritized over the needs of others, and the family as a unit over other forms of association. Mrs Redwood articulates this in response to questioning about how they as a couple square their choice of private education for their children with their active membership of an opposition political party.

Mr Redwood: . . . the political party of which we are members have no particular hang-ups about private education. OK, the party policy is

141

in favour of comprehensive education rather than selective education. But the party [. . .] has always been one of freedom of choice for individuals, and therefore if that is a way in which any individuals choose to spend their money, well that's fair enough [. . .]

Mrs Redwood: I basically don't think it's fair, but I think at the end of the day Bruce and I always agreed that the children, the family comes first. I suppose that's rather wet really but that's what we feel. If politics interferes, that has to go.

(Mr and Mrs Redwood, 31–3)

Similarly Mr Yew, talking about his children's private education, says that it is something that is contrary to his principles as a socialist (he came from a working-class family and was formerly a strong trade unionist). However, he says, "When it comes to a clash between your politics and your family . . . you put the family first".

Almost all the couples say that they have discussed the possibility of private education, and their reasoning for their choice, whether for or against it, is constructed in terms of the future labour-market *advantages* for the children (calculative, "quantity" reasoning) and the individual personalities and needs of the children ("quality" reasoning). They thus follow the preferred design for a rational decision, though the accounts are almost all far longer than those for other decisions, and sometimes occupy several pages of transcript. Those who opt for private education see it as providing future benefits in terms of access to higher education and good jobs, and above all to having the character and habits that will lead to success, in competition with children who have not had these advantages.

Ms Blackthorn: . . . I don't think it [private education] necessarily produces a better-educated child, but it's the advantage of confidence. I think there's often far more discipline, I think there are quite a lot of advantages. I think they are more advantaged in society, rightly or wrongly, therefore one wants to do the best for one's children.

(Ms Blackthorn, 32)

Mr Lime: . . . I have strong views on education, and I believe that you should do the best for your family, whether that is morally or implicitly right or wrong, I do tend to put on one side on that particular occasion. Seeing what it's [private education] done for my first batch [children by first marriage], who've turned out so far extremely good and quite well balanced, and obviously there are benefits. I feel sorry

142

for all the ones who haven't had the benefit of what they've had . . .

(Mr Lime, 15)

Mr Mahogany: I think a lot of the success of a business is sort of the people you're mixing with. You try to keep up with them don't you? If you're going to a council school and all your friends are farm workers, maybe you'll only want to be a farm worker . . .

(Mr Mahogany, 21)

Mr Redwood: . . . I would hate either of the boys to have fallen into a situation where they got in with a group of friends where working at school became in some way uncool, I mean I've seen it happen to children of friends of ours [. . .] Because hopefully I can afford the fees it's a risk that I don't particularly want to take.

(Mr Redwood, 19)

Mrs Quince: . . . So I think we possibly thought that he would have a better opportunity in the private sector. Whether we're right or wrong I don't know, but we'll find out at the end of the day, won't we?

(Mrs Quince, 21)

Those who decide for state education do not adopt a different design in their reasoning; rather they argue that the advantages claimed for private schools are illusory and that money spent in this way is not well invested. They then go on to give "quality" reasons why their children's experience of state education has been beneficial and has contributed to their all-round development and to the quality of family life.

Mr Palm: Well, we've both been teachers so I think we probably know as much about the level of teaching and education as most parents and perhaps more than most parents. It doesn't seem to us that private education offers by and large better teaching. In fact in some cases in [city] that I know of, markedly worse teaching is available than in state schools [laughter], but I can understand how people from a modest background might say to themselves, this is an advantage we can give our children. Er, I mean, we have perhaps, because of our background don't have a problem about contacts. Um, we already are part of a political elite [laughs] if I can put it like that, and an educational elite, and don't particularly worry that our children won't know the right people, which I think is important if you have just got your fingers on a career ladder. Also perhaps we are

143

confident about our children's academic ability [lists achievements].
I think the people who fear that unless they do everything possible
for their children they might just not get onto the next ledge. That's
not a problem for us particularly. (Mr Palm, 22–3)

Mrs Sycamore: We were always quite content with the education our
children were getting [. . .] I mean, if that's the way they [parents
who opt for private schools] choose to bring up their children, that's
up to them. I don't think it makes their children any better or any
worse than mine. In fact my children know more of the real world,
even if it is working in a factory spraying resistors, my children have
got more values than theirs have. (Mrs Sycamore, 25)

Mrs Box: . . . they didn't particularly want to go to private education.
She has friends who are privately educated, so there's no barrier
there. And we felt they could be in state education, and we could
actually . . . we feel that the whole environment is crucial, and we
feel that we give them a pretty good grounding, and we back them
up at anything they want to do, if they want to go on trips, or they
need things, we have an extensive library here, and everything. And
if we privately educated I think a lot of stuff would go out the win-
dow. We try and have a holiday and do nice things, theatre and stuff,
and one's bound up in sport, and the other's bound up in music, and
I think actually they are two pretty well-balanced kids. And that's
not totally our doing, it's . . . they see the world in quite a good light,
I think, in a very rounded version, and I think state education is good
for that actually. I think it enables them to live with everybody, not
just one particular class . . . (Mrs Box, 10)

These detailed accounts of decisions (both Mr Palm's and Mrs Box's
might be described as *more than morally adequate*, being so well articulated
as almost to undermine their credibility as pieces of spontaneous talk)
suggest a carefully worked-out and rationally constructed decision making
process between the couples. Certainly there is much evidence here of well
rehearsed discursive moral regulation of the household, based on agreed
versions of what is best for children. However, other couples' accounts of
decisions suggest that this is more provisional than it seems, and that events
can change decisions. Mrs Quince says that it was the discovery of her son's
high ability that influenced them to choose a private school.

Mrs Quince: They both started off in the state system, did extremely

well, we were very impressed with the way they were being taught
in primary education [. . .] I think, to be honest, that the reason why
we decided to do something about Maurice was that he was actually
getting very high marks for everything he was doing, and he was
getting thoroughly bored. We looked at this and went and talked to
the headmaster, and he said, "Well, he's got quite a lot of ability and
he's actually being held back a bit".   (Mrs Quince, 21)

Mrs Willow gives a very lengthy account of their changes of mind on
this issue. Originally happy with their children's state schooling, they were
alarmed that their second daughter was found to have "learning difficulties" because of "short-term memory loss", but that she was given very little
help over this. They therefore opted to send her to a private school and,
disillusioned by this experience of the state system, did the same for their
son (the youngest). However, he disliked his school and their elder daughter resented the fact that she was the only one left in state education. At
this point her husband's firm relocated to the city, and they took the opportunity to choose private schools that they considered suited the individual needs of all three – a process Mrs Willow describes as "I could maybe
right some of the wrongs that I'd made earlier with the children". This
section of the transcript runs to six pages.

Mr and Mrs Hazel have recently decided to send their eldest daughter
to a private school.

Mrs Hazel: Well, basically it was an emotional thing, she was very
     depressed at school, and hadn't been doing anything at all, and she
     was very concerned and daunted by the boys in her class, and hav-
     ing worked in a comp. for five years, very aware that certain types
     of girls of very academic but very quiet personalities don't get their
     fair share of attention, and don't achieve their potential in some
     respects.

Q: So are you generally, though, pro or anti private education?

Mr Hazel: I think it's a false argument, I mean one is interested in
     choice, and seeing the contortions one's friends are going through,
     while good practising socialists, in order to make . . . to make sure
     that they get the school of their choice. I mean the so-called equal-
     opportunity state system would have you in fits of laughter [. . .]
     This is false to say that we've opted for private education, we have
     opted for a period of a minimum of six months for a private school

to give daughter the choice of whether she wishes to continue there. If she does not wish to continue there we shall use the state system quite happily. [. . .] I am a complete individualist, I don't believe in the state as such, I obviously believe in social organizations and groupings and that side of things, but I ain't voted for it on the one hand, and I ain't going for it on the other.

(Mr and Mrs Hazel, 32–3)

Retrospectively, Mr and Mrs Laburnum, too, question the wisdom of their decision, in this case to send their son to a private school. As we have seen (pp. 62–3) they describe it as an "unmitigated disaster".

Mrs Laburnum: It did teach him a few things, but I mean, he was thrown out actually in the end, but we put him somewhere else because he was right in the middle of exams, and that's been even worse [. . .]

Mr Laburnum: So I think the first [state] school would probably have been all right if we could have just hung in there for another two terms . . .

(Mr and Mrs Laburnum, 31)

These examples suggest that the carefully reasoned versions of their choices over education given by the majority of couples are generalized guidelines, and that actual decisions are often taken in the wake of events or developments that are inherently unpredictable. These *ad hoc* versions are "rational" in so far as they continue to be constructed within the dual-accountability framework of individual competitive advantage and personality, but they show that the guidelines do not always prescribe actual choices, however detailed and morally adequate the accounts given.

Conclusion

This chapter has focused at some length on the "rationality" of decision-making, because this was one of the main issues for our research. We have seen how interviewees combined "quantity" and "quality" reasoning in accounts of their individual decisions, as a design feature of their answers, but in pithy and cryptic ways. The terms used, especially in relation to values, were indexical, and remained indeterminate until put into a context of everyday life. While they provided order, predictability and commit-

146

ment for meaningful communication and action, their reasoning neither linked these elements in a formally logical way nor gave rise to "rules" that would prescribe actions and choices.

The cobbled-together nature of reasoning and decision making was even more apparent from the joint interviews, in which couples had much greater difficulty in sustaining versions of "agreements" and "joint decisions". It was argued that this reflected the need for autonomy and flexibility in the face of the contingencies of family life; hence even those who could identify "rules" they agreed on went on to describe apparent breaches in these. Of course, such accounts constituted a reinterpretation of the "rules", and hence a repair in the local order of family life, creating a new "reality" that was stable enough for practical purposes.

In the final section we analyzed the issue to which couples gave prominence as an index of family priority – children's schooling. While all sought to show how their decisions would equip their offspring as well as possible for adult life, and argued strongly that either private or state education would do this, there was some evidence that their choices were more provisional than they seemed. However, this topic also indicated that something else was going on in these households: parents were investing (both materially and emotionally) in their children's futures. Even though this was only dimly reflected in the accounts, they were choosing to use their resources in a certain way, in the expectation of a "return" on them. This brings us back to the economic analysis of rationality in Chapter 5. In the next chapter, we will see whether it is possible to reintroduce this theoretical perspective into our analysis.

References

1. R. Hilbert, *The classical roots of ethnomethodology: Durkheim, Weber, Garfinkel* (Chapel Hill, NC: University of North Carolina Press, 1992), p. 56.
2. D. Lawrence Wieder, *Language and social reality: the case of telling the convict code* (The Hague: Mouton, 1970).
3. M. Weber, *Economy and society* (1922; ed. G. Roth and C. Wittich, New York: Bedminster Press, 1968), p. 8.
4. Ibid., p. 25.
5. Ibid.
6. J. Elster, *The cement of society* (Cambridge: Cambridge University Press, 1989).
7. M. Hollis, "Moves and motives in the games we play", *Analysis* **5** (2) (1990), 59.
8. Ibid., p. 61.
9. B. Hindess, "Rationality in modern society", *Sociological Theory* **9** (2) (1991),

216–27.

10. J. Heritage, *Garfinkel and ethnomethodology* (Oxford: Polity, 1984), p. 256.

11. E. Schegloff, "Repair after next turn: the last structurally-provided defence of intersubjectivity in conversation", *American Journal of Sociology* **97** (5) (1992), 1295–1345.

12. M. Redley, "The rational and the irrational in interview accounts of making a decision", University of Sheffield, 1993.

13. H. Young, *One of us: a biography of Margaret Thatcher* (London: Macmillan, 1989), p. 5.

14. B. Jordan, S. James, H. Kay & M. Redley, *Trapped in poverty?* labour-market *decisions in low-income households* (London: Routledge, 1992).

CHAPTER 7

Investments, Power and Autonomy

In the previous chapter we may have strayed too far for the comfort of some readers (especially those with a background in economics or philosophy) from the issues of rationality and decision making raised at the start of this part of the book. Much as we might admire the artful dexterity of Mr Hazel's rendering of the switch to private education for their eldest daughter ("six months to give her the choice of whether she wishes to continue"), they may wonder what this, and the other rhetorical practices analyzed, have to do with rational decisions, in markets or the moral sphere.

In this chapter, we aim to bring together the rational choice explanations of household relations discussed in Chapter 5 and the processes of moral regulation identified in the last chapter, to see whether any kind of synthesis of the two is possible. We want to look at the long-term commitments that these couples have made to each other – to share their lives, accumulate property and raise children – and the implications these have for their decisions. This requires us to develop an analysis that deals in economic concepts (investments, pay-offs, opportunity costs), political relations (power, subordination, resistance) and sociological processes (moral constraint, order, responsibility).

Although there is very little direct evidence of it in the interview talk, the couples' lives seemed to reflect a strategic approach to jobs and property that was largely taken for granted. This took the form of gradually accumulating assets (a job for one or both partners with pension rights and perks, an owner-occupied house, savings, insurance policies, etc.) and equipping their offspring to embark on a similar process of accumulation. The fact that no such strategy was outlined in the interviews may mean that it was part of the common-sense framework in which decisions were made, rather than implying an absence of strategic thinking and behaviour.

The couples' shared concern for their children's achievement of educational advantage was indicative of the forward-looking nature of their partnership. Hence the strength of their mutual commitment should perhaps be gauged not so much by the discursive moral regulation of everyday domestic life and their *ad hoc* decision making, but by their sustained joint projects of parenting and home-making. These required long-term bonds of reciprocity, based on promises and trust.

This notion of a shared "moral economy" of the household, engaging as a strategic unit in the market economy of employment and property, has to be set against the individual decisions of many of the respondents. Our analysis must also deal with the small minority of households in which neither partner gave a "career" account of their labour-market decisions, and the man explicitly disclaimed a "career" with cumulative job assets. It must show what happened when something went wrong with a "career" – how the other partner reacted when a "career" seemed to be foundering. And it must look at the difficult issue of separation and divorce – something hardly mentioned by the interviewees and not a specific focus of our questions – and at why a tiny minority had never married, and why only two women said they chose to make provision for themselves in case their partnerships broke up.

What we are addressing, therefore, is whether there are strategies behind the cobbled-together reconciliation of "quantity" and "quality" reasoning displayed in the interviews. We are looking for a way of discovering some "underlying rationality" in the co-ordination of choices over labour supply and household sharing that the interviewees' accounts reveal. How much do individuals choose to commit themselves to partnership and parenting, and what (if anything) do they keep in reserve, as it were, as a hedge against the failure of their joint enterprise?

To tackle these issues, we are also required to analyze power relations in the households. The asymmetric nature of the rôles and responsibilities and the unequal accumulation of "job assets" (referred to by Mrs Fieldmaple, see pp. 36–7, but by no other woman respondent) have implications that form the basis of feminist theory on the family. What do these accounts reveal about the way domestic power is exercised and resisted?

Our analysis in this chapter is crucial to our claims that our research study can contribute to theory on decision making. It rests on the notion that how individuals *invest* in what they make of themselves in the labour market and in what they prioritize in family life can be explained in terms of long-term strategic bargaining. This means that – following Popkin[1] –

we treat agents' decisions about whether to use their time and energy in commercial or domestic activities as choices between alternative allocations of scarce resources, and individual agents as if they are calculating short-term and long-term expected returns. Each individual's calculations and predictions takes account of his or her partner's investment strategy, and attempt to reply to it in such a way that each of the couple maximizes his or her utility, given the other's strategy, over a life-time of partnership.[2] We try to show that this explains women's investments in care rather than career, when account is taken of such factors as their probability of outliving their partners by several years.

However, this involves women in short- and medium-term choices that give them smaller pay-offs than men (the equivalent of the Nash equilibrium in a Battle of the Sexes game where they get the lower score).[3] More significantly, it is not clear that women's strategies take account of the risks of divorce. And women's position during their children's dependence is especially vulnerable, given their reliance on income from men's careers. Hence this economic explanation needs to be supplemented by an understanding of how trust and mutual commitment are sustained within asymmetrical rôle relationships.

This is where our analysis of the partnership code and the moral regulation of decisions is relevant. The interactional order of everyday family life allows women, in spite of their structural disadvantages, some autonomy and scope for resistance to power. Drawing on the work of James C. Scott,[4] we show how women's interpretations of agreements and decisions can diverge from men's, and how this enables them to pursue their interests within subordinate rôles. We go on to demonstrate how the requirements of the interactional order – for the production of selves, for meaningful communication and reliable structure – facilitate the development of autonomy, through the exchange of ritual respect in partnership.

Investments

With the notable exception of Mr and Mrs Mahogany, who gave an impressive account of their long-term investments in their farm, leading to a five-fold increase in its acreage and a corresponding growth in income, these interviewees did not describe their decisions in terms of joint strategic planning. Yet beneath the apparently haphazard moves and choices in their accounts there was – to judge by their currently fairly comfortable circumstances – a certain direction and purpose. In the vast majority of these households, at least one of the partners had gained enough incremental increases in salary to provide a more-than-adequate income, some fringe benefits and the prospects of income for retirement, and in most this was supplemented by the additional earnings of the other partner. All had maintained mortgage payments on an owner-occupied house, and many had savings, insurance policies and membership of private welfare schemes. This implied an *investment strategy* – long-term planning, which may have included some short-term sacrifices, for the sake of future gains. Even though many of these benefits were built in to the jobs that "careerists" had taken, the fact that they had sustained their employment in such positions represented a kind of investment decision.

Yet these investments by the partners were by no means symmetrical. Despite their virtually identical educational backgrounds, the men had invested far more heavily in "careers" (by staying in the same jobs, seeking promotion, and so on) and the women had invested much more of their time and energy in the household. What we seemed to be seeing was men following an *economic* investment logic, maximizing their "job assets" (in terms of current income for some, but long-term security for most), and the women making *moral* (non-market) investments in the family, a collective system of mutuality and sharing. This, of course, gave rise to inequality of power – for instance, in decisions over where the family should live (see Dr and Mrs Conifer, p. 106) – and women's investments were at risk if separation or divorce was threatened.

Did this imply two quite different kinds of economy – a "moral economy" of the household, involving sharing and reciprocity, where interests were seen as mutual, and outside this a market economy where the male careerist pursued competitive advantage? Were women – by choice, or through being socialized into altruism, or by the exercise of male power – making their decisions only by reference to the good of the household and without an eye to self-interest? Were men making two kinds of decision, the one as individual actors in the competitive economy, and the other as co-operative members of households, or were they translating strategic household decisions about the family's welfare into choices about their own labour supply and investment behaviour?

Recent anthropological theory has rejected the distinction between two spheres of decision making (market and non-market), pointing out that individuals must always choose between investing in communal welfare systems of mutual aid or in assets that give a return in money. Popkin shows that peasants' behaviour can be explained by postulating that they attach opportunity costs and pay-offs to collective infrastructural projects and private commercial enterprises,[5] planning and investing throughout both the crop cycle and the life cycle, and allocating their resources between communal and private schemes according to predicted risks and returns.[6] His analysis of investment strategies may be valuable for our study of better-off British couples. The decision whether to invest in "career" or in "family" might be seen not as a choice between non-comparable alternatives, but as one between alternative uses of scarce resources, where the choice depends on a calculative prediction of individual benefits.[7] Can the same investment analysis be applied to the decisions by men and women over how much of their time, energy and material resources to devote to the accumulation of job assets, and how much to household relationships of care and mutual support?

Investing in careers

The most striking fact about the labour-market positions of male and female interviewees was that, despite almost identical levels of education, men on average earned three times as much as women. We wanted to see whether this reflected an investment strategy – did men "make more" of their initial qualifications in "career" terms partly because women's supportive rôle in the household represented a vicarious investment in their success? In other words, did women choose to invest their resources in the household because they got a better return on the combination of pay-offs from this activity and from the long-term benefits of male careerism (pensions, perks, private welfare schemes) than they would from investing in their own "careers"?

In the interviewees' accounts, there were no noticeable differences between men's and women's versions of any education they had up to first degree level where degree studies were undertaken immediately after schooling. Both men and women gave versions of subsequent education and training (college based or distance learning) as long-term investments in qualifications that allowed future advancement (including promotion to more senior posts). Another group of male "careerists", those in insurance, accountancy, estate agency and other commercial occupations, gave far more instrumental accounts of gaining professional qualifications while working their way up in their organizations. Those in commercial management posts appeared to be earning a "job rent" – a premium for staying

DECISIONS

with their firm that went to "insiders" and took the form of high salaries and fringe benefits. Hence they placed a high value on security and continuity.

Mr Willow: I'm security-conscious, I suppose. I've got lots of brothers who've been all over the world and done all sorts of things which I haven't, I've been stuck in the same job because I've got this basic need for security [. . .] I think one of the attractions, one of the benefits, of working for an insurance company is [. . .] that there's a subsidized mortgage as part of the package.   (Mr Willow, 7)

These two kinds of investments – improving job qualifications and seeking a job-rent through continuity within the same organization – were (in principle at least) open to both men and women, yet a large majority of men made some such investments in their "careers" and only a small minority of women did so. Of the latter, most were teachers, and two of these (Mrs Dogwood and Mrs Birch) did not want to leave the classroom for more managerial posts, while two others (Mrs Pine and Mrs Palm) were considering leaving teaching for research or further (non-career-orientated) study. Yet most of the women described their earlier work experience, before they had children, as being of a kind that could have developed into a "career" if they had invested in this, rather than in the family, and in their partner's advancement.

The striking feature of women's accounts of this moment in the family life cycle is that, although they describe the decision to have children as a choice, there is little or no discussion of the implications of giving up a job with good prospects and rejoining the labour market either in a different (often manual or secretarial) rôle or at much reduced salary, status, hours, etc. This is particularly marked for those women who moved away from London, following their partner to the South West, at the same time as starting a family. Mrs Hemlock says she "didn't make the effort" to keep in touch with her London publishing contacts.

Mrs Hemlock: But we had this funny situation of life before and life after the children, because when we came down here I got pregnant, and so the life before [this city] is one thing, and then life after . . .
                        (Mrs Hemlock, 1, 12)

Mrs Laburnum was also in publishing in London when her husband applied for a job that involved a move to this area.

Mrs Laburnum: No, we just thought we'd give it a whirl really. [. . .]

154

Anyway, I was about to have a baby, and that seemed like a good idea,
I suppose you think it might be something new and different . . .

(Mrs Laburnum, 4)

Both these women (and some others, such as Mrs Box and Mrs Maple)
acknowledge that there is a trade-off between the advantages of living in
the South West of England and the lack of work opportunities in their
occupation. However, even those who were already based in the area seem
to accept the "career break" with childbearing as natural and inevitable,
and only Ms Blackthorn (who was a single parent) develops an argument
for better child care provision. Why do so many of the women interviewees invest so little in their own employment assets and settle for work that
can easily be reconciled with child care and domestic responsibilities?

Economic theory, supported by some research, explains this phenomenon in terms of employers' investment strategies. Continuous employment allows investment in "human capital" through on-the-job training
and experience:[8] skills are developed cumulatively. However, human capital
deteriorates quickly when the employee leaves the labour market, even for
quite a short period.[9] Because women are required to take breaks for
childbearing, it follows that (in the absence of active policies to combat
this effect) they are therefore the obvious choice to be child-carers also.
Research by Mincer in the early 1960s[10] suggested that men invested 10
times more in job training than women; his explanation of this was that
investment decisions by couples anticipated those of firms. In the 1970s
he advanced the hypothesis of a three-stage pattern in married women's
employment related to the family life cycle.[11] In the first, women who anticipated a period of child-rearing would acquire less job training than other
men and women with comparable education. In the second, such job-related skills as had already been acquired would deteriorate, and no new ones
would be gained, but instead women would invest in non-market productivity (presumably voluntary and community work, as well as domestic
skills). This "specialization" provided a rationale for the division of labour
in the household. Finally, women would return to continuous employment
after their children became more independent, because the incentives to
invest in job-related skills were re-established, though inevitably the potential returns would be lower, given the shorter period to retirement.

Only one of the women in our sample perfectly fits this pattern. Mrs
Fieldmaple, a graduate, did little to develop her educational attainments into
marketable employment assets; she was involved in playgroups when her
children were at the preschool stage, and worked in a junior post in a vol-

155

untary organization for a while; then she decided to get a professional qualification as the children reached secondary education and, having tried a
teaching course, which she disliked, she has now started to train as an
occupational therapist. Many others vaguely echo such a pattern, but the
variations are too wide for us to adopt this explanation. First, demand-side
factors work unevenly across the occupational range. It was far easier for
those who had previously worked as teachers (like Mrs Palm and Mrs
Dogwood) to get back into the labour market in mainstream or promo-
tion-stream rôles quite soon after having children than it was for women
in commercial occupations. Yet a few of the latter (Mrs Lime, Mrs Sycamore, Ms Blackthorn) did make strenuous efforts to maintain their labour-
market links and avoid the "skills decay" factor, even on reduced hours and
salaries. Secondly, the relative ease of combining teaching with caring for
children of junior school age attracted a number of women (Mrs Pine, Mrs
Pear, Mrs Hemlock) to retrain as teachers, and others (Mrs Birch, Mrs
Silverbirch) to improve their qualifications at this stage. Yet there are also
a number of trained teachers (Mrs Elm, Mrs Redwood, Ms Whitebeam) who
have not returned to this work, despite having secondary school age children in the case of the latter two. Thirdly, a large number of women seem
to be committed to part-time employment (Mrs Beech, Mrs Teak, Mrs Oak,
Mrs Hazel, Mrs Quince, Mrs Rowan, Mrs Elder, Mrs Chestnut, Mrs Cedar)
or craft work (Mrs Laburnum, Mrs Maple, Mrs Alder) despite the fact that
in many cases the pay is very low, or they are not apparently getting full
value for their qualifications or past experience.

Thus we are driven to looking more deeply at partnership for the analysis of investment decisions. These variations seem to cast doubt on the generalization from survey evidence that women returners to the labour market could quickly restore their earning power; [12] this was true only for teachers. The rest earned a small fraction of their partners' salaries, yet they chose
to work. Is there any theory that can make sense of such diversity?

Investment and partnership

Economic models of partnership are of limited use to us in our search for
a convincing analysis of investment decisions by couples. Samuelson's family consensus model [13] cannot tell us how the preferences in a "family welfare function" are derived or how couples evaluate and modify decisions.
Becker's altruistic model [14] (in which each partner's utility depends partly
on the other's consumption) does not help us handle conflicts of interest

or investment in separate (independent) resources. Most co-operative su-
per game models[15] are rather crude and do not allow for the asymmetrical bargaining power of the partners arising from their different rôles in
reproduction.

However, the idea of bargaining games between partners over a long
period[16] does seem to capture some aspects of the partnership decisions
we are trying to analyze. We need to show how asymmetrical bargaining
positions at the point in partnership where these interviews occur can
account for much larger investments by the woman in family and in the
man's career than in her own career; but if this is the "standard case" we
must go on to show why some men do not appear to develop careers and
some women do. At this point our analysis reverts to the assumptions
about rational agents (calculating utilities and probabilities) of game-theoretical explanations, and suspends the criticisms (in terms of the normative aspects of partnership) developed in our subsequent discussion. However, these will be reintroduced at a later stage (see conclusions to this
section, and the rest of this chapter).

Allowing for the facts that a woman lives (on average) six years longer
than a man[17] and that she is on average two years younger than her partner on marriage,[18] she stands to benefit from a career man's pension by
double his pay-off. Given that the retirement age in Britain is currently 65
for men, and 60 for women, and that men live on average to 73 and women
to 79, the average man's pay-off for his pension contributions is 8 years,
and the average woman's is 16 years (on his pension, given she is 63 when
he retires). Thus a game-theoretical representation of partnership as a life
cycle bargaining game might show the woman's optimum strategy as follows. She knows in advance that she stands to get double the long-term
pay-offs from her partner's career that he does, but only if their partnership endures up to his retirement. It is therefore worth her while to protect his career by being "supportive" (taking responsibility for children at
the expense of her paid work rôle), even if this means accepting smaller pay-
offs in the short to medium run. This model shows why it would pay Mrs
Conifer to move to this city with her husband, or Mrs Pine to move to the
Midlands with hers, sacrificing their work satisfactions and networks of
friendship and support. Dr Conifer and Dr Pine have around 20 years apiece
of career ahead of them, but both indicate that they may well return to the
areas favoured by their partners (Scotland and Devon respectively) for retirement. Thus Mrs Conifer and Mrs Pine have reason to believe that their
post-retirement pay-off will be even larger, since their first preference of

place to live would enhance the return on their investments in their partners' careers, measured in terms of likely years of survival.

Taken in isolation from the rest of our analysis, the paragraph above sounds very crude. However, taken in combination with the demand-side factors already mentioned in the last section, it seems to offer a plausible model of domestic rôle taking and decision making. Employers discriminate between men and women over their investments in human capital; the labour market is highly segmented, and in Britain and Europe the number of secure well paid full-time jobs is falling, while the number of insecure, low paid, part-time jobs is rising.[19] In Chapter 9 (p. 219) we will introduce an analysis of the labour market as a social institution in terms of a bargaining game between "insiders'" and "outsiders", which offers an explanation of why women do not collectively challenge the advantages enjoyed by men as holders of job assets from "insiders" careers. One part of the reason why well-qualified women as a group of "outsiders" do not attempt to bid down the "job rents" paid to men, by offering their labour power for lower salaries, is that such women usually are (as household partners) the indirect beneficiaries of men's job assets. They have invested in their partners' careers by being "supportive" during this phase of the family life cycle.[20] Given the current (discriminatory) structure of the labour market, the two strategies (man's career, woman's non-career) are the best replies to each other when account is taken of the life-course, including retirement.[21]

Hence the investment logic of women's rôle in partnership could be seen as similar to any other investment strategy – a small sacrifice of short-term pay-offs for a large gain in long-term pay-offs. However, the difficulty occurs in the medium term, because it is there that the woman's greatest sacrifices may be required and that the risks are greatest:[22] the man may decamp or his career may founder. Hence women face a shifting choice of options the further down the road of childbearing (and away from a career of their own) they go. What seems like a complementary, parallel and rational carriageway in relation to the man's career choices may turn out to be a cul-de-sac of lone parenthood or a diversion towards bankruptcy.

Ms Blackthorn's experiences in her first marriage are instructive. She moved home repeatedly, following her husband's career moves, when her children were young.

Ms Blackthorn: . . . there was no stability for me, I could never put myself in a position where I could think about what I wanted to do. And that just got worse and worse. Basically I think, the feeling in retrospect is that for a very long time I had to put everything on hold and I didn't particularly want to. But I didn't feel that I was in a position to do otherwise [. . .] we'd been there probably five months when my husband left. So then I had Daisy, 12 months old, and Alex was 7. So that then put me in a position that, basically I had to go back to work . . .   (Ms Blackthorn, 30)

Once driven into a local optimum (choosing to stick with their partner's career moves and decisions at key points) women may then find that it is too late to go back and be forced to start from a very disadvantaged position in the direction of building a career of their own. Alternatively, they may recognize the signs that their investment in their partner's career is shaky and take steps to strengthen their own job assets by investing more in their own career. This seems to be what Mrs Silverbirch is doing. As her husband's estate agency business has run into trouble, she has been investing in her teaching qualifications and increasing her earnings.

Q: Did you consider yourself a career teacher, or . . . ?

Mrs Silverbirch: Not initially, no, but I suppose I am considering it
     more now. I'm currently doing an M.Ed. to try and improve my
     qualifications.   (Mrs Silverbirch, 9)

She goes on in her individual interview to explain that most of her husband's salary from his "second job" goes on his living expenses or into the business, so she earns their income for all household expenditure except the mortgage. Hence she is attending to such issues as her own pension; and in the joint interview she makes it clear that she no longer sees her husband's "career" as a sounder investment than her own.

Q: . . . So how do you do your budgeting between you? Do you have a
     joint account or separate?

Mrs Silverbirch: No, we don't trust each other, not with joint accounts,
     do we dear? [laughs] We have a completely separate account [. . .]
     We don't even share the same bank [. . .]

Q: So what then is your [husband's] part, so what are you spending
     on?

Mrs Silverbirch: He pays the big bills.

Q: I'm assuming then there's quite a large differential between your
     two incomes?

DECISIONS

Mr Silverbirch: [indistinct]

Mrs Silverbirch: I seem to be catching up actually, sir. When I'm going for Deputy Head, then you'll be in for a [indistinct].

Q: This is something you're going to apply for, or you're working towards?

Mrs Silverbirch: Oh I will do, but not for another three or four years, when he's [son's] a bit older [. . .] when he becomes [. . .] a bit more independent I shall have a lot more time.

(Mr and Mrs Silverbirch, 21)

Similarly Mrs Birch, although she disclaims career ambitions, has recently taken a degree, and completed other courses, to improve her teaching qualifications. She makes it clear that her expectations of the pay-offs from her husband's "career" have been much reduced and more is required from her employment assets (he has recently taken a pay cut as director of his own small brewery).

Mrs Birch: As I've said, I enjoy the teaching, I wouldn't want to do anything else, but yes, all of a sudden I am tied to it [. . .]

Q: In terms of planning for your retirement, what sort of issues are on the agenda? [. . .]

Mrs Birch: We haven't actually planned for retirement, no. [. . .] obviously over the years the fact that Adrian has changed jobs drastically has meant that any retirement schemes he's belonged to have either been cashed in or added to one another, something like that. We realize that our prospects for retirement are not as rosy as they could be [. . .] Certainly, I mean although my salary is hardly magnificent, it certainly is enough to live on, and that's always been in the background that no matter what else happens there will always be that and of course the property as well . . .

(Mrs Birch, 4–5)

What we seem to be seeing here is these women reinvesting in their own job assets, and adjusting their expectations of the pay-offs from their husbands' assets. But there are also examples in the texts of women coming to the rescue of their husbands' "careers" when they were in trouble. Mrs Beech, for instance, had her small baby looked after by a friend while she ran her husband's solicitor's practice, when he was becoming stressed and overstretched, until it was possible to close it; meanwhile he got employment elsewhere. Now Mrs Beech jokes that she is well off in the rôle of part-time worker, and rejoices that society sanctions her staying at home with the children (see p. 110–11).

These medium-term dilemmas for women (appearing during the dependency of their children and hence before they are free to change course) are not easy to capture in game-theoretical models. What men and women make of themselves in relation to partnership and family is relative to each other's self-making; although the ethic of self-making is individualistic, the activity is not solitary. Martin Hollis points out that games against nature are parametric – based on probabilities – but games with people are different.[23] Jill has to work out what Jack does in relation to what she does, and so on.

The agents of rational choice theory, aware of each other's calculative and predictive rationality but able only to communicate through their actions, and pursuing strategies based on beliefs about what each other will do, can be shown to be incapable of choosing in ways that benefit them both in the simplest of games.[24] Although it is possible to devise ways in which they may be able to co-ordinate their choices (by gaining a "reputation" for reliability,[25] by "promising"[26] or by "joint precommitment"[27]), all these are either inconsistent with the assumptions of the theory or import elements from other games.[28] This kind of rationality turns out to be unable, on its own, to model long-term games of partnership in which co-ordination depends on postponed gratification and trust. Everyday agents – whether they are Popkin's peasants or these British couples – have to find *reasonable* ways of co-ordinating their decisions to ensure that their long-term investments produce the expected results. Although there is no "moral economy" in which decisions are totally non-calculative, reasonable co-ordination requires moral regulation.

So the investment logic of this kind of strategy can be successfully managed to its conclusion only by something other than the "rationality" of economic theory. Hence our analysis at this point tries to complement the explanations offered by economic models (bargaining theory) with the interpretations available from a sociological understanding of the accounts. We need to see how the trajectory of these partnerships over time creates mutual expectations that are normative and how these are handled in everyday life. The Conifers and the Pines do not explicitly calculate the consequences of their partners' preferences in the asocial, abstract, utilitarian manner of rational choice and game theory; they try by empathy to anticipate and influence them.

161

Dr Conifer takes photographs of his new job location in a vain attempt to soften the blow of the move; Dr Pine does the shopping when he gets home for the weekend; both talk about retiring to the area they know their partners prefer. By cultivating joint projects, shared activities and "quality of life" priorities, they seek to build mutual trust and commitment to their joint future plans. Hence they encourage the expectation that the long-term pay-offs will make these short-term sacrifices worth while, they seek to create links between their decisions over career and the context of partnership, making the trajectories of their joint lives explicit, and binding themselves to these forms of co-operation (rhetorically at least). Joint pre-commitment is thus the attempt to overcome the paradoxes and problems posed by a bargaining-theory version of the life-time partnership game.

Jobs, rôles and the regulation of dependence

By looking at accounts of employment decisions and partnership during the period of children's dependency, we are therefore analyzing the mid-point in a life-time relationship, whose characteristics can partly be explained in terms of a rational-choice bargaining game, and partly be understood in terms of negotiated normative commitments. But there is clearly another dimension in the interview accounts of this stage of partnership – power. Too many women face difficult issues over how to reconcile the needs of children, the development of their own labour-market rôles and the demands of their partner's careers to conceal this aspect of the relationship. Even though there is a kind of taboo on talking about separation and divorce in the interviews, the very few women who mention this topic display considerable concern about the disadvantages of their situation. To read the accounts of women facing unexpected changes in their lives brought about by their partner's pursuit of career advantage – Mr Hemlock's sabbatical year abroad, Mr Yew's firm's move from London, Dr Pine's move to the Midlands – is to become aware of their relative powerlessness in the face of these men's control over the household's destiny. Even a sudden setback in a hitherto successful career – such as the reduced profits of Mr Redwood's solicitors firm, recently declared – makes the implications of women's dependence painfully obvious. Mrs Redwood is an occasional piano teacher.

Mr Redwood: Yes, we came back from that partners' meeting and we
    were . . .

Mrs Redwood: . . . suicidal . . .

Mr Redwood: Yes, you've obviously got to talk about it and . . . It's very difficult to try not to over-react, if you like.

Mrs Redwood: Well, I worry more than you do about it.

Mr Redwood: Well, you worry more than me about it because you're not the one that's in control of it.

Mrs Redwood: That's right.

Mr Redwood: In a sense . . .

Mrs Redwood: That's right, and I just see this overdraft. But the nature of the way that it works . . . we've always had an overdraft and I see this going up and up and up, it does worry me, but . . .

(Mr and Mrs Redwood, 39)

Feminist theory links male power with the systematic extraction of unpaid services from women; patriarchy in these households seems inextricably linked with men's job assets.[29] In feminist political theory, the marriage contract is one in which woman becomes part of her husband's property, and the right to domestic privacy is the right of each man to be left alone to oppress a woman.[30] Women's civil and political rights in the public sphere mask their subordination and exploitation in the private sphere, where male domination is seen as part of the "natural" (prepolitical) order.[31] Men's employment assets give them access to property (including employment and pension rights), which allows them to exercise power through women's economic dependence.

Since the feminist analysis of male power suggests that this is ideologically constructed as being of biological or psychological origin, we should not be surprised to find little rational justification for, or argument against, women's subordination. The fact that there was little interview talk about power in partnerships, and an absence of feminist discourse in women's accounts to male interviewers, is only to be expected. In this section, we want to analyze what is said about dependence and independence, and how the tensions over these dimensions of partnership are regulated by the couples. Because so many of these issues were taken for granted within the standard division of rôles and responsibilities between men and women, the moral regulation of dependence and independence was most overt and articulate in the joint interviews with couples where the man had rejected the concept of "career" in his version of his employment decisions. It is on these that we now focus.

Mr Hawthorn and Ms Whitebeam both give "non-career" accounts of their work (his as a contract civil engineer, hers as a trainer on an employment training scheme). They are asked why they choose to use different names.

Ms Whitebeam: When the children were younger I did stay at home and was with the children and I know there was a certain amount of resentment in me at playing that part, and some resentment in Steve in having to be the breadwinner for all the year, and I think now that I work and he works, it feels a bit more like we can be independent in certain things that we do, and also because the children are independent, there aren't those restrictions. [. . .]

Mr Hawthorn: . . . the man's part of it in the traditional rôle is that he has to go out and bust a gut earning a living, particularly if he is the sole breadwinner, and that applies with working-class men to long hours or very hard physical work, which is what I see on construction sites, and it also applies to middle-class men who get very involved in career-orientated things. And it's like I observe quite a lot of men who appear to want a wife who stays at home and keeps up that end of things, whereas they're working their arses off at work, bloody killing themselves. That doesn't actually appeal to me. I think the other thing is that for a lot of men they're actually pretty much incapable of looking after themselves because they got married too young; it's like they left their mothers to marry their wives who look after them: and I didn't marry to have someone look after me, I would much rather be independent.

(Mr Hawthorn and Ms Whitebeam, 29–30)

Both partners make the connection between male careerism, female dependence and the constraints of gender rôles, but the outcome of their rejection of this relationship is that he gains in "independence" (for instance, to go and work on his old mill in France when he is between contracts) and she contributes more income to the household, "try to get more of an equal balance", but not for him to do more of the child care (he says "I don't have anything to do with the children"). So their attempt as a couple to avoid the "tendency to fall into traditional rôles" (Ms Whitebeam) is constructed in terms of his autonomy within non-advancement-orientated employment and her contribution to household income. It is Mr Hawthorn's "independence" in this sense – and not Ms Whitebeam's escape from reliance on his earnings or his contribution to child care – that is at stake in the moral regulation of these issues between them.

Much the same interaction is evident in Mr and Mrs Pear's account of their plans to readjust their labour-market commitments. Up to now, he has been the main provider of household income through his post of senior technician in a college (see p. 129). She teaches drama, music and movement to people with learning difficulties and pre-school children, and in her individual interview she agonizes about whether she should now pursue this as a full-time "career". She says that she "promised" her husband that he would have his turn to do self-developmental projects as their children became more independent. In the joint interview they are asked about the things they do outside work.

Mr Pear: Well, we sometimes do joint projects, don't we?

Mrs Pear: Yes, you sometimes do stuff with me.

Mr Pear: Well, there's environment things, there's being a parent governor of the school . . . [indistinct] the woodcraft folk, and then there's just lots of little projects and doing the allotment, doing the house.

Mrs Pear: But it has actually become more of an issue just lately, hasn't it? Because I think Ronald is beginning to feel that you want a more creative outlet, you've had enough?

Mr Pear: I've had enough of doing the house. I've had enough of coming back and thinking: what shall I do tonight, I'd really like to make a drum tonight, but the skirting boards all need rubbing down with caustic soda, and I always end up doing the skirting boards. So the sooner I get that out of the way I can make the drums.

(Mr and Mrs Pear, 25–6)

It seems that here too Mr Pear is claiming more autonomy than his rôle as main earner allows, even though his own version of his employment decisions is strongly self-developmental and anti-careerist. He and Mrs Pear appear to agree that he has discharged his responsibilities as major provider of income, and even as unpaid labourer in home improvements. This puts him in a strong position to press home his claim for greater self-developmental scope outside work.

Mr Pear: A friend of ours is an educational psychologist, and it's when you make a decision in your life, a major decision, and you make the decision because of persuasion, or pressure, or conformity, rather than making the decision because it's an intrinsic part of yourself: and to do that you "murder" part of yourself [. . .]

Mrs Pear: Yes, we've got used to that kind of convenience with your job, but I always have felt that you suffered through not really fulfilling yourself.
(Mr and Mrs Pear, 31–2)

These couples construe the man's rôle as "breadwinner" as a source of unwanted constraints for him, rather than of power in their partnership, and Mrs Pear in particular experiences a strong sense of obligation to take her turn in this rôle. However, both Mr Hawthorn and Mr Pear did provide all or most of the household income when their children were young, as did Mr Palm, whose partner took over his job in a "rôle swap" they both described as mutually advantageous.

These issues are quite differently regulated in the joint interview with Mr and Mrs Maple. Mrs Maple has been quite a successful craft worker, but for some time she has not been expanding her business because of the birth of their child (now aged 7 – see p. 81–2). Mr Maple has done some decorating work and other casual building work, but has recently trained to be a teacher; he is planning to move to London to do his probationary teaching year. In his individual interview, he describes his past antipathy to careerism and his (somewhat ambivalent) change to a career orientation. In the joint interview, the couple are asked about this:

Q: One of the things you [Mr Maple] mentioned last week is that you had this sort of anti-work attitude, and I was wondering where you got this attitude from, and why it sort of changed?

Mrs Maple: [laughs]

Mr Maple: It's easier to talk about why it's changed, I think, so perhaps I'll start there.

Mrs Maple: Where did you get the attitude from in the first place?

Mr Maple: Well, I'll do the easy bit first. It's partly changed under pressure from Maggie – I think I did touch on that last time – you know, she's basically getting fed up of doing all the work over the years – fair enough. But having been given a boot up the arse, I do actually quite enjoy the job that I'm heading towards at the moment, so I've actually discovered a fulfilling job I suppose, which a couple of years ago I didn't think existed. So, having been pushed in that direction, I'm quite satisfied in some ways with the job that I'm headed towards. Is that enough?

Q: I'm sort of wondering if you were swept along on this sixties sort of . . . ?

Mr Maple: I think that's partly it, I did grow up in the kind of subculture – I mean looking back on it, I wasn't thinking like this at the time – where you really did just live for today, I guess.

Mrs Maple: Yes, but you were allowed to carry that on to the age you are . . .

Mr Maple: That was the cosseting of my middle-class background . . .

Mrs Maple: No, no, no, no. You were allowed to carry on with vaguely that attitude because I was also paying for you to not work.

Mr Maple: Yes, all right.

Mrs Maple: So I'll make you admit that.

Mr Maple: Yes, I suppose that's the point really. It's quite a good point that it's not so much where it came from but how come it lasted so long. Because most of my contemporaries at school were just as happy-go-lucky as me at the time, but ended up in fairly stable jobs for one reason or another.

Mrs Maple: They're all stinking rich now. [laughs]

Mr Maple: Well a lot of them are, yes. [laughs]

(Mr and Mrs Maple, 33)

What is particularly interesting about this exchange is that the two partners are analyzing his move into teaching within different frameworks. He tries to account for it as a negotiated reciprocal decision made in the context of her discontent with the rôle of main earner (rather like Mrs Pear saying that she is taking over this rôle to relieve her husband's frustration) but with his sense of obligation reinforced by her "boot up the arse". But Mrs Maple will not let him get away with this. Her analysis is in terms of long-term strategy in a bargaining game: she has been "suckered" into the breadwinner's rôle, and she can force him into it only by refusing to co-operate until he makes a move to take over this responsibility. With considerable forcefulness she rejects his account ("No, no, no, no") and substitutes one in which his anti-work orientation and his non-career were possible only because of her willingness to earn enough to support the household. Hence in her version, he was able to sustain his "happy-go-lucky" practices as a free rider solely through her responsibility and work orientation. This passage would not be conceivable in a joint interview with a male "careerist" and a female "non-careerist": no man in our sample would discredit his wife's version of a morally adequate non-career in this way. This gendered difference in what constitutes a morally adequate account cannot be explained in this case purely in terms of child care responsibility, since Mr Maple was primarily responsible for this while his wife was working. Moreover, this moment of disagreement – in which Mrs Maple briefly undermines his account of the transition from "non-careerist" to "careerist" – is sustained for longer than any of the other disagreements between couples in the joint interviews. Mrs Maple is asked how she put up with him for so long:

Mrs Maple: Oh dear. Well probably very badly, I don't know. Half the time I reproached myself about being angry about it, and the other half of the time it was the opposite really. He did work on and off, but it was always me, I always paid; even though my work was really precarious, it was a lot more secure than anything he ever did. That's why this future thing of him taking over all the bills and that, I won't believe until I see it. [. . .] I think personally, now that you're sitting here I can say this, he's still very laid back about it, and when the pressure gets on he will change his attitude because he's learning – he said to me the other day he spends his money three times over. I'm the cautious one about spending because I've always been in control of the money, and I think it will turn around, when he starts earning he'll be very cautious. I don't know, maybe he won't [. . .] It's sort of a transition that's been forced on us, but it's probably the best way. And the next six months are going to be really tough – for me to relinquish the responsibility and for him to take it on.

Mr Maple: It sounds like a punishment.

Mrs Maple: Well it is. You take it as you like [laughs] – but you take it and you sort it out.

(Mr and Mrs Maple, 34–5)

Mrs Maple's account of the "transition" is couched in the rhetoric of her husband "learning responsibility" – rather as if he is a child who is still to be socialized into an adult rôle. He, in his turn, reinterprets this in a game-theoretical way: he is being punished for his defection in the prisoner's dilemma of partnership, and in the iterated version of the game she is playing Tit for Tat. It is perhaps an insightful comment on the nature of partnership that she retorts, "You take it as you like". Partnership is indeed ambiguous: it can be interpreted as a game between bargain-hunting rational egoists, who will defect and exploit at every opportunity (her retrospective version), or as a co-operative, negotiated series of transitions, based on reciprocity and fairness. It is not until near the end of the joint interview that the "moral" frame of partnership is restored and trust-orientated discursive regulation resumed.

So there are strategic games going on in these partnerships, even though they are only recognized as such in times of crisis, such as Mrs Conifer's moment of truth, Ms Blackthorn's hour of need, and Mrs Maple's well-aimed kick. But power is a complex feature of relationships. Traditional, taken-for-granted patriarchy has its responsibilities, which Mr Hawthorn, Mr Pear and Mr Maple would rather avoid. As soon as traditional rôles are challenged and women step into "breadwinner" and "careerist" rôles, men have opportunities to pursue long-term strategies of a new kind, which Mrs Maple now resists. The partnership code is a way of regulating the conflicts inherent in asymmetrical power relations. This is the subject of the final section.

Power and autonomy

These issues need to be addressed within a broader theoretical study of power and resistance to it. What our interviews displayed was the everyday practice of power relations. In making sense of this, we found the work of James C. Scott of great value. His original study of a peasant community in Malaysia and his subsequent broader critique of the dominant ideology thesis both analyze power relations as rooted in class and capitalist production but pay close attention to the resistance practices of subordinates.[32] He shows how these employ the repertoires of the powerful against those in authority, and use "the weapons of the weak" (defection, absenteeism, go-slows, minor sabotage, pilfering) against their oppressors. When Mrs Beech says that she "is onto a winner . . . because society accepts the fact that women stay at home", she is self-consciously borrowing from the ideology of women's subordination and turning it to her advantage: it is in her interests to reinforce hegemonic appearances rather than challenge the dominance of men. To what extent were women interviewees maintaining a public posture of compliance, while covertly pursuing their own ends, and subverting male power in small but subtle ways?

The clearest account by a woman of how she handled the expectation that she would be home based in a "supportive" rôle while her husband pursued his career comes from Mrs Willow. She had not greatly enjoyed her work as a nurse before she married, and gave it up when she had children, as he expected her to do.

Mrs Willow: I feel in lots of ways it wasn't very fair to Max, because I think that I had always implied that I was quite happy to stay at home and that I wasn't a career-minded person, because to be totally honest I had never really enjoyed work very much [. . .] and I was always quite keen to get off duty. So I think the thought of giving up work was quite inviting, so I don't think I had led Max to believe I was a career person at all. So, his reaction to me working was probably quite predictable, but I hadn't realized that he would feel like he did.

Q: And his reaction was? I know he wasn't very happy with it, but I mean how did he argue that?

Mrs Willow: He didn't argue it. He doesn't argue very often. He looked pained. Yes, it just was a bit difficult at times. In fact it went on for quite a long time if I'm honest. I put it down to his mid-life crisis, or male menopause, but it was very difficult for a while. I mean I used to go to work and then come home and change my uniform very quickly, so that he wouldn't know that I'd been to work. He did know I'd been to work, and he did know that I was going to work, but it was as though I was pretending I hadn't been to work . . . I'd be standing at the kitchen sink when he came in and I'd break my neck to get there. And I realize now with hindsight that I was just making it worse, I mean I just didn't have the nerve to say, "Well let's sit down and discuss it, why are you behaving like this and why am I behaving like a child?" [. . .] I probably think that he thought that he wasn't giving me enough money or he wasn't supplying a good enough standard of living . . . And it wasn't really anything to do with that at all, it was just the feeling of I wanted to do something a little bit else, and the independence it gave me not to be his wife but [. . .] and besides . . . then I started to spread my wings a bit more and I suddenly realized that having come up the scale quite a bit, and as a student never quite succeeded, to passing exams and realizing I could do it . . . but as a practice nurse I suddenly realized that people had tremendous faith in me and that I could do it and I went on and did other training and when I was asked I got to start lecturing and teaching, and by going and doing other courses I suddenly found out that, certainly in the world of practice nursing, most people know who I am, because I teach a lot and write articles. And it just suddenly was like a light switching on, somebody had valued what I was doing in a way, and I suppose it just snow-balled and it's difficult to stop doing it. (Mrs Willow, 37–9)

This sounds as if it is beginning to develop into a feminist critique of patriarchal domestic relations, but it does not. Mrs Willow instead pays tribute to the security her husband's job and income have provided, saying they enabled her to develop her interests and abilities:

Mrs Willow: Oh, I'm sure it's been the security of being able to do it the way I've wanted to do it, rather than feeling I've got to work. And I wonder in a way if that's why I enjoyed going back to work, because I didn't have to, whereas before when I'd worked, as a student and before we were married, I'd had to work because else we wouldn't have been able to afford to have lived [. . .] And so I wonder if, because we were financially quite happy and comfortable, and I didn't have to work, whether that, the perverse way my mind obviously works, meant I quite enjoyed working. (Mrs Willow, 54)

And again in their joint interview she demurely plays the part of the grateful wife, graciously acknowledging her partner's protection and his enabling rôle.

Mrs Willow: . . . I certainly feel that I couldn't have done it without the security of having a good base. In fact in a way it's been a luxury to be able to do it, because I felt confident that the home base, the family, and my marriage, hopefully, is secure [laughs]. And I don't think I could have done it without that security . . .
(Mr and Mrs Willow, 68)

Mrs Willow's "secret" excursions into the labour market, her unwillingness to challenge her husband's expectations of her domestic rôle directly, and her statement that her achievements are attributable to the "security" his job and property give her are all typical of the practices that Scott identifies with subordinate groups.[33] He points out that, when the weak do protest about the abuse of power by those with authority over them, they often complain of the lack of *dignity* and *autonomy* accorded them.[34] This part of his analysis is rather underdeveloped in his work, but is important for our understanding of passages like this, in which Mrs Willow says that she wanted "something a little bit else" and "some independence" yet seeks this within a relationship in which her husband's career and assets still take priority. We need to analyze this "autonomy within domination" more closely in order to make sense of the interactional order of partnership.

Mrs Willow's version of partnership is one of reciprocity within asymmetrical power relations. Her coy acknowledgement of her dependence on his career assets is her part in the ritual courtesies of such a relationship; he in turn pays his respects to her achievements in her field (see p. 34). Their mild complaints about each other's expectations in their individual interviews are politely modified, and Mrs Willow defers to her husband's position as the head of the household. All this seems to relate as much to the "face work" of the interactional order that we analyzed in Part I (Ch.3) as to any bargaining strategy over power. It is through the skills and competencies of these rituals that partners understand each other and communicate mutual recognition, as when Mrs Willow "repaired" the rift between them over her taking a job. In conflicts such as that one, there is a dialogue, largely in the terms of the dominant ideology of gender – but, as Scott points out, such hegemonic discourses are in a sense "an invitation to a structured argument", in which "the basic terms . . . are shared but the interpretations follow wildly divergent paths in accordance with vital interests".[35]

As we have seen, this seems to be the case with the partnership code: its indexical terms allow the partners to interpret it within a context, and hence it gives them the autonomy to choose in ways they can retrospectively justify (as prioritizing the family) but which are in line with projects and interests of their own. Resistance practices are not strictly strategic (except in Scott's sense of avoiding the risks of confrontation). The important point is that reciprocity is not just a contingent feature of patriarchal or any other power relations; it is a necessary condition for the communication on which the interactional order is based. The best way for Mrs Willow to pull off a creditable performance of herself is to keep up her husband's appearances (to sustain his "face" by avoiding giving offence). Formal power relations require the rituals of "giving face" in interactions to be asymmetrical (in terms of authority and deference) but the principles of mutual commitment still apply. Dominator and dominated have an interest in saving each other's face.

This makes the few instances of open disagreement between the partners in the joint interviews particularly interesting. As we have seen, these are heavily concentrated in the interviews where the man had no career assets (Mr Maple) or where these were depreciating (Mr Birch, Mr Silverbirch, pp. 116 and 119) or where the man gives a "non-career" account of his work but describes the woman's as a "career". Mr Larch and Ms Plum have a lengthy disagreement about whether her "career" was a success, which is ended only when the interviewer tactfully reminds them of their mutual commitment to "teamwork".

Other couples whose divergent interpretations of the code become overt are generally able to resolve their differences by the small teases and in-jokes that characterize partnerly interaction, but it is almost always the woman who finally defers to the man's version. After Mrs Lime has exposed her husband's lack of help with domestic chores by saying how she does all these, even after a day's work, he resorts to the jokey interactive ploy of saying "poor old thing". The dialogue continues:

Mrs Lime: Yes, but I more or less cooked before, when we were both working [full time] anyway.

Mr Lime: I'm the occasional cook, aren't I? I do a mean chilli, and occasionally we have people round, but I'm somebody who just messes up the kitchen completely, you know; it takes four hours to boil an egg. I quite enjoy doing it, but Liz predominantly looks after the house.

Mrs Lime: Well, it's just like most men, bloody hopeless really! [laughs]

Mr Lime: That's what we like to think . . . we're not hopeless, we're just downright lazy.

(Mr and Mrs Lime, 34)

The large variations in the patterns of labour-market decisions by these couples are therefore analyzable in terms of long-term bargaining strategies but an everyday partnership order that allows women considerable scope for autonomous decisions and men a good deal of flexibility in interpreting their responsibilities. The counterparts of Mrs Beech's leisurely chats with friends and Mrs Willow's secret sallies are Mr Hemlock's year in Europe and Mr Hawthorn's mill in France – rather weightier and more extensive undertakings. But on the whole women have a more varied portfolio of voluntary and communal activities and self-developmental employment than men, and this is what leads Mr Pear, Mr Teak and Mr Larch to insist that it is only by rejecting "careerism" that they can be really autonomous in their choices of how to combine paid and unpaid work.

The more accepted political interpretation of autonomy within partnership – the quest for independence through the accumulation of individual job assets by women – occurs in only a minority of households, and even here there are only two who give versions of these choices that question the dominant discourses of gender relations. Mrs Fieldmaple's critique of her husband's pension scheme, and the risks for herself in the event of their marriage breaking up, stands out as the only such account of making separate provision for retirement. Ms Blackthorn, too, gives as her reason for having a separate bank account and other financial arrangements the possibility that her fairly new relationship with Mr Spruce might break up, as her first marriage did. But all the other couples give versions of their decisions in which autonomy is sought through the individual interpretation of an apparently consensual (but importantly indexical) code, which enables them to accommodate their divergent interests.

Conclusions

This chapter is crucial for our overall analysis of decision-making by the interviewees. In it we have argued that lifelong partnership choices can be explained in terms of investments in job assets and property and in the family as a system of care. Men's and women's decisions over how to allocate their resources between these uses are clarified by bargaining theory, because this helps us see that women's long-term strategy can be analyzed in terms of higher pay-offs over the duration of their lives, achieved by sacrifices in the short and medium term.

However, the everyday order of partnership relies on negotiating decisions within rôles in which power is unevenly distributed – especially at the point in partnership at which these interviews occurred. Our analysis of power relations in the household emphasizes that reciprocity in partnership is as much about ritual respect in interaction as about a system of sharing resources, or a code of moral conduct. The partnership code allows women enough autonomy to pursue their own purposes and interests within the relationship, while men also have considerable scope to interpret their responsibilities. It sustains an interactional order that provides the appearance of stable and trustworthy relations, reliable enough for practical purposes.

So far, our analysis has focused fairly narrowly on these households, trying to make sense of how the accounts relate to each other, and the relationships between the couples' decisions that they reveal. In the final part of the book we will consider what kind of society these household relations construct – the forms of citizenship revealed in these accounts.

References

1. S. Popkin, *The rational peasant: the political economy of rural Vietnam* (Chicago: Chicago University Press, 1979).
2. M. Hollis & R. Sugden, "Rationality in action", *Mind* **102** (405) (1993), 9.
3. Ibid., p. 9, and B. Lyons, "Game theory", in *The theory of choice: a critical guide*, S. Hargreaves Heap, M. Hollis, B. Lyons, R. Sugden, A. Weale, Ch. 7, especially p. 109 (Oxford: Blackwell, 1992).
4. J. C. Scott, *Weapons of the weak: everyday forms of peasant resistance* (New Haven: CT: Yale University Press, 1985); *Domination and the arts of resistance* (New Haven, CT: Yale University Press, 1990).
5. Popkin, *The rational peasant*, pp. 25–36.
6. Ibid., p. 37.
7. Ibid., p. 251.
8. G. S. Becker, "Investment in human capital: a theoretical analysis", *Journal of Political Economy (Supplement)* **70** (1962), 9–49.
9. J. Mincer & H. Ofek, "Interrupted work careers", *Journal of Human Resources* **17** (1982), 3–24.
10. J. Mincer, "On the job training: costs, returns and some implications", *Journal of Political Economy (Supplement)* **70** (1962), 50–79.
11. J. Mincer, *Schooling, experience and earnings* (National Bureau of Economic Research, 1974); J. Mincer & S. Polacheck, "Family investments in human capital: the earnings of women", *Journal of Political Economy* **82** (1974), S76–S108.
12. M. Corcoran, G. Duncan & M. Ponza, "A longitudinal analysis of white women"s wages", *Journal of Human Resources* **18** (4) (1983), 492–520.
13. P. A. Samuelson, "Social indifference curves", *Quarterly Journal of Political Economy* **70** (1956), 1–22.
14. G. S. Becker, "A theory of marriage: part I", *Journal of Political Economy* **81** (4) (1973), 813–46, and "A theory of marriage, part II", *Journal of Political Economy*, **82** (1) (1974), S11–S26; and *A treatise on the family* (Cambridge, MA: Harvard University Press, 1981).
15. See, for instance, M. Manser & M. Brown, "Marriage and household decision making: a bargaining analysis", *International Economic Review* **21** (1) (1980), 31–44.
16. Lyons, "Game theory", pp. 112–29.
17. Office of Population Censuses and Surveys, *Population Trends* (London: HMSO, Au-

tumn 1992), Table 12, p. 62.
18. Ibid., Table 21, p. 72.
19. G. Esping-Andersen, *The three worlds of welfare capitalism* (Oxford: Polity, 1990), ch. 8; C. C. Harris & L. D. Morris, "Labour markets and the position of women", in *Gender and stratification*, R. Crompton and M. Mann (eds), 86–96 (Oxford: Polity, 1986).
20. For a life-course perspective on women's rôles in labour market and household, see J. Brannen, "The resumption of employment after childbirth: a turning-point within a life-course perspective", in *Women and the life cycle: transitions and turning-points*, P. Allatt, T. Keil, A. Bryman, B. Bytheway, 164–77 (London: Macmillan, 1987); also (in the same volume) S. Yeandle, "Married women at midlife: past experience and present change", pp. 117–34; J. Mason, "A bed of roses? Women, marriage and inequality in later life", pp. 90–105. See also J. Burgoyne, "Change, gender and the life course", in *Social change and the life course*, G. Cohen (ed.) (London: Tavistock, 1987); A. Bryman, B. Bytheway, P. Allatt, T. Keil (eds), *Rethinking the life cycle* (London: Macmillan, 1987).
21. J. Finch & D. Morgan, "Marriage in the 1980s: a new sense of realism?"in *Marriage, domestic life and social change: writings for Jacqueline Burgoyne*, D. Clark (ed.) (London: Routledge, 1991).
22. D. Clark, "Changing partners: marriage and divorce across the life course", in *Social change and the life course*, G. Cohen (ed.), pp. 106–33; M. MacLean, "Households after divorce: the availability of resources and their impact on children", in *Give and take in families*, J. Brannen & G. Wilson (eds) (London: Allen & Unwin, 1987).
23. M. Hollis, "Moves and motives in the games we play", *Analysis* **50** (2) (1990), 51.
24. Hollis & Sugden, "Rationality in action", pp. 8, 21.
25. D. M. Kreps & R. Wilson, "Reputation and imperfect information", *Journal of Economic Theory* **27** (1982), 253–79.
26. D. Gauthier, *Morals by agreement* (Oxford: Oxford University Press, 1975).
27. E. Van Damme, "Stable equilibria and forward induction", *Journal of Economic Theory* **48** (1989), 476–96.
28. K. Binmore, "Bargaining and morality", in *Rationality, justice and the social contract*, D. Gauthier & R. Sugden (eds) Hemel Hempstead: Harvester Wheatsheaf, 1993).
29. C. MacKinnon, *Feminism unmodified* (Cambridge, MA: Harvard University Press, 1987).
30. C. Pateman, *The sexual contract* (Oxford: Polity, 1988).
31. S. Moller Okin, *Women in western political thought* (Princeton, NJ: Princeton University Press, 1979).
32. Scott, *Weapons of the weak*, and *Domination and the arts of resistance*.
33. Scott, *Domination and the arts of resistance*, pp. 85–107.
34. Ibid., pp. xi-xii, 5–8, 112–15, 210.
35. Ibid., pp. 100–102.

Part III: CITIZENSHIP

CHAPTER 8

A Property-owning Democracy?

In this third part of the book, we analyze how the interviewees' individualistic accounts of their decisions and their practices of partnership influenced their construction of their relations with their fellow citizens. Although the research interviews were not focused on citizenship, the accounts reveal a good deal about their interpretations of their entitlements and obligations as members of a political community. The priority they gave to self-responsibility and family had important implications for their descriptions of wider society and their responsibilities towards others.

These questions are of considerable significance because of the changes that have taken place in British society since the beginning of the 1980s, partly through government policy. Our aim in this concluding part is to see how better-off couples – the material beneficiaries of many of these changes – described their position in the wider community, their political interests, their affiliations with groups, organizations or parties, and their commitments to private and collective welfare systems. We also wanted to analyze how they accounted for their own good fortune, and whether their versions of this provided evidence of how they construed the misfortunes of others.

Our methods of analysis in this part of the book extend the scope of those already used to analyze agents' identities and how couples coordinated decisions. We employ the concept of *interpretative repertoires* to examine how interviewees justify their advantages, include or exclude the needs of others in their accounts, and identify issues as public ones where political values and collective responsibility are at stake. These repertoires are "broadly discernible clusters of terms, descriptions and figures of speech often assembled around metaphors or vivid images . . . They are some of the resources for making evaluations, constructing factual versions and performing particular actions".[1] In describing their labour-market decisions, the interviewees anchored these in the context of a particular kind society, with themselves located in a set of social relations. Some topics prompted comments on the political implications of decisions, others did not. Their accounts "are organized in specific ways which make a particular reality appear solid, factual and stable".[2]

As we saw in Chapter 3, the interviewees were often required to account for how they managed situations of uncertainty and change, including an interpretation of their responsibilities in threatening and unpredictable circumstances. Behind these events in their personal lives lay much larger changes in the world economy and the political order. The British government's radical attempts since 1979 to alter the balance between private property and collective social rights and to restructure the agencies of public administration can be understood as a response to global issues about citizenship and nation states. Some time in the mid-1960s, the expansion in world trade, the rise in international corporations and a new international division of labour began to erode the post-war institutional structures of both Western capitalist and Soviet bloc socialist states. In the case of the latter, the symptoms of this process were dramatic – economic sclerosis followed by political collapse – but among the advanced capitalist states they were more subtle and varied. While some corporatist social democracies (like Sweden) were able to go on juggling with rising taxes, tighter wage and price controls and expanding welfare provision, right into the 1990s most European states sought refuge in a larger trading bloc (the EC), sacrificing large parts of their long-cherished systems of national economic management and social protection. The British government was both bolder about dismantling its (always rather unsuccessful) corporatist institutions, and more cautious about losing its political sovereignty, than its EC partners were: in the euphoria following the collapse of the Soviet and East European regimes, it claimed to have discovered the elements of a sustainable social order within the new global economy – the "property-owning democracy".

At an institutional level, the Thatcher years in Britain saw a self-conscious experiment in reconstituting social relations, breaking old loyalties and bonds (especially to collective systems and public agencies) and strengthening new ones (based on commercial enterprises, private property and family self-reliance). The government's strategy consisted in the rhetorical and structural re-articulation[3] of group interests, away from universalistic state provision and towards individual self-reliance and household mutual responsibility, leaving a residual public sector to regulate the poor. At a political level, this relied on creating a coalition of voters who defined themselves as economically secure – "comfortable Britain", the two-thirds society[4] – against those with an interest in redistributive policies by expanded welfare provision. More subtly, it also required the government to convince people like these interviewees that they were better off, despite an overall level of taxation that remained constant and their increased personal liability for a range of welfare goods previously provided out of this taxation.

These changes have redirected social scientific theory to the concept of citizenship, as a membership category that transcends class and other distinctions. Attention has turned back towards T. H. Marshall's analysis of the protective capsule of rights (civil, political and social) that gave all citizens a common status – "a kind of moral if not material equality"[5] – in the post-war social democratic order of the welfare state. Critics of the government's strategy point out that new institutional systems neither adequately protect those most in need nor create common interests between economic groups; instead, new welfare schemes (such as stricter work tests for the unemployed) reinforce conflicts of interest between taxpayers and the poor, and institutionalize the situation of an excluded "underclass".[6] Proponents of the strategy look for new forms of "active citizenship" to legitimate the advantages of the better-off, and new ways for poor people to be "reintegrated" into mainstream society by processes of re-education (if necessary compulsory) into "the social obligations of citizenship".[7]

In this chapter, we look at the idea of a "property-owning democracy", and at how the interviewees' accounts constructed their ownership of property, their democratic responsibilities and their place in the polity. In the next section, we locate the concept of property-ownership as a basis for citizenship in the liberal tradition of theory of a democratic polity. We go on to analyze the kinds of property most relevant for citizenship in contemporary Britain, and to examine how the interviewees interpret their access to these assets. Following the work of those social theorists who identify regular jobs and their attendant assets as the most important forms of property in modern polities, we see how interviewees' accounts of their tenure of such jobs (their entitlement through the processes of what they have made of themselves) exclude reference to issues of power, justice or democratic participation. The repertoires of contemporary British individualism do not construct property within a discourse of active membership of a local community. The implications of this are analyzed through Tocqueville's theory of democratic citizenship.

However, some interviewees do draw on a *collectivist repertoire* to interpret events within their sector of the labour market. Many of those employed in the public sector give accounts that include rhetorical resistance to government policies, within social democratic discourses of collective provision. Others summarily reject private welfare systems as inconsistent with their (implicitly collectivist) values. However, our analysis shows that these collectivist rhetorical constructions are deployed within individualist accounts, and display confusion and bafflement over how to translate these discourses into effective action as citizens. Only in their work-places, as public sector employees, defending their jobs and established practices, do they see opportunities for actions that express collectivist goals.

In the following section, we analyze interviewees' accounts of their children's futures. One reason why they attach such importance to decisions about schooling is that they see it as essential for their children to gain access to higher education. They construct obtaining a degree as the minimum requirement for achieving the status of job-holder within a desirable career. Even if they acknowledge that their offspring may not want such a job, they describe a degree as a necessary condition for "real choice" of an alternative pathway. The individualist repertoire thus serves to demand high educational achievement, even though many of the interviewees with well paid jobs had few qualifications when they themselves left school. However, it does not link these discourses with ones of equality of opportunity or social justice for "others" who lack family advantages.

Individualist accountability, as we show in the final section, does not require these interviewees to take account of the welfare of others in their choices over public and private welfare. They describe their decisions within the frameworks of "career" and "family", not social citizenship. Some paradoxical consequences of these choices will be analyzed in Chapter 9.

Property and democratic community

We wanted to analyze how the individualist repertoires used by these couples to interpret their lifestyle choices to us and to regulate their daily interaction with each other described their relationships with their fellow citizens – and especially those less fortunate than themselves. The key terms of the new British model of citizenship are "property" and "democracy", and we wanted to see how (if at all) interviewees made links between them. Our general conclusion, which will be set out in this chapter, is that they could not make satisfactory links within the cultural resources available to them – liberal individualist repertoires – and that this has important implications for the analysis of citizenship in North America, where liberal individualism is already the dominant discourse of social relations, and Europe, where it is being increasingly adopted.

So far in this book we have emphasized the *ad hoc*, do-it-yourself, improvised nature of the interactional order created by these couples, through which they sustained the sense of a stable social and material reality, sufficiently serviceable for everyday decision making. However, the repertoires they used to do this were not arbitrary or conjured up out of nothing; they were culturally produced, sustained and developed, through the shared discourses and practices of a political community. Hence we must briefly trace the origins of the liberal individualist tradition, particularly in relation to its two key elements, property ownership and democracy.

The tension between these two dimensions of liberalism was clearest in the writings of John Stuart Mill.[8] He recognized that the notion of a political community implied shared resources, and that the gradual progress towards democracy that he advocated depended on the development of common interests between classes, and hence the relative decline of the political significance of property. Yet he was writing in a tradition in which property was central to the whole construction of a stable social order, and was built on 17th-century theories of possessive individualism.[9] In Locke's political thought, property was the basis of citizenship because all – even the poor – benefited from the growth in productivity that private ownership allowed.[10] Hume argued that property was a necessary social institution, not only because of scarcity of resources, but also because of human beings' limited benevolence (individuals could feel "affection and tender regard" only for a few others, and especially their families, not for all other members of their community).[11] The liberal tradition since Mill can be read as a debate between those (like Alexis de Tocqueville,[12] T. H. Green[13] and his followers, William Beveridge[14] and John Rawls[15]) who thought that Hume's limited benevolence could be extended (and democracy strengthened) by a judicious mixture of moral education, political participation and social engineering; and those (like Herbert Spencer[16] and more recently Friederich von Hayek[17] and Robert Nozick[18]) who thought that the "spontaneous" order of property entitlements, markets and families provided a more reliable and sustainable basis for prosperity and social order.

Democratic theory has always included a tradition of criticism of property relations and of this basis of liberalism. Marx insisted that no *real* democracy was possible so long as private property (and hence class conflict) persisted. Bourgeois constitutions split off the private individual's pursuit of particular interests from the citizen's commitment to the common interests of the political community.[19] Feminists argue that the "fraternal contract" between men (as "heads of the households") excludes the private realm of the family, and hence bars women from citizenship in the public sphere, treating them as part of men's property.[20] Hence the cultural legacy of liberal individualism consists of a strongly contested debate, with one pole represented by ideas of property, privacy and family, and the other by community and democratic citizenship. In drawing on these cultural resources and unresolved conflicts, the interviewees were, in effect, entering that debate.[21]

This was particularly clear in Tocqueville's classic study of *Democracy in America*. He analyzed the roots of democratic participation in the practices of small-town voluntary associations and the political culture of small farmers and traders. Unlike earlier republican theorists, such as Rousseau, he thought that good government depended not on the civic virtues of citizens but on "a sort of refined and intelligent selfishness",[22] which allowed Americans to recognize that their own private interests were inextricably tied in with the interests of the community, and thus that they should be active in collective decision making. Tocqueville argued that this was the main factor in preventing the young polity with its strong tendencies towards an egalitarian mass society from becoming (by default) a centralized elected tyranny. He warned that individualism and the pursuit of wealth pulled citizens away from the public sphere and towards "the circle of family and friends",[23] and in this "little society" to "leave the greater society to look after itself".[24] The doctrine of economic self-interest was the enemy of democracy, because it led citizens to believe they can leave government to others and withdraw from public life. He painted a vivid picture of a culture in which the individualist feels nothing for fellow citizens: "in the end, each nation is no more than a flock of timid and hard-working animals with the government as its shepherd."[25]

What do these interview transcripts reveal about the tensions between retreat into a "small circle" of property and family and democratic participation in community and voluntary organization? This question is, of course, highlighted by Mrs Redwood's and Mr Yew's almost identical "confessions" (see p. 142), echoed by Dr Conifer, Ms Blackthorn and Mr Lime, that their decisions to choose private education for their children set aside their political principles and sense of social justice. The prioritization of family, picked up in the title of this book, seems to be precisely that narrowing of citizens' locus of identity, perception of interest and commitment to membership of which Tocqueville warned.

Yet some caution should be exercised before this interpretation is adopted. First, the very nature of property has changed over the centuries. Whereas Locke was writing primarily about ownership of land, and Tocqueville about small stores and workshops, these interviewees (except for the Mahoganies and Mr Birch) own very few productive resources. In an employment-based economy, access to property (houses, shares, insurance policies, entitlements to private welfare provision) lies in the secure possession of a good job (and its attendant perks and pension rights). In recent years, it has been argued that *regular jobs* constitute the most important assets, giving economic advantages and potential for domination. For instance, Philippe Van Parijs has calculated that such job assets provide by far the largest sources of wealth in modern societies, as well as access to other forms of property.[26] This analysis is echoed in social theory on class, exploitation and power.[27]

The interpretative repertoires of individualism allow interviewees to account for their possession of jobs as part of their descriptions of what they have made of themselves by their own development of their talents. Since men own the vast bulk of job assets among the interviewees, this section focuses on their accounts. They are not required to demonstrate awareness of how competition for such jobs disadvantages women, black people or members of the younger generation by the form of accountability that characterizes individualism. Even when men who give "career" accounts acknowledge that as "insiders" their progress through promotion to better-paid posts with more fringe benefits is almost automatic, they do not see themselves as called on to account for their entitlement to these advantages (as compared with the claims of "outsiders" like low paid or unemployed people). Responsibility for what they have made of themselves is thus interpreted as implying entitlement to any job assets they succeed in gaining.

Mr Ash's account of his career as a solicitor provides an illustration of the individualist repertoire.

Mr Ash: I'm being admitted as a partner on 1st November.

Q: Congratulations.

Mr Ash: Thank you. I would have to say that my prospects with the firm are extremely good [. . .] When you start off on your legal career you tend to see partnership as the ultimate goal.

Q: And it comes quite early in a career if you do well, does it?

Mr Ash: Yes, I think if you do well you can expect to be offered a partnership, say within five to eight years of occupation.   (Mr Ash, 2)

Mr Linden describes his pathway, from a clerical post in the civil service to a managerial one in an insurance company, in terms of the development of a range of skills.

Mr Linden: . . . what I actually wanted to do was develop my own skills,
and I wanted to broaden out into the man-management, the training, the people-training skills, management, development and those
type of skills, which I hadn't done a great deal of, but had many advantages. One was that it enabled me to develop *me*; and two, it gave
me lots more prospects, because now my next job doesn't have to
be in insurance any more. If you're a technical trainer then you're
limited to the industry that you're in, but when you get into man-
management, the organization is irrelevant.   (Mr Linden, 26)

Mr Hazel describes his university post as if it were his property – he is
entitled to do whatever he wants within it.

Mr Hazel: I'm "self-employed", I can do what the hell I like, and I do
what the hell I like.

Q: So, when you say you're "self-employed" . . . ?

Mr Hazel: Well, in a sense this is a slightly absurd way of putting it,
but effectively I have a limited number of students, I can write me
own courses, and I can do what I like . . .   (Mr Hazel, 6–7)

Other men give accounts as if their job assets, accumulated over their
careers, were a form of tradable property rights – for instance when they
discuss the decision whether or not to take early retirement, or move into
self-employment at some point in their careers. Mr Oak is talking about
his work as a teacher.

Mr Oak: I've toyed many times with the idea of going "point seven-
five" and having more time to do freelance and be here with the children . . . I suppose when I retire – I might well, retire early – but it
depends whether these freelance ideas are things I want to pursue
. . .   (Mr Oak, 19, 21)

Mr Spruce is about to become a partner in the firm of quantity surveyors that employs him. But in the longer term he plans to take early retire-

ment and set up in a gallery or bookshop in France. He needs to "farm" his job assets with this in mind.

> *Mr Spruce:*   But what I want to do is set myself up financially, because I think I would want to get something out of what I've been doing for the last 20 odd years. And I think I would attempt to secure that over the next 10 years [. . .] You attain sufficient equity to release an income. It's an annuity situation.   (Mr Spruce, 64)

This passage has some echoes of Mr Birch's and Mr Alder's accounts of how they used redundancy payment rights from their jobs to set themselves up in business, and Mr Lime's of how he plans to draw an income from his business for early retirement. But significantly Mr Spruce adds that his plans "would not deter me from attempting to influence the practice". In other words, the relevant locus for collective decisions is the *enterprise* (public or private) for these property rights. Hence perhaps the drift from an economy made up of independent producers to one based on large firms changes not only the nature of property but also the relevant site for decision making and collective interests.

> *Mr Spruce:*   . . . because I think the only way I can have a say in the way that the practice is directed in future is to be an equity partner or an equity shareholder, because I can only influence it to a certain degree now. I can make suggestions, but for my voice to be heard I have to be in that forum.   (Mr Spruce, 7)

Thus the individualist repertoire places the job-holder in a context of participating, with a group of peers, in decisions about the firm. But how are relations with the wider community constructed? Here Mr Ash's account is instructive. He explains why they moved to the area, after commuting for a time from a town some 35 miles away, where his wife still works.

> *Mr Ash:*   It was all part and parcel of the whole partnership. They [the partners in his firm of solicitors] took the view that in order to connect you, in order to be a partner in a firm in [city], then one has to involve oneself in the local community as well, and one couldn't take an active part in the community living in [the other town]. So therefore they offered the partnership on the basis that I would move down.

> *Q:*   When they say that, "an active member of the community", what does that really mean?

Mr Ash: Yes, that's right. Getting to know people, so that when people think, "Oh, we want a solicitor", and they know somebody down
the road, it will be a way of bringing in business.

(Mr and Mrs Ash, 9)

This account constructs the link between professional status and community involvement in economic terms – as a way of "bringing in business"
– rather than through the democratic processes or citizenship responsibilities that might characterize the repertoires of a Tocquevillian version.
Job assets are the fruits of what one has made of oneself, and they are linked
with obligations to firm and family, but not to fellow citizens of a democratic polity. In no account is such a connection made.

To assess citizenship in the "property-owning democracy" in terms of
the accountability adopted by job-holders is therefore to study self-responsible economic agents who call each other to account by the canons of
business efficiency, and mutually responsible family members who absorb
– as far as possible – the costs of caring for themselves and each other. This
is what Raymond Plant has called a "nomocratic" rather than a "teleo-
cratic" version of citizenship.[28] It rejects the idea of a political community
with shared purposes and common values, in favour of a society whose
rules are designed to allow each individual the maximum freedom to pursue his or her own version of the good life, consistent with others' equal
freedom. This is the kind of society promoted in the writings of Hayek and
Gray[29] among modern advocates of neutral laws to secure equal liberty,
but recognizable also in such diverse liberal theorists as Rawls,[30] Dworkin,[31]
Sandel[32] and Charles Taylor.[33]

Many of the interviewees' accounts are exemplary by these criteria, and
the common features of their accountability to the interviewer – explaining what they have made of themselves and how they put the family first
– are, after all, definitive of this kind of citizenship. Yet there is a remaining puzzle over how we are supposed to recognize a good property-owning *democrat* (as opposed to a fascist, racist, sexist, or any other form of
authoritarian, or someone with no commitment to any particular form
of collective decision-making process) in these accounts. Clearly a liberal
upholds those laws that give equal freedom to *all* citizens, and this perhaps
requires respondents to give some evidence of commitment to equality of
opportunity. But what *active* commitments does good citizenship entail –
and in particular, how do good property-owning democrats describe their
attempts to influence collective decisions and the quality of life of their
community? Do these interviewees see themselves as answerable for these

187

shared aspects of their lifestyles in any way, and do they influence their decisions over work and the family?

This question opens up a fundamental ambiguity in the British government's version of citizenship. If equal liberty and the rule of law are such paramount principles, we would expect their active promotion to be *the* first purpose of political activity. In so far as a public sphere of shared commitments and actions could appear in such a society, it would consist of those collective processes that upheld such norms. We might expect really important issues of public policy to be subjected to constant scrutiny by property-owning democrats, rather as they were disputed and defended by Tocqueville's small-town Americans. Thus we might look for the emergence of *public issues* in the accounts, especially those affecting the life-chances of individuals – issues in which equal liberty or equal opportunity are crucially at stake. Presumably, a good *democrat* would be equally concerned for the just treatment of each fellow citizen, and for the influence of all fellow citizens on key decisions over these issues. To be committed to democracy is not, of course, to seek consensus or compromise; it would be consistent with championing democracy to be fiercely partisan on such questions, but the defining characteristic would be an insistence that decisions be based on public debate and maximum participation (at least by voting) in the collective choice.

Yet many public pronouncements of ministers and ideologues of the property-owning democracy seem to suggest instead that the public sphere should contract, leaving as many issues as possible to the market or the family. Indeed, the version of "active citizenship" promoted by government ministers is much more about private, charitable good works for the "less fortunate" than about participation in issues of collective concern. The public duties of citizenship seem to be discharged by those who obey the law, pay their taxes and vote at elections. The interpretations of individualism displayed in these interviews indicate how the key terms, phrases and images of this repertoire are well suited to discourses of privacy, personal responsibility, exclusive property and the competitive struggle for advantage, but do not easily construct issues as ones of public concern, or recognize the significance of individual decisions for the common good.

It is indicative of the invisibility of public issues that might signal democratic concerns in these accounts that we are unable to select a topic through which to show how these respondents emerge as citizens. To suggest, as Giddens does, that this is because "lifestyle politics" have transcended "emancipatory politics"[34] is an interpretation that does not emerge from our reading of our data. These interviewees have many concerns and fears about the impact of forces beyond their personal control and that they recognize as involving matters of collective rather than individual choice. They are worried about the security of their own employment, the solvency of their enterprises, their children's futures, and the country's social fabric; they do not imagine that these are issues for them alone.

> *Mr Elder:*   . . . we're in a very deep recession [. . .] and the professions are being quite badly affected, and nobody is absolutely secure [. . .] I'm realistic, I've actually queried my position, and although they've turned round and said there's nothing on the cards at the moment, they will not give me my normal three months' notice – if I was made redundant I would be called in and asked to leave. [. . .] And any of my colleagues at my level would be treated in exactly the same way.   (Mr Elder, 17)

> *Mrs Palm:*   . . . you see there's an awful lot of question marks about both our futures, because I know I'm good at this job but it may not be there to be done, although my boss talks about, you know, perhaps we would go freelance, but it's a huge question mark over that, and I can see the possibility that I have an interim when this job finishes and maybe I'll get a temporary contract or something just working in school . . .   (Mrs Palm, 33)

However, what does not emerge from the interviews is a coherent account of how matters of collective choice can be influenced by the actions of citizens, individually or in concert. It is as if they have internalized the paradox of citizenship in a "property-owning democracy" – that the public sphere is minimized as government "targets" a narrow range of issues and needs, and political activity becomes futile. Although interviewees recognize questions of social justice, where public policy should be at stake, they do not translate these into public issues over which their views and actions are described as relevant. Instead, they construct private "solutions" as best they can.

Collectivist repertoires

Although all the interviewees (men and women) adopt a form of accountability that can be characterized as individualistic and use these interpretative repertoires to describe their labour-market decisions, there are some – mostly public sector employees – who use another repertoire to answer specific questions. We call this the *collectivist repertoire*, and it refers to a range of social democratic institutions – the welfare state, public sector terms and conditions of employment, trade unions – and draws together phrases and images from the traditions of the Labour Party, the social services, full employment policies, and social solidarity. What is noticeable about the way this repertoire is deployed is that the interviewees use it in response to specific questions about issues (such as private welfare schemes or the reforms of education and social services), often signalling this by the use of terms that indicate a temporary shift from narratives of self and family.

However, the use of these repertoires does not give those who deploy them an easier way to link accounts of their decisions and actions with discourses of active citizenship or democratic participation. Indeed they experience a particular kind of trouble – which is not evidenced by those who stay within the individualist repertoire – in linking their rhetoric of collectivism with a version of how their actions and decisions address the issues they identify. Thus a certain kind of collective issue becomes more "visible" within their accounts, but they do not construct means of acting to be effective in relation to these issues. Only teachers, giving accounts of what they can do to resist government education reforms, claim that they can have significant influence.

This trouble in giving accounts of how to be a good *social* democrat (in terms of the institutions and traditions of the Labour Party) seems to be linked with the structures of the welfare state. The politics of universalist social services can scarcely be compared with Tocquevillian democratic participation. The distinct rôles of contributor (taxpayer), service provider (staff member) and service-user (beneficiary) are defined in such a way that contributors cannot readily give service, providers cannot do much to raise funds, and beneficiaries can usually neither contribute nor give service. It is difficult for taxpayers, who seldom use services, to give an account of how they can support the welfare state, or staff who work in services to say how they can increase its resources – even when a household contains a taxpaying man with social democratic sympathies, and a woman employed within a public agency.

This paradox emerges clearly in some interviewees' accounts of their opposition to government policies over the welfare state, and their difficulties in finding an appropriate expression for this in their rôles as taxpayers, service providers or users.

Mr Oak: . . . this is a very strange view, I don't think we actually pay enough tax. I don't think tax rates are high enough in this country to pay for the things we actually need to be a civilized society. So tax isn't something we're likely to avoid actually. In fact we have some very funny stories here; Trevor [Mr Teak, who shares house] actually trying to pay capital gains tax for doing half-years and finding it was too difficult to do so. Me actually trying to pay my income tax on royalties – I earn £2000 or £3000 a year on books – and it can be incredibly difficult to actually pay the tax at times . . .

(Mr Oak, 24)

Mr Fieldmaple: . . . with health care, it's a matter of principle as much as anything. I mean, not being entirely satisfied with the National Health or the state education system necessarily, but as a matter of principle not, not wishing to take them [children] out of that [. . .] just the fact that those, the state should provide those things and they should be improved, and that it's not going to improve them by taking our children out of it. I mean it doesn't necessarily improve it by leaving them in, I know [laughs] but it's the principle of the more people that do support it then the more likely it is to be supported by government funding. (Mr Fieldmaple, 26)

Mrs Pine is an experienced teacher, about to follow her husband's work move.

Mrs Pine: When we move to [Midlands] and I give up my teaching job here, I will probably find it difficult to get another teaching job, because in this experience of local school management I would be an expensive teacher to employ. Because I'm at the top of the scale, and previously that didn't matter [. . .] now when schools have a certain budget and they have to organize it as well as they can [. . .] they might choose to employ a newly qualified teacher for £12,500 or £12,000. So there will be problems about getting a job.

(Mrs Pine, 17)

However, some teachers and those involved in training for teaching do describe active campaigns against the government's policies for restructuring and re-regulating their work.

Mr Hazel: We'll have to get in there fighting to try and make sure that what is implemented in schools is both viable and reflects what we believe in, it's as simple as that. [. . .] Never stop fighting. We always win, even with this government we've won again. I actually believe that if you fight hard enough . . . if it's something completely bonkers, at some point in the process of informing the people taking decisions, there will be mechanisms whereby common sense will prevail.

(Mr Hazel, 18)

Mr Dogwood is a trade union official in a teachers' union.

Mr Dogwood: What the 1988 Act has done is to set school against school with competition. In other words, education within a local authority is not now a corporate enterprise where you all steer in one direction. Education, like the Health Service too, has become fragmented, where you're actually in competition [. . .] In other words, the market place prevails. These are the things which I am not very happy about . . . In other words, the kind of control that teachers had over learning has now been taken away, and increasingly so.

(Mr and Mrs Dogwood, 36)

The way the collectivist repertoire is deployed here reveals some of the rhetorics and practices among "producer groups" in the social services that the government seeks to discredit. Reference to a "corporate enterprise" and "teachers' control" smacks of a professional and political elite who, with the collusion of the public sector trade unions, have excluded citizens from the decision-making process and have determined their own policies and practices. The welfare state was, in this view, quite unlike Toqueville's public sphere of citizens' participation and democratic self-rule. It was an oligarchy, paid for by taxpayers with no influence and consumed by passive recipients of its paternalistic prescriptions.

Hence the part of the liberal tradition to which the British government appeals can readily criticize the rhetoric of collectivism, and the practices it sustains, as inherently undemocratic. Margaret Thatcher's political strategy was to expose "social democracy" as a set of organized interest groups – public sector professionals, trade unions and Labour politicians, especially at local level – committed to monopolizing power and excluding the wider public from influencing decisions. Since this coalition used corporatist processes and local government agencies to expand its own resources by spending ordinary citizens' contributions, it followed (on this analysis) that democracy could be increased, and citizenship enhanced, only by cutting back the powers of these institutions and interests. The British government's reforms of the social services in the period 1988–91 were presented as a strategy for making these groups more accountable to taxpayers for their stewardship (in terms of value-for-money and effectiveness). Since then, the introduction of Citizen's Charters for the public services has also attempted to make them answerable to the public as consumers, rather in the way that shops are for the quality of what they sell. Hence government policies aim to substitute the repertoires of individualism for those of collectivism in the accountability of those who are employed in the social services.

Children's futures

Although the individualistic repertoire avoided these "troubles", it did involve the interviewees in constructing some paradoxes, which were not apparent to them but emerged from our reading of the transcripts. As we showed in Chapter 6, children's education was of paramount concern for the couples. Although they reached different conclusions over the merits of state and private education, they all gave carefully constructed accounts of their decisions over this choice. In this section, we will demonstrate how their concerns over their children's futures focus on the almost unanimous claim that higher education is a necessary condition for access to the kind of employment that will allow them to become the property-owners of the future – holders of job assets or the assets that flowed from these. However, although the accounts reveal awareness of questions of justice and public choice at stake in the allocation of job assets (the interviewees do not pretend to believe that the labour market is like a market for commodities, or that a purely meritocratic system prevails), nevertheless their children's future job prospects do not emerge as a public issue. They act as parents to do their best for their individual children, but they neither speak nor act as citizens to try to influence collective decisions about the future of their children's generation.

As has already been noted, several male interviewees (Mr Cedar, Mr Willow, Mr Linden) had high salaries despite leaving education with only a few "O" level passes; however, all of these agree with Mr Cedar (see p. 31) that the time when this was possible has passed. Their own children will require much more qualifications for the same level of jobs.

Mr Rowan: In the 1960s, early seventies, when I started work and
    when I changed jobs, it was never a question of what "A" levels you

had, it was only "O" levels. If you had "A" levels it was a bonus. And now I've seen things change where I work now, because [. . .] now you've got to have nothing less than a 2.1 degree to come in as a trainee.
(Mr and Mrs Rowan, 29)

Mr Elder: At the time when I started with the firm, you didn't have to have a professional qualification to actually get on [. . .] Whereas now the emphasis is totally different. If I wanted to start within the firm and move up in terms of the management structure, I would have to have a degree before I could even get in. (Mr Elder, 7)

The perception that jobs such as the ones that "career" respondents hold will in future require higher education is translated into the accounts of their aspirations for their children; this is as much true of women's as of men's versions, and about daughters' education as about sons'. In the accounts, the notion that children may not want to pursue professional or managerial "careers" is canvassed, but usually as an option for them to take after they have equipped themselves for the possibility of a well paid job. Hence manual work becomes a "choice" rather than something that is forced on them by the lack of qualifications for employment that gives access to property assets.

Mr Linden: If Reub [son, aged 4] went to school and he got a degree in whatever and then decided he wanted to be an ice-cream salesman then my view would be, he's being an ice-cream salesman because that's what he wants to do, not he's selling ice creams because that's all that is available to him. And I think that's quite important.
(Mr Linden, 35)

Dr Conifer: He [son, aged 7] certainly has great promise as an engineer. I say that quite seriously, because he figures things out that seem to me quite extraordinary for a 7 year old, in the engineering side, engineering in its broadest terms. But if he turns out to want to be . . . that's fine.

Mrs Conifer: A carpenter . . . if he was happy to be, I would like to see them contented in what they do. (Dr and Mrs Conifer, 27)

Mr Palm is asked about his ideas over his two daughters' (aged 16 and 14) futures; the younger one (Beatrice) has just wandered into the room and then out again.

Q: Is it important to you that they do higher education?

Mr Palm: Yes.

Q: Why?

Mr Palm: Well, I think . . . let me modify that. Um, Rose is I think very
academic, and in a conventional sort of way, and I think she will
derive an enormous amount out of it, and . . . um . . . Beatrice is different. Beatrice is the younger, she is a very good mathematician, for
instance, but is not – I'm sounding a bit unfair on her – but as I say
she is not steady, but she's not as conventional as her elder sister, um,
she wants to run an ice-cream parlour. I'm very happy about that,
but I think she ought to be properly trained – I mean I think she
might go to polytechnic and read economics for instance, and her
mathematics might be part of that, for instance.   (Mr Palm, 21–2)

If ice cream represents the polarity of unconventional, non-career-orientated choice, being a vet seems to represent the high-status option (especially for girls), requiring lengthy education and training, and a career
that combines scientific knowledge with ecological caring. Several of the
parents who mention possible careers for their daughters give this as their
favoured one.

Mrs Rowan: She's [daughter, aged 12] been wanting to be a vet for a
long time.

Mr Rowan: She'll either be a vet or she'll go to some sort of medical
clinic.   (Mr and Mrs Rowan, 29)

Mr Mahogany: Well the daughter [aged 12] . . . I just want her to do
what she wants to do really. She doesn't know herself quite. She's
interested in being a vet and wouldn't matter to me either way so long
as she's happy in what she does, I think that's quite important.
                                              (Mr Mahogany, 20)

Dr Conifer: Caroline [aged 10] wants to be a vet. She's certainly pas-
sionately keen on natural history, and she's clever, so she could be.
                                                  (Dr Conifer, 26)

However, interviewees are not under any illusions about the fact that
competition for places in higher education is fierce, and they see it as their

responsibility as parents to gain every possible advantage for their children (including private schooling) to help them succeed against others. It is here that they most clearly indicate the tension between their consciousness of issues of equal opportunity and social justice, and their commitment to giving their children preferential access to job assets (see also Mrs Redwood, Ms Blackthorn and Mr Lime, pp. 142–3).

Dr Conifer: . . . what is worrying us, we're coming to the decision point with our eldest, with that it looks to us that if we stay here, particularly here, then the only option we have to make sure she gets the best she needs is to send her to private school. [. . .] Well, I think it's . . . because there are no alternatives in [city] of the same, or even adequate calibre. [. . .] We're socialists [laughs] and don't believe in private schools [. . .] (Dr and Mrs Conifer, 25–6)

Mr Larch: Yes, well, from experience Melissa will probably want them sent to a private school [laughs] [. . .] my previous wife [. . .] was always against private education as well. It's like all these socialist councillors, Mrs [name] – she said, "Private education is appalling"; yet one child went to [boy's private school] and one went to [girl's private school]. (Mr Larch, 24)

Some of the respondents go further than Mr Lime (who feels "sorry for the others" who do not get it) and argue that private education allows their children to escape from the influence of those others who might distract them from their quest for higher education and labour-market advantage.

Mr Redwood: . . . I would hate either of the boys to have fallen into [. . .] a group of friends where working at school became in some way uncool . . . (Mr Redwood, 19)

Mr Mahogany: . . . there's a lot of farmers' sons went to the school I went to, the private school, which . . . I think a lot of the success of a business is sort of the people you're mixing with. You try to keep up with them don't you? If you're going to a council school and all your friends are farm workers, maybe you'll only want to be a farm worker . . . (Mr Mahogany, 21)

Hence in these parts of the accounts access to higher education and good jobs emerges as the most important element in securing children's futures (and thus of "putting the family first"). Yet all the respondents see this as involving their children gaining advantages over others; they disagree only over whether private schooling confers such advantages, and whether it does so unfairly. What is missing from the accounts is an attempt to describe what might be done about any injustice that is recognized, or how the life-chances of the "others" might be better protected. Equality of opportunity and equality of citizenship do not emerge as public issues in these versions of access to higher education and good jobs. Instead, we have accounts of how to do the best for one's own children in a situation of scarcity of both these resources. The political dimensions of the problem are bracketed, even by some (Mr Yew, Dr Conifer) who describe themselves as socialists. Some of the paradoxes of individualism will be pursued in more detail in Chapter 9.

Choice and the welfare of others

Thus, in describing how they chose between public and private welfare systems, the interviewees did not attempt to take account of the welfare of others without their advantages. This omission can be traced to the nature of their individualistic accountability. They gave versions of their decisions and actions in which they showed what they had made of themselves and how they had put the family first. Being primarily accountable in these terms, private sector "careerists" described occupational welfare as part of their accumulated job assets, and the self-employed described health insurance much as they would house insurance. Those who have invested their employment skills in the public sector tended also to use public welfare systems. The exception to this, as we have seen, was education, where more active decision making was required and the moral stakes were higher. But none of this required them to account for their views on other people's welfare, unless (as in the case of Mrs Redwood, Mr Yew or Dr Conifer) they acknowledged a conflict between these and their choices in relation to family members – in which case they put the family first. Commitments to the welfare of others (whether in terms of collectivism, environmentalism, religious groups, charitable works or professional ethics) were not part of the respondents' primary accountability in these interviews.

This had two consequences. First, because of this accountability framework, actions that benefited others (or involved the construction of common-interest systems with others) were in a sense "optional extras" in all the accounts except those of the Oaks and Teaks (who pooled all their resources and hence always referred to each other's welfare). Even Mr and

Mrs Palm, who pulled off a coherent socialist version of their decisions, and Mr and Mrs Pear, who constructed an environmentalist one, gave accounts within such a framework. Secondly, welfare schemes that could be located in an account of what one had made of oneself and of putting the family first needed little further justification, and were presented as part of the rationale of such decisions rather than as requiring legitimation in their own right.

This can be clearly seen from several interviewees' accounts of the health insurance cover they get as part of their "package" of occupational benefits (job assets).

Mr Elder: Well, I get a company car. As a senior manager it's quite a good car, the value I suppose is about £15,000 or so, if you were buying new, [. . .] mine's a Bluebird 2x Turbo, so it's the top of the range. That's probably worth £2500 to £3000 in terms of value to my salary. I get permanent health insurance . . .

Q: What's that for?

Mr Elder: Permanent health insurance is not BUPA, that's the private medical insurance – I get that and that's for the family – I get permanent health insurance where, if I was off work for a long period of time with a serious illness or I was in a major car accident say [. . .] the health insurance comes in to pay your salary for you [. . .] after three months or six months, whatever that might be. [. . .] That's more or less the package I get [. . .] plus of course you get the firm's pension scheme [. . .] So the whole package together is probably worth somewhere in the region of about £32,000.

(Mr Elder, 14)

Q: And what about private medical insurance, do you have that?

Mr Box: Yes, that's provided as part of a fringe benefit with my employment.

Q: And does that cover your wife and children?

Mr Box: Yes, and the children as well, yes, yes.

Q: And what about a car, do you have that as a . . .

Mr Box: Yes, yes, I have a car and that's another benefit that the firm pay up to a certain amount for repairs, and tax and insurance on my wife's car as well, yes.

(Mr Box, 19)

These accounts (which are replicated in the interviews with other male "careerists" in private sector employment) are in sharp contrast with those of public sector employees. Since the latter do not have occupational health insurance as part of their fringe benefits, they would have to take an individual decision to opt into a private scheme, but they say that they reject this option – often without elaboration.

Q: What about things like private medical and health insurance?

Dr Pine: No, we don't believe in that. (Dr Pine, 7)

The interviewees who give the most elaborate replies to questions about private health insurance are self-employed men. This is because they are not within any occupational scheme, yet their households are – in most cases – largely dependent on their insecure incomes. Mr Lime's account indicates the sensitivity of the topic of insurance for this group of respondents, since the moral adequacy of their version of setting up their own business depends on demonstrating that they are putting family first by investing heavily in this. The sometimes heretical Mr Lime takes this issue very seriously.

Q: And do you have private health insurance?

Mr Lime: Yes.

Q: That's for yourself and for your family?

Mr Lime: Yes. I don't know if you want to ask the reason why . . . it's always a comfort to know – I mean I realize that if there's an emergency, an emergency is a devil for private health, and the National Health Service is very good at dealing with emergencies, and not so good at dealing with the routine stuff where you've got to wait on a list or whatever. And I actually decided, for fairly selfish reasons, because I thought if I've got to work hard and be the breadwinner as such, I don't want all the hassle of being worried if one of my family ever needed some kind of operation which they wouldn't get on the NHS. So it's really for my own peace of mind actually.

Q: And presumably your life is insured?

Mr Lime: Yes.

Q: And is Liz's life insured?

Mr Lime: Yes, for obvious reasons. If, heaven forbid, anything happened to Liz, that would probably have a bigger effect on me than me dying. I mean everything would be paid for and she'd be OK, but conversely I would still have Katie and would have to do something with her. I think when you start a business one of the people you see more than anybody are the insurance people because they obviously see you as a prime target for selling their wares. And in fact quite rightly so, because the more things you can say, "Yes, they've been sorted", you can now forget about them, put them in the background and hope you never need them. But they are there in the eventuality . . .

(Mr Lime, 11–12)

Mr Beech, a solicitor in partnership, is also detailed in his description of decisions over insurance, and accounts for this in terms of his family.

Q: [. . .] Do you have a private health plan?

Mr Beech: Yes, I do.

Q: And life insurance for yourself?

Mr Beech: Yes, I've got private health cover, accident cover.

Q: Are these for you or for the whole family?

Mr Beech: The private health is for the whole family, accident cover is on myself, and I have numerous policies in one form or another, whether straight term assurance or endowment policies or pensions on my life, and Sally has a number on hers. I mean, if I were to die, Sally would be a wealthy woman, probably the only way she'd ever be a wealthy woman.

Q: And these are things that you both decided to subscribe to as your family's grown, are they?

Mr Beech: Yes, I suppose we have. I've always had a number of policies, with . . . even before we had children, so that if anything happened to me Sally could survive relatively easily, or at least get a good kick up the ladder to begin with. Since we've had children we've added more and more really. (Mr Beech, 5)

Mr Larch, who is self-employed but not a "careerist", sees the topic of insurance as an opportunity for demonstrating his moral adequacy in terms of putting the family first.

Q: Do you have things like private insurance?

Mr Larch: Yes, Melissa and myself are both under separate private schemes because Melissa is 15 years younger than me, so if we went together it would be a lot dearer than two separate ones. So we've got separate private insurance.

Q: And that covers medical insurance?

Mr Larch: Medical insurance, yes, and private dental insurance. Having said that, I only started since Melissa had Kirk, because the chances of something happening to me are far greater than to Melissa, and so I thought it would be hedging against disasters like illness and what-not. Death – oh, I've got life insurance too. I took out a life insurance which would give Melissa a lump sum if I dropped dead. (Mr Larch, 23)

However, not all this group of male respondents considered health insurance a good investment. Once again, Mr and Mrs Mahogany account for their decision with systematic economic logic – and on the basis of alarming experience. Mrs Mahogany had twice been treated for malignant tumours when her children were very young, and their son (now aged 10) had glandular fever and had been in hospital for some time in recent years. However, they are not in a private medical insurance scheme; they paid for Mrs Mahogany's treatment outright. They are asked how they came to decide to pay for this out of their business account.

Mrs Mahogany: That was probably your decision, you didn't hesitate at the time, and I thought it wasn't much good to argue against that [laughs].

Mr Mahogany: It wasn't just the health, it was the fact that she was probably worrying about . . . we were both worrying about it a bit, and the sooner it was dealt with the better.

Q: Was it expensive?

Mr Mahogany: Well yes, nearly £1000 a time, wasn't it? Just at that time we weren't that flush with money, but we thought health was more important than the next building or whatever it was we were doing.

Q: But when your son was ill, I can't remember whether that went through the National Health or . . .

Mr Mahogany: National Health.

Mrs Mahogany: Oh no, his was an ongoing glandular type thing.

Mr Mahogany: We didn't see any advantage where he was concerned to have private . . . in fact we thought the facilities would probably be better . . .

Mrs Mahogany: I think the care in hospital was probably better on the National Health. And in fact I've had a minor varicose vein operation done since at the hospital, the [name], and the care is just as good, it's just the speed of getting in, I suppose.

Q: Each time you've had to get in and have something done, you've paid for it, the operation or whatever other treatment. You haven't insured? You've done it.

Mr Mahogany: I think we thought about insurance, didn't we? We were wondering about . . . with that sort of treatment, whether we could, but you probably would have been [indistinct]

Mrs Mahogany: Yes, [indistinct]

Mr Mahogany: The premium was so high that unless you go in fairly regular you're better to do it just when you need to go in and pay.

(Mr and Mrs Mahogany, 40–41)

Here Mr and Mrs Mahogany pull off a "rational" account of their choices in terms of the design feature identified in Chapter 6, combining calculative economic reasoning with "quality of life" (psychological wellbeing) reasoning over how to decide between the three systems – collective (NHS), to which they subscribe automatically, insurance and direct payment. Mr and Mrs Mahogany, with access to a large business account, have made an investment decision to use collective provision for everything except a serious illness that requires quick treatment, and that – as a high-risk life – their premiums would make the insurance scheme uneconomic. Others who have recently moved into self-employment, and whose businesses are struggling, are unable to give such an account. Mr Birch indicates awareness of the sensitivity of this topic as an index of the overall moral adequacy of his account.

Q: [. . .] Do you have an insurance policy for your family?

Mr Birch: No, that's really not all that well covered at the moment, I'm aware of that. That's one of the things I lost when I left the larger company that I worked for, so . . . living dangerously at the moment.

The mortgage is covered, that's about it.

Q: Is that something you're likely to do in future?

Mr Birch: Oh yes, yes. I have so many competing advisers – you probably don't know, when you start out with that sort of situation, starting a new company, you'll get six or seven different people coming along giving you conflicting advice about what you should and shouldn't do. Possibly for this reason, I haven't actually chosen any one of them yet, but I'm aware that there's a need to do that.

(Mr Birch, 12)

Commercial medical insurance also poses a special problem for the one male "careerist" in the private sector with a serious health problem in the family. Mr Quince cannot get full cover because of his wife's long-term illness and disability.

Q: Now you mentioned medical costs, so presumably you have a private health insurance scheme for the family?

Mr Quince: Well, actually I do for myself. I haven't extended it to the boys, and of course no-one would look at her [my wife], so you can't get these things unless you take them out when you're young and healthy.

(Mr Quince, 6)

Mrs Quince echoes this in her interview.

Mrs Quince: Medical insurance, no, I don't have that because I had a series of major operations and in fact have got what they call an ileostomy which is a stoma, and they won't actually insure me because I'm too high a risk I think.

(Mrs Quince, 19)

Despite the variety of choices over health care that they describe, all these versions have a common accountability framework, which excludes discussion of the effects on others of their decisions or relegates this to an "optional extra" in the accounts (only Mr Fieldmaple talks about the collective consequences of individuals choosing commercial health schemes, though others employed in the public sector give briefer indications of their rejection "in principle"). This relegation of the needs of others, or the consequences of "putting the family first", will be further analyzed in the final chapter.

The variety and flexibility in the use of commercial and public welfare systems in these accounts is striking. Although certain patterns follow from the nature of the main job-holder's employment (such as the private sector employees' membership of occupational health insurance schemes, and public sector employees' rejection of them), the common accountability framework shared by all these interviewees allowed them to construct versions in which all these elements were combined in ways that could be readily justified as allowing them to make something of themselves and put the family first. Within this framework, no coherent prioritization of others' needs or account of the collective consequences of individual decisions was necessary – or indeed, to judge by the acknowledged contradictions in some of the interviewees' versions, possible.

A final example sums up the complexity of the patterns revealed in the interviews. Mr Elm has recently set up as a self-employed accountant, and his wife runs a small occasional nursery class; both work from home. They are active in a Christian church, which promotes community and informal co-operation. They also employ a member of the church, who is currently unable to find employment in his occupation (as a librarian) to help in Mr Elm's business.

Mrs Elm: He's an employment trainee . . . Rory and another chap in the church said, "We could employ you between us" [. . .] He's inputting into the computer. (Mrs Elm, 10)

However, Mr and Mrs Elm are also claiming a social security benefit (family credit) because of his low declared earnings from his new business.

Mr Elm: . . . our standard of living has stayed the same but instead of being financed by a large firm of accountants it's now being financed by the [bank's name]. The main effect is the overdraft's higher [. . .]

Q: But you weren't claiming family income support, so in a sense that tells me you must be on a low income, yet you're simply saying that you're not . . .

Mr Elm: We have a high standard of living. We draw £1300 a month, which is not poverty . . . (Mr and Mrs Elm, 6)

In this account, Mr and Mrs Elm are living on the far frontiers of the mixed economy of welfare, with their combination of small business entrepreneurialism, Christian communal mutuality and two public welfare schemes (employment training and family credit). They may indeed have pushed the flexibility of welfare pluralism a little further than ministers intended with their claims for the latter.

However, if flexibility is the advantage of these new combinations of systems, what are the collective consequences of the decisions we have analyzed in this chapter? It is to these social policy implications that we turn for our conclusion.

Conclusions

In this chapter, we have started to analyze the way in which citizenship in a "property-owning democracy" is revealed in these accounts. There is ample evidence that respondents were aware of the changes from a social democratic polity, in which social rights to universalistic services formed one of the main elements of common membership, to a different kind of order, where families were required to provide more for their own from their private resources. There was also evidence that they recognized that issues of social justice were at stake, particularly in competition for higher education and good jobs. Yet the way they were able to deploy the interpretative repertoires of individualism led to an absence of accounts that identified such issues as public, as requiring collective solutions, or as demanding their active commitment to the protection of equal opportunities and processes of procedural and substantive fairness. Their reconstructions of their decisions were morally adequate legitimations of their property advantages (in terms of individualistic accountability), but said little to link these with the collective decisions of a democratic system.

References

1. M. Wetherell & J. Potter, *Mapping the language of racism: discourse and the legitimation of exploitation* (Hemel Hempstead: Harvester Wheatsheaf, 1992), p. 90.
2. Ibid.
3. J. Torfing, "A hegemony approach to capitalist regulation", in *State, economy and society*, R. B. Bertramsen, J. P. Frolund Thomsen, J. Torfing, 35–93 (London: Unwin Hyman, 1991).
4. R. Lister, *The exclusive society: citizenship and the poor* (London: CPAG, 1990); Frank Field, *Losing out: the emergence of Britain's underclass* (Oxford: Blackwell, 1989).
5. T. H. Marshall, *Citizenship and social class* (Cambridge: Cambridge University Press, 1950), p. 56.
6. R. Dahrendorf, *The modern social conflict: an essay in the politics of liberty* (London: Weidenfeld & Nicolson, 1988); B. Jordan, *The common good: citizenship, morality and self-interest* (Oxford: Blackwell, 1989); D. J. Smith (ed.), *Understanding the underclass*

(London: Policy Studies Institute, 1991).

7. L. Mead, *Beyond entitlement: the social obligations of citizenship* (New York: Free Press, 1986).

8. J. Stuart Mill, *Principles of political economy* (1848) in his *Collected works*, ed. J. M. Robson (Toronto: University of Toronto Press, 1967), Book 2, Ch. 1, Sec. 1–3.

9. C. B. MacPherson, *The political theory of possessive individualism: Hobbes to Locke* (Oxford: Oxford University Press, 1962).

10. J. Locke, *Second treatise of government* (1698; ed. P. Laslett, Cambridge, Cambridge University Press, 1967), Sec. 33–7, 45–50.

11. D. Hume, *A treatise of human nature* (1745; ed. L. A. Selby Bigge, Oxford: Clarendon Press, 1888), pp. 494–5.

12. A. de Tocqueville, *Democracy in America* (1835–40; ed. J. P. Mayer & M. Lanner, London: Collins, 1968).

13. A. Vincent & R. Plant, *Philosophy, politics and citizenship: the life and thought of the British idealists* (Oxford: Blackwell, 1984).

14. W. Beveridge, *Full employment in a free society* (London: Allen & Unwin, 1944).

15. J. Rawls, *A theory of justice* (Oxford: Clarendon Press, 1972).

16. H. Spencer, *The man versus The state* (1884; London: Penguin, 1969).

17. F. A. Hayek, *The constitution of liberty* (Chicago: University of Chicago Press, 1960).

18. R. Nozick, *Anarchy, state and utopia* (Oxford: Blackwell, 1974).

19. K Marx, *Critique of Hegel's doctrine of the state* (1845) in *Karl Marx: early writings*, L. Colletti (ed.) (London: Penguin, 1975), pp. 87–8.

20. C. Pateman, *The sexual contract* (Oxford: Blackwell and Polity, 1988).

21. M. Billig, *Arguing and thinking: a rhetorical approach to social psychology* (Cambridge: Cambridge University Press, 1987), Ch. 7.

22. Tocqueville, *Journey to America* (1831; ed. J. P. Mayer, New Haven, CT: Yale University Press, 1962), p. 211.

23. Tocqueville, *Democracy in America*, p. 569.

24. Ibid.

25. Ibid., p. 899.

26. P. Van Parijs, "A revolution in class theory", *Politics and Society*, **15** (4) (1987), 453–82.

27. B. Jordan, *The common good*, Ch. 4.

28. R. Plant, "Citizenship and the civilising process: a political science perspective", in *Citizenship, Civil Society and Social Cohesion*, Bryan S. Turner (ed.), 202–58 (Swindon: ESRC, 1991).

29. Hayek, *The constitution of liberty*; J. Gray, *Liberalism* (Oxford: Blackwell, 1982).

30. Rawls, *A theory of justice*.

31. R. Dworkin, *A matter of principle* (Cambridge, MA: Harvard University Press, 1985).

32. M. Sandel, *Liberalism and the limits of justice* (Cambridge: Cambridge University Press, 1982).

33. C. Taylor, *The sources of self: the making of modern identity* (Cambridge, MA: Harvard University Press, 1989).

34. A. Giddens, *Modernity and self-identity: self and society in the late modern age* (Oxford: Polity, 1991), Ch. 7.

CHAPTER 9

Social Policy Implications

Our analysis so far has been mainly concerned with making sense of these interviews as individual and joint accounts of identities, decisions and citizenship. But what sense do they make collectively? We have shown how the interviewees discursively construct an everyday interactional order, and how their decisions reflect long-term bargaining strategies (over rôles and investments) with each other. But does the sum total of these represent a collectively rational set of choices? Should social policy be guided by them, or should it seek to modify or mould them in the name of social justice or economic efficiency?

These couples were selected to represent social groups who gained most from the processes of change in the 1980s. Whereas the bottom 10 per cent of the population in Britain stood still in real terms in that decade, the rest saw an average rise in living standards of one-third, the best-off netting the largest gains.[1] But such measures are rather crude. Our study of the poorest people in the same city[2] showed that most gave themselves some room for manoeuvre by bending the rules on income tax and social security claims – doing some occasional undeclared work for cash. By the same token, perhaps some of the gains made by households such as the ones in this study were illusory. If they were caught in a cycle of paying more and more for previously collectivized services, or supporting their offspring through greatly prolonged dependency, were they really better off than before?

Conducted soon after the end of the Thatcher decade, the interviews bear the mark of its leading figure. Although there is nothing brashly acquisitive or crassly complacent in the accounts, they none the less reflect many of the themes and discourses of the era – individualism, family responsibility, choice, welfare pluralism. Without any active endorsement of selfishness or greed, they offer little by way of a critique of property, inequality or competition. They respond to the government's incentives (reduced tax rates, relief on mortgage interest payments, or changes in the law on pensions) with little comment.

In this final chapter we will investigate whether their accounts reveal any perverse consequences of individualism and the prioritization of family. We will look at effects (acknowledged and unacknowledged) of their decisions, particularly in terms of gender and intergenerational relations. Do the cumulative consequences of millions of such choices sum together into outcomes that are individually advantageous, or do they collectively frustrate individuals' intentions? How do they affect wider social relations, and the quality of life in households and the community?

In the 1980s, critics of social democracy mounted a fierce attack on collectivist social policies that focused on how to divide up the economic cake rather than on how to enlarge it. Trade unions pursuing their collective interests limited resources for investment; high tax rates for redistribution blocked entrepreneurial initiative; the cushion of social protection dulled ambition and effort; worst of all, collective benefits and services rewarded idleness and improvidence in the name of "social need".[3] Liberal individualists insisted that it was only by releasing the energy of self-interest and the spontaneous order of markets and families that a dynamic spark of growth could be rekindled in complex advanced economies.[4]

However, this ignored a simultaneous critique, which drew attention to the social limits to growth. Not everything most desired by citizens in such a polity was either a pure private or a pure public good. In conditions of affluence, scarcity, overcrowding and pollution could combine so that goods acquired "social" or "positional" characteristics.[5] While it was rational for any individual to invest the necessary resources to acquire such goods, if all did so the majority of such expenditure would be wasted. Just as in a crowd one person's decision to stand on tiptoe (for a better view) justifies the energy expended, a similar decision by all others frustrates everyone, and renders each action wasteful.[6]

The British government claimed that its economic policies in the 1980s led to faster growth, at least for the second half of the decade. But this growth did not increase the supply of certain key economic assets. Employment expanded, but the number of secure, well paid, full-time jobs contracted.[7] Money poured into the domestic housing sector, but the number of available houses grew more slowly than the number of households seeking them.[8] Thus a kind of overcrowding phenomenon affected both these spheres. In employment, more people, with better educational qualifications, sought fewer good jobs. Many who invested much in degrees or postgraduate studies were disappointed in the pay-off from their invest-ments.[9] In housing, larger borrowing drove up the price of the existing stock, until the price collapse of the early 1990s left many mortgagees with negative equity.

The same phenomena could also affect public goods, like the enjoyment of a pleasant environment. If too many people flocked into a desirable part of a city, or an attractive rural area, it could lose much of its amenity value. The prestige associated with living in an affluent area could be offset by the costs if it became a target for crime. All these issues demanded some form of collective measures – not necessarily those associated with social democratic institutions, but ones not available through any kind of individual self-inter-ested choice that took no account of the positional nature of these goods.

The strategy of the British government largely ignored these problems: ministers insisted that decisions should be made by individuals and fami-lies. Using a rhetoric of anti-collectivism that emphasized the unintended effects of social democratic policies, they built their political support through "negative brokerage" – promising to keep taxes down and prop-erty values up, where their predecessors had tried to build coalitions through focusing hopes of redistributive and regulatory measures on a rational, foresightful state.[10] Part of their case for individual economic decision making and family responsibility rested on discrediting govern-ments' claims over the planning and management of society's welfare.

However, even a self-proclaimed radical individualist like Mrs Thatcher could not govern without some resort to those twin instruments of regimes that seek to influence collective outcomes, *education* and *social engineering*. The former is a shorthand way of referring to the attempt by officials to widen benevolence (what Hume called "tender regard for others") by in-creasing awareness of the collective hazards of narrow self-interest. For instance, the British government conducted a vigorous, if crude, campaign to educate the public over the risks of HIV infection and to modify sexual conduct. Social engineering refers to attempts to influence attitudes and behaviour and hence avoid seriously suboptimal outcomes – by the selec-tive manipulation of material incentives and penalties. Here, of course, the British government used these to reward individualism and penalize col-lectivism, for instance by offering local authority tenants substantial dis-counts to buy their houses but forbidding councils to spend the proceeds on replenishing their dwindling stock.

In examining the social policy implications of these accounts, we will therefore be looking at the interaction between individual decisions and collective results. This should reveal whether any of the interviewees' choices are individually rational but cumulatively wasteful, because of the positional characteristics of the goods at stake. Although it is beyond the scope of this book to analyze collective solutions to the problems that emerge, we will provide some tentative suggestions about how these might be alleviated. We will argue that the educative and social engineering policies of the British government have reinforced a number of the perverse consequences of individualistic choices, and that policies that offset or reverse these are now needed in the name of both economic efficiency and social justice.

The central argument of our concluding chapter is as follows. In the "property-owning democracy", the key economic asset for households in this income range is the possession of at least one secure well paid job. Couples pursue a strategy of using the advantages that flow from these job assets to ensure that their offspring in turn gain every competitive edge that will help them to secure such a job. This focuses on getting them the best possible education, and those who believe that this is to be found in the private sector are willing to pay quite heavily to get it. But these strategies and choices ignore the positional nature of both jobs and education. The overcrowded scramble for good jobs is fierce precisely because these are scarce, and competition drives up the "price" (in terms of educational qualifications).[11] Couples have to support their offspring for longer, simply to ensure that they are not disadvantaged in competition with others. Furthermore, the higher the numbers that "pay twice" by choosing private education, the smaller the premium (in terms of positional advantage) this confers.

The scarcity of good jobs has effects on relationships within the household also. Most couples opt for a strategy in which the man becomes a "careerist" and the woman a secondary earner, so she can be "supportive" and sustain his career. Although we have seen that the everyday code of partnership allows women considerable autonomy, this depends on the survival of their relationship: divorce reveals an enormous discrepancy in power and resources. Furthermore, young people's prolonged dependence, and difficulties in gaining access to secure employment, have major implications in terms of power relations. Women and young people do not directly challenge adult male power (though they develop the everyday resistance practices analyzed in Chapter 7); some hypothetical explanations for this are discussed in the second section of what follows.

These strategies and decisions are in line with government rhetoric and the structure of incentives and penalties that has been established by its policies. Yet collectively they largely frustrate individuals' intentions and cause them to bear the costs of wasteful uses of resources. Each "careerist" is forced to seek more advancement, and keep (usually) his job for longer, in order to support offspring through a longer period of dependence (and to bear the increased costs of higher education, with reduced maintenance grants). But with *all* "careerists" doing this, access to good jobs for their offsprings' generation is blocked for longer, so the vicious circle of prolonged dependence is given an extra twist.

In the sphere of housing, another aspect of this trap is recognizable. Households increased their borrowing in the 1980s, and a large proportion of this went into owner-occupied houses, whose prices rose considerably faster than general inflation, denying the new generation entry into this tenure.[12] With the enforced rise in interest rates at the end of the decade, the housing market collapsed. Although this helps younger people with jobs to become first-time buyers, the interaction of economic factors and a set of government housing policies leaves many couples in their parents' generation with properties worth less than their mortgages, especially if they bought their houses in the previous five years. This hinders any plans they may have to move into smaller houses for retirement or to release capital to assist their offsprings' purchase of housing.

Given the present structure of incentives and costs, it is hard to see how these socially wasteful uses of resources could be diminished. Individual rationality leads to collective frustration in ways dimly recognized by these interviewees, who seemed at times as trapped within the quest for advantage as the respondents in our earlier study were in poverty. The individualist repertoires in terms of which they construct their choices, and the family priority through which they regulate them in partnership, readily legitimate such decisions, but tend to obscure the collective results of their choices. Only fairly radical, long-term measures to make collective, common interests more visible, and to provide incentives for greater equality and sharing, would be likely to release them from the unintended consequences of their choices.

Job scarcity: crowding and screening

In his classic study of the *Social limits to growth* (1976), Fred Hirsch illustrated the concept of *positional goods* by reference to top jobs, education and housing, all of which are relevant in the analysis of these accounts.[13] A generalized rise in standards of living satisfies certain material needs, but it causes "congestion" in those spheres where personal welfare is linked to having advantages over others. Hirsch pointed out that the utility associated with being a leader, having a superior education, or owning an exclusive property were all vulnerable to a crowding effect. Following Harrod's distinction between "democratic" and "oligarchic" wealth,[14] Hirsch defined a positional economy, relating to "all aspects of goods, services, work positions, and other social relationships that are either (1) scarce in some absolute or socially imposed sense or (2) subject to congestion or crowding through more extensive use".[15] He went on to ask what happened when the material economy grew but the positional economy remained confined to a fixed size.

The situation in Britain in the 1980s was rather more extreme than the one analyzed in his model. Hirsch pointed out that collective systems, compulsorily imposed on all, could manage some aspects of the crowding phenomenon. In the social democratic era, collectivization of economic life (the public sector) expanded partly in order to deal with congestion in the positional economy; it allowed previously oligarchic spheres to be "democratized", at least to the extent of permitting a larger-entry higher education, secure and statusful employment and decent housing than would have been possible under conditions of private sector competition between individuals. But the Thatcher government dismantled many of these collective systems, deregulating the labour market, abolishing much employment protection, reducing educational and training grants, and cutting social housing provision. In effect, the institutions for "managed crowding" in the social democratic era were swept away, and the positional economy was again laid open to the effects of individual and household decisions.

As we have seen, many male "careerists" among these interviewees benefited from the open access to well-paid employment of the era of collectivization. Like John Major, Mr Chestnut, Mr Cedar, Mr Rowan, Mr Elder, Mr Mahogany, Mr Linden, Mr Willow and Chief-Inspector Sycamore all left school at 16 or younger, with "O" levels or less. They recognize that the same would not be possible today (see pp. 193–4). Furthermore, in many different ways, the positional nature of their (now well paid) jobs is re-emerging, as collective systems for employment protection dissolve and competitive forces re assert themselves. One symptom of this, of course, is the commercialization of the professions, of which several interviewees complain. But some respondents recognize that crowded occupations can quickly be thinned out once competition is allowed in. Mr Redwood sees this happening among solicitors with increased commercialization and fewer professional controls.

Mr Redwood: It's not beyond the bounds of possibility that the legal profession will change in such a dramatic way that I may, as all lawyers may, have to make choices as to whether or not that's the sort of change that they can make, and they'd want to make, or whether they are going to [. . .] go away and try to look for something different.   (Mr and Mrs Redwood, 42)

In several commercial fields, such a process of thinning is already well under way. Mr Box describes the situation in his architects' practice:

Mr Box: We are all, and I mean all the profession, virtually all are suffering some way or another [. . .] we're all moving back a step at the present time, in terms of salary, and some are suffering with redundancy of course [. . .] We as directors agreed that we would take a 10 per cent cut, and that's affected other senior staff as well. That's been a fairly recent decision [. . .] it's only just happened really, and no, we're in a slight fool's paradise at the moment because we arranged finance mainly by selling some of our extraneous life policies that we'd accumulated over the years to pay for alterations to the house here and also a holiday [. . .]. It may well be our last family holiday . . .   (Mr Box, 15–16)

Mr Laburnum describes a similar situation in publishing:

Mr Laburnum: I don't feel at all secure at the moment, to be quite honest, because publishing is going through an extremely bad, difficult period [. . .] of recession, of complete change, I think. I've never known it to be anything like it, so we are having to be quite judicious at the moment [. . .] I think eventually we'll change the shape of the company, which may mean that I might go off and do other freelance activities probably linked to publishing . . .
                                                                                        (Mr Laburnum, 11–12)

In the most competitive, commercial enterprises, congestion in higher management is cleared by reducing staff and increasing responsibilities.

Mr Cedar: . . . the company's been taken over a couple of times and obviously [. . .] they'll often change the structure of the company [. . .] they'll change boundaries and they'll even change the numbers of people they have doing jobs, so all of a sudden . . . if you take the job I'm doing now, there were seven people doing this job, they've now cut it down to three. [. . .] We normally change about every 18 months [. . .] My job isn't secure. That's the downside of the job. I mean the package I get is exceptionally good, it is very good. But in terms of job security then that doesn't exist, I live on my results and my ability to convince my directors that I know what I'm doing and I've got control of the situation. (Mr Cedar, 1, 5)

In other occupations, early retirement eases congestion.

Q: Have you thought much about retirement?

Mr Poplar: The option's always there if the economy hits a very sticky patch. Again, in local government, you're guaranteed your pension after 50, which is a big difference. (Mr Poplar, 3)

In all these different ways, the accounts reveal that senior "career" posts are being transformed back into "oligarchic wealth", after a period of "democratization" through collectivist processes; their positional status is re-established. This is sometimes achieved through intensification of work demands, sometimes through reduction of rewards, but either way the effect is to thin out the number of job-holders and to give positional benefits to those who remain.

Simultaneously, the "price" of access to such jobs is increased by *screening* – the raising of qualifications for entry and the increase in obstacles to promotion to senior posts. Here again, we have already seen that interviewees recognized this process at work (see Mr Rowan and Mr Elder, pp. 193–4, Mr Cedar, p. 31). This contributes to their determination that their children will receive higher education, even if they themselves did not (see pp. 193–6). They are willing to make whatever sacrifices are necessary (in their view), first to get them into higher education, and then to support them through this and professional training. These sacrifices are greatest for those who see private education as advantageous in gaining a university place.

Mr Quince: . . . we don't spend very much outside those basic items: mortgage and children. We don't spend virtually anything on holidays for ourselves, clothes, furniture, jewellery, china or any of those things . . .

Q: So if you weren't paying the school fees would you be spending money on these items?

Mr Quince: Yes, we'd be living better than we do.

Mrs Quince: Yes, we'd probably have holidays. I mean we would have holidays, rather than at the moment where children have been given opportunities at school and we feel having embarked on that sort of education, we'd be silly to let those go by. So yes, we tend to look towards those things . . .   (Mr and Mrs Quince, 27)

Those with offspring already at university or college comment on the costs of maintaining them.

Mr Hemlock: . . . our daughter doesn't get a grant this year, it may be that when they're both there they might get a small grant. Jane is already in [southern city's name] which is expensive, and Sam may well be in London, which is also expensive.
(Mr and Mrs Hemlock, 32)

The prospect of these expenditures cast a shadow over some of the accounts.

Q: Have you made financial arrangements for the maintenance grant for your eldest who is starting his "A" levels?

Mr Fieldmaple: No, we almost got around to it in the last few months, thinking that the way things were going [. . .] if he is going to go to university, that the cost of that has increased rapidly, and whether we are going to have enough to support him or not, so we almost got into a financial plan of some sort which would have provided that, but what we actually looked at showed us that we were probably already too late to start investing for that, we should have thought about it four or five years ago maybe, because the plan that was offered didn't really provide any benefit until just about the time that he finished the three year course, and OK, it would have been OK for my daughter who's next, but so, no, we would rely on savings and interest from savings . . .   (Mr Fieldmaple, 27)

Mr Box: Yes, don't remind me [laughs]. Have we made any provision for that? The answer's no.

Q: So how are you going to do it?

Mr Box: Well, to be honest, we haven't given it any detailed thought. We just feel that, particularly with my wife working, that we'll be able to manage it. If she wasn't working, then I doubt whether there'd be any grant available anyway, and we'd just have to manage, but I'm not quite sure how we'd do it.   (Mr Box, 17)

These interviewees would not contemplate letting their offspring down: the moral adequacy of their accounts, as responsible parents, depends on doing everything possible to equip them for a good job. Mr Rowan, himself threatened with redundancy from his accountancy firm, tells how he and his wife would sell their house rather than take their daughter out of private schooling (see p. 64–5); they would live in their caravan. They go on to commit themselves to supporting her through seven years of higher education if she decides to be a vet (see p. 195).

Yet there are contradictions at the heart of the accounts. Careerists' own versions of the changes within their occupations reveal the rising price of positional goods, both through thinning the crowded environment of higher posts and through screening for higher qualifications. Despite all the effort and sacrifice, their offspring may well be disappointed in the return on their investments. By 1993, the number of unemployed graduates stood at 8956. In the post-Thatcher economic environment, position counts for more, but the expenditure of resources of those who compete unsuccessfully for positional goods constitutes a considerable waste.

There is an even more conspicuous anomaly over women's labour market rôles. The female interviewees' earnings, and their work responsibilities, are spectacularly below the expected return on their educational qualifications and previous employment experience. Yet the accounts of parental investment in daughters' education are every bit as ambitious as those for sons, with higher education the normal expectation. Is there not a contradiction between women's acceptance of a secondary labour-market rôle on the one hand, and their aspirations for their daughters on the other?

Gender and generational relations

Although women with extensive educational qualifications or previous experience of responsible posts describe their decisions to do low paid, part-time work in self-developmental terms, and as chosen for their flexibility and intrinsic interest, they none the less recognize that they are receiving small pay-offs for their years of study or training. In some cases, this relates to the self-employed status of their partners: Mrs Laburnum and Mrs

Alder both do part-time craft work and (for tax reasons) are "employed" in the family firm to do the books. Mrs Elm, a graduate and trained teacher, does the same for her husband's accountancy business, while running an occasional nursery class. Others give family reasons for choosing to do work that is badly paid and has few fringe benefits. Mrs Cedar's secretarial job is below the tax and social security contribution thresholds.

Mrs Cedar: In a way I'd like to work more hours, but whatever I do it has to be fairly flexible, because I've got no-one to leave the children with if they're ill, and so until they're old enough to be here without me around . . .   (Mrs Cedar, 17)

Mrs Elder earned more than her husband before they had children. Now she works one day a week as a typesetter.

Mrs Elder: Yes, I enjoyed that, but then we didn't have any children, and I think that changed it.   (Mrs Elder, 1)

Mrs Poplar was a probation officer, but now does secretarial work. She is asked why she took this.

Mrs Poplar: I've got secretarial qualifications anyway, and experience [. . .] Mainly because I left the probation service to have a family . . .   (Mrs Poplar, 7)

This has important consequences, as we saw in Chapter 7, for power and dependence in the household. Although women have considerable autonomy within the everyday order of partnership, their long-term bargaining strategy (to sacrifice medium-term for long-term pay-offs) succeeds only if the partnership remains intact. Mrs Conifer, who was in "a weak bargaining position" over her husband's move south (see p. 106), recognizes her reliance on his pension, because hers is not adequate.

Mrs Conifer: I had this very naive notion that you could pay into a pension scheme . . . if you had the money you could pay in when you're not working, but of course you can't, you have to be working to pay into a pension scheme. So no, I'm not very secure as far as my own pension is concerned, just hoping I've still got Andrew to fall back on financially [laughs].   (Mrs Conifer, 43–4)

The same unease is signalled by Ms Plum, whose art studio is heavily subsidized by Mr Larch. They are not married, and he has had several previous marriages and cohabitations.

Ms Plum: . . . My opinions have changed, because I didn't think it used to matter. But since having children, I think that it does matter, and I think that I feel insecure to a large extent because we're not married. That's from my point of view. And I feel that the children will, particularly the boy – not so much the little girl – will share that insecurity when he realizes. (Ms Plum, 13)

Ms Blackthorn's experiences reinforce this: after the breakup of her marriage, she was forced to claim income support for a time, and struggled to make her way in the labour market. Why then do women opt for an individual strategy in partnership that is apparently not in the collective interests of women, as workers or as partners?

Of course, although these interviews do not reveal this, exactly the same question could be posed about young adults' position. Why do they put up with being "screened out" of good jobs for so long, especially when these are held by older people with fewer qualifications? These questions are the political ones of the positional economy (analyzed in the previous section). Positional job assets are virtually monopolized by the "careerists" among these interviewees. Yet there are almost as many "non-careerists" as "careerists" in the economy as a whole, if low paid subcontract, casual and self-employed workers (mostly men) are added to part-time workers (mostly women).[16] And there are a great many more "non-careerists" in society as a whole if all those outside the labour market are added in. Why do all these (unemployed, sick, disabled, retired) not make common political cause with women and young people for a collectivized redistribution of the fruits of the positional economy, currently the "oligarchic wealth" of a group made up mostly of men?

A third way of asking the same set of questions – and one often addressed by economists – is to enquire why the labour market does not clear itself. Why do all these well qualified women, doing badly paid part-time work, not offer themselves for the jobs done by careerist men, but at slightly lower wages? And why do not others, currently unemployed, in turn offer themselves for other jobs elsewhere in the economy, and so on until all underemployment and unemployment are eliminated? The American economist Robert Solow points out that neither efficiency wage nor insider outsider models (which are the accepted economic theories of differential wages and conditions) can explain why individuals do not bid for positional assets.[17] He postulates an equilibrium strategy in which labour-market behaviour is governed by norms of non-competition between insiders (job-holders) and outsiders.[18] Outsiders act as if they are playing a Prisoner's Dilemma super-game, in which employers will pay only a reservation wage (so low that workers will be indifferent between working and not working) if anyone offers to work at less than current (non-market-clearing) rates. Hence they are best off by "sitting tight" – unemployed or in low paid part-time employ-ment – partly in the hope of eventually getting an insider's job and partly out of fear of destroying the oligarchic wealth of the positional economy.

Solow's theory of the labour market as a social institution is aimed at explaining why all marginal workers may have a strategic interest in not challenging the *status quo*, by offering to work for less than job holders do. But in the case of "non-careerist" women interviewees in this study, they have an additional strategic reason for not seeking short-term gains at the expense of their long-term investments in their partners "careers". If breaches in the norm of non-competition threaten insiders' positional ben-efits, they stand to lose more from the destruction of their share of men's job assets (particularly their pensions) than they will gain from improved access to better employment.[19] Their interests as members of a coalition (or class) with substantial "rents" from job-holdings outweigh their inter-ests in redistribution. Hence, collectively, women in higher-income house-holds have a dual interest in maintaining the positional economy from whose pay-offs they are excluded. In so far as they do form part of a po-tential coalition of outsiders, their best strategy is to sit tight on the mar-gins of the labour market. In so far as they, as individuals, have an indi-rect stake in job-holders' positional goods, their best strategy is to support their partners in maximizing their positional benefits.

But this ignores the extent to which their offspring run the risk of re-maining outsiders in the longer term. As Solow points out, the equilibrium in his supergame holds only as long as outsiders believe they have a good prospect of gaining positional advantages in the future. Everything these couples say suggests that they believe their children will get good jobs if they study and work hard, even thought they will have to wait much longer than their generation did when they were young. Hence they are willing to absorb the costs of longer dependence, including the possibility of some intergenerational strife within the household. Mr and Mrs Alder have two late teenagers and a younger daughter.

Q: Do you have any thoughts about . . . the oldest children could well be leaving home within the next few years . . .

Mr Alder: HOORAY !!!

Mrs Alder goes on to describe competition between them for rooms within the house:

Mr Alder: I'm sure we'll reach a compromise again which will be noted as me having my way [laughs]. I actually view the children leaving, especially going to university, as more of a financial burden.

Q: This is because you'll be contributing to grants?

Mr Alder: Yes, bound to . . .   (Mr and Mrs Alder, 48)

This passage allows a glimpse of the power implicit in intergenerational as well as gender relations in these households. Mr Alder, a self-employed builder who will not train his son because of the potential conflicts between them (see p. 131), goes on to explain how he has to budget for his children's long-term dependence on his earnings. Issues of parental authority and the younger generation's resentment of dependence appear only dimly in these accounts, as in Mr Alder's confusion over his own reactions to his son becoming a man. But behind these snapshots of family life lurk larger issues about relations between the generations. Are these parents' individual strategies over investments in their offspring collectively rational? Will they give their children eventual access to positional goods in the labour market?

Clinging on: trapped in advantage?

One of the ironic features of the accounts is that those men with positional job assets were almost without exception keen to cash these in by taking early retirement; but many reflected that they could not do so because of the escalating costs of the prolonged dependence of their sons and daughters. The costs of maintaining them through higher education were the heaviest aspect of this burden. The aim of this expenditure was to equip them for competition for the positional goods of the labour market – good jobs. But the number of such jobs was diminishing (on their own accounts of their occupational environments) and the competition for remaining positional goods was driving up their "price" (in terms of ever-higher qualifications). The only way in which the positional economy could be opened up to a new generation was through retirement. Yet these men could not retire for some time yet because they were paying to support their offsprings' quest for the higher qualifications that their positions now demanded.

Mrs Pine: . . . Edward talks about retiring early, but you know there is the possibility that we will be funding our children in education for another seven years, and none of our children will get a maintenance grant, we'll have to finance them. And when you're thinking of giving up £6000 of your taxed salary, it is actually a lot of money [. . .] I suspect that when it happens it will be a shock, and it will actually limit other kinds of decisions. (Mrs Pine, 24)

Mr Redwood: . . . it always sounds a bit optimistic, but I would quite like to be able to retire at 60.

Mrs Redwood: That's hopeful, isn't it?

Mr Redwood: Yes, but realistically I think that with financial commitments and the school fees and university and all the rest of it, I think 55 is too optimistic and really none of the pension policies are . . . I mean I would like to retire at 60 . . .

(Mr and Mrs Redwood, 51)

Mr Lime: I've paid off all the money I owed – I took out insurance policies for [three children by first marriage], but they've all been paid off now. I wouldn't be too worried about [cost of private education for daughter aged 20 months] . . . we could probably afford it now because by the time she goes to school the other three will be out of my hair . . . (Mr Lime, 16)

Thus these job-holders' accounts begin to suggest a vicious circle. These are accounts by people, some of whom were *not* advantaged by their childhoods (who went to state schools, which they left without qualifications, and who missed certain early chances to gain positional goods and career advantages), yet even so had made something of themselves. In their striving to ensure that their offspring are better equipped for competition than they were, each contributes to a system of relations in which the stakes are bid ever higher – in which the favoured ones need more qualifications, resources and assets to gain even the same advantages as their parents have enjoyed. The paradox of putting the family first is that – from the very nature of positional goods, and from the structure of a society that allows these assets to bestow such advantages – not all who strive can gain them. "Making something of oneself" is comparative and positional; this is a feature of individualistic societies that distinguishes them from traditional ones organized through "mechanical solidarity". Thus there is a "ratchet effect" that raises the stakes for such goods in a meritocratic and competitive system. As all are better equipped and resourced than were their parents' generation, the effect is that even some well qualified and generously resourced individuals will fail to make anything much of themselves, to the great disappointment of their and their parents' expectations and the frustration of their sacrificial efforts. Indeed, if their daughters adopt the same non-competitive bargaining strategies as their mothers, in the labour market with men in general and in the household with their partners, they will not get any positional returns on these investments.

Our study of labour-market decisions in low-income households was published under the title *Trapped in poverty?*, and addressed the notion of structural and systematic disadvantage. It was tempting to call this section, or even the whole book, *Trapped in affluence?* because of these perverse consequences of individualistic decision making. This would have been a catchy but misleading title. The couples in these interviews were not affluent, except by relative standards. Few of them enjoyed luxurious lifestyles; far more exercised considerable restraint and self-sacrifice for the sake of their children. The paradox of their lives was not the constraint associated with riches, but the self-defeating pursuit of advantage. Putting the family first implied that they had to take every step available to give their children a better chance of making something of themselves than other people's children enjoyed. Without any ill-will towards others, the logic of their choices must always tend towards giving their offspring a headstart – more learning capacity, better concentration, more practice, better facilities, more resources, a favourable environment, more qualifications, more confidence, more contacts, more social skills – over others who would also be striving to make something of themselves.

Being trapped in the quest for positional advantage is partly a consequence of government social policies. Strict controls over expenditure on state services have held back improvements in some services and led to deterioration in others. As more parents have become anxious about a perceived decline (publicized by ministers critical of the teaching profession) in standards of state schooling, more children are withdrawn and placed in private education. But the higher the proportion who take this option, the more the marginal premium of advantage for each private pupil is reduced, because of the positional nature of the goods sought.

Housing is another aspect of the positional economy. In the 1970s and 1980s, couples like these were able to occupy a powerful position in the housing market by borrowing as much as they could afford early in their partnerships and "trading up" over time. [20] The rationale for this is presented in the interviews in terms of spacious and commodious accommodation for children's needs, but larger houses also conferred positional command over exclusive resources of space and security, and a shrewd investment. As funding flowed into the domestic housing market, house prices consistently rose faster than the general rate of inflation, so couples like these were doubly rewarded. [21] The government gave them tax relief on mortgage interest and inflation made their positional housing assets grow, while their mortgage repayments remained constant (i.e. shrank in relative terms).

Many respondents acknowledge that they have done well from these processes. Those who got jobs offering home loans at low interest as perks (Mr Willow, Mr Linden, Mr Yew) were among the largest gainers, having bought houses before they were married. Others recognized the advantages they gained over others who entered the market later.

Dr Pine: . . . because a mortgage taken out 20 years ago is a trifling amount compared with what people are paying today. So in that sense we don't have to worry financially because our mortgage is now relatively low.   (Dr Pine, 17)

Mr Palm: . . . I think [in the 1970s] we had a mortgage of about £7,000 . . . At the moment we pay £77 a month mortgage [. . .] it was diminishing quite quickly [. . .] with the inflation of the middle seventies.   (Mr Palm, 13)

Others wished they could have bought sooner than they did.

Mr Dogwood: Yes, it was a source of regret to both of us that we hadn't managed earlier to buy a property. If we had done, if we'd done it five or six years earlier we would have been in a lot stronger position financially.   (Mr and Mrs Dogwood, 27)

Chief-Inspector Sycamore: . . . how prices were leaping ahead of us at that stage at a phenomenal rate, and the house prices were increasing faster than you could sort money for a deposit . . .
                                                   (Chief-Inspector Sycamore, 39)

Yet these positional advantages are gained partly at the expense of their offsprings' generation. The latter face a far higher hurdle to get into the housing market because of the rise in the relative price of housing: they have to earn and save more to get a foot on the ladder. Hence these individual decisions (to maximize borrowing and positional housing assets), though individually rational, collectively disadvantage the next generation. The "people today" who have to pay so much more (Dr Pine) will soon be his own children.

Anxieties about the possibility that their offspring will need substantial financial assistance to get into owner-occupation surface only fleetingly and jokingly in the accounts.

Mr Hazel: Well, if I hit the jackpot again this year [with royalties for a book], which I might or might not, we might buy a house for the kids.

Mrs Hazel: It'll have to be a very small one.

(Mr and Mrs Hazel, 46)

Of course, since the interviews were completed, the rise in interest rates caused a fall in British house prices, which has allowed some members of the younger generation (those with secure jobs) to gain access to owner-occupation. But this has also made it harder for the parental generation to sell their large houses, as several planned to do for retirement, and thus release capital for their offspring. This in turn contributes to the trap, keeping the interviewees' generation of "careerists" in their jobs for longer than they planned, and blocking the new generation from the positional assets that they seek for them.

Managing congestion

Why should these issues be of concern for social policy? Our analysis of the interviewees' accounts shows how the individualism of making something of oneself and putting the family first can produce a stable order of partnership and parenting, and a long-term bargaining strategy for investment decisions, the domestic division of labour and support during retirement. This order is sufficiently flexible to allow considerable variation: it can accommodate socialists like the Palms and environmentalists like the Oaks and Teaks, as well as allowing sufficient autonomy to satisfy the less conventional aspirations of "non-careerist" men and much self-developmental scope for women. So long as it can eventually give enough of a new generation access to the positional economy, why should not the individualism and family orientation of the "property-owning democracy" survive as the basis for citizenship in the next century?

We have shown in this chapter that unmanaged congestion in the positional economy can lead to decisions that, though individually rational, are collectively wasteful and frustrate individuals' intentions. This becomes an issue for social policy when the effects of such decisions limit the growth of the material economy or cause social strife. In the United States, health care provides the example. Competition for positional advantage in health care has driven up the price to a point where it both blocks investment in productive industry and leaves millions of households with no means of covering their health costs. By contrast, although in Britain the better-off have always been able to get some positional health goods (quicker and more extensive treatment) through private medicine, occupational insurance and cultural factors, congestion has hitherto been managed in such a way as to prevent an escalation in the costs of health care.

In the case of housing, British policy has been much less successful. In the "property-owning democracy", owner-occupied houses are rhetorically constructed as positional goods and policy is – through tax regulations, legislation on tenure and assistance to buy from local authorities – directed towards raising aspirations for ownership without a corresponding increase in the supply of homes. The deregulation of credit in the mid-1980s contributed to a rapid inflation in house prices, as borrowing to finance purchase and improvements rose steeply.[22] In the early 1990s it has become clear that fluctuations in the housing market are now an important factor in Britain's inability to achieve steady economic growth. Unless congestion is managed, competition between households for positional goods will continue to distort other sectors of the economy and reduce overall efficiency.

Crime and security are notoriously problematic areas of public policy in the United States, and increasingly also in Britain. Security is discursively constructed in terms of weapons, guards, alarm systems and exclusive property, rather than the management of a congested social environment through communal civic culture and orderly sharing. In the United States, the carrying of guns as positional assets for personal security contributes to high murder rates; in some parts of Britain, carrying knives has led to positional competition and an escalation of wounding.[23] Increased expenditure on guards, video systems and alarms adds to the positional economy in security, but does not reduce overall crime rates. It also creates a structure of institutional interests in positional goods (such as the American Rifle Association) and a security industry, which act as obstacles to alternative systems for managing the social environment.

However, the key economic asset in all advanced economies is secure, well paid employment, and the bulk of this chapter has been devoted to analyzing the positional aspects of the labour market. We have also shown throughout this book that the household – through the partnership code of "supportiveness" and long-term bargaining strategies between couples – does provide a system for managing congestion. Institutional features of the labour market and the household mesh together to ensure a large measure of non-competition by women and young people for predominantly male job assets, and that most of the costs of long-term competition (via education and training) for these positional goods are absorbed by households. So long as enough young people are willing to delay entry into the positional jobs economy, and enough women to be excluded from it, this system is sustainable.

Of course, there are many other households (such as the ones we analyzed in our previous study) that are more systematically excluded from access to good jobs. They make up the growing sector of households with no job-holder, where all members are either insecure, low paid marginal workers, or long-term claimants. The "property-owning democracy" relies on better-off households to act in such a way as to take no account of their interests, leaving these to the residual social services. So long as women and young people adopt the non-competitive strategies identified in this chapter and rely on benefiting (as dependants) from the job assets of adult men, there is no need for government policy to take poor citizens' claims for increased employment and income too seriously. Their political significance can be measured in terms of their potential for disorder, crime and disruption, rather than their productive capacities.

Hence the questions for social policy raised by this study concern the interaction between a number of features of individualism and family prioritization. Are its systems for suppressing competition by women and young people for male job assets sustainable in the longer term? How much more of the rising costs of "screening" for the positional labour market will households be prepared to bear? Will the distorting economic effects of a government's tax treatment of housing finance outweigh the political advantages? Will public concern about crime and security cause an escalation in punishment (for instance, the return of the death penalty) or a reassessment of how to manage congestion in the labour market and the social environment?

The other side of these questions is the declining effectiveness of social democratic methods of managing congestion. Because of rising relative costs, the use of public service employment to widen the availability of secure jobs is no longer sustainable. Individualism itself reduces the scope for substituting public goods for positional ones. Systems that allocate "standard rations" or require undifferentiated sharing violate the requirements of choice and domestic consumption in what selves make of themselves and how they put the family first. Hence socialist parties increasingly develop rhetorics that embrace various forms of individualism for the sake of electoral support, but lack the policies to harness this to new programmes for efficiency and justice.

Marrying efficiency and justice

The electoral failures of the British Labour Party have occurred despite evidence of public concern over issues of social policy – unemployment, health, housing and education. These interviews too revealed the gap between a desire for a better-managed social environment and the individual actions that could achieve this (see pp. 191–3). As was shown in Chapter 8, concerns do not emerge as public issues, requiring citizens to engage with others to discover democratic solutions. Instead, individualist repertoires focus on personal responsibility for the welfare of households, and the perception of unsuccessful management of congestion through public policy (whether seen as mistaken market-mindedness or failure of collectivist solutions) increases the pursuit of positional goods. Individualism encourages citizens to be responsible for themselves and their families and to leave unfortunate others' problems to the state.

This study also gives clues about why feminism's project of equal opportunities in the labour market has stalled. Women will not compete with men for positional assets so long as they believe a non-competitive strategy can allow them to contribute best to their children's future prospects. If this belief is well founded, the "property-owning democracy" will indeed be a model for future citizenship. If it is not – and our analysis in this chapter suggests that it is likely ultimately to prove wasteful and self-defeating – then governments will promote economic efficiency and social justice only by exposing the perverse consequences of this strategy and providing an institutional framework that promotes another. In other words, if non-competition by women and young people leads older male insiders to cling on to positional goods (despite stress and resentment) and forces able outsiders – both female and from the younger generation – to put their energies and talents to less productive uses than their capacities would allow, then this outcome is neither just nor efficient.

In Britain, both the major political parties are reviewing their social policy programmes with the avowed aim of discovering a coherent set of principles to define the social rights and obligations of all citizens.[23] In practice, this focuses on the social security budget, which at £80 billion amounts to more than any other two categories of public spending added together. Our research study indicates that the present structure of opportunities and incentives (tax reliefs on private pensions, the National Insurance Scheme, means-tested student grants) reinforces a strongly gendered division of work rôles and makes invisible the linked issues of access to and exit from the labour market. It encourages households to maximize the job assets of the male "head" and obscures the inefficiencies and inequities of this strategy.

The debate about social citizenship has hitherto centred on the duties of the poor, and especially whether they should have an obligation to work for benefits. It has been conducted in abstract terms that take little account of citizens' practices. This study provides evidence of how better-off couples interpret their rights and responsibilities, and how they make decisions. It indicates their willingness to make sacrifices to give their children future advantages, and how this overrides other considerations – such as responsibilities towards a wider kinship network or towards other members of their political community. It shows how these priorities are derived from an individualistic ethic but constructed within the context of welfare pluralism as lifestyle choices, largely without reference to collective consequences. This gives important clues about the gap between survey evidence of concern about social welfare issues and voting behaviour.[24] As Mr Yew and Mrs Redwood say, in a choice between family and politics, they put the family first.

This challenges the social policy programmes of both the major British parties. For the Conservative government, it warns of possible future problems, similar to those experienced by the Bush administration in the USA. There, a combination of falling incomes and rising health care costs led to a sudden disillusion with market-minded policies. In the same way, middle- and higher-income groups in Britain could come to resist further burdens on household resources, especially if their children's labour-market prospects look gloomy.

But the challenge for the Labour Party is more fundamental. Now committed to strengthening individual social rights and promoting choice,[25] it needs to find ways of making the collective implications of household decisions more transparent. This would involve accepting the unpalatable fact – confirmed by this study – that National Insurance no longer provides a universal structure of opportunities and incentives, linking the economic decisions of all citizens within a common framework of rights and responsibilities. Just as our research on poor households showed that they chose work by reference to means-tested benefits, so this study demonstrates that better-off couples frame their decisions in relation to occupational and private systems. Hence the Labour Party's social policy choice is between abandoning the pretence of universalism and common social citizenship (accepting a "targeted" benefits system or moving towards negative income tax), or taking the risk of proposing more radical measures.

One proposal is to make the tax–benefit unit the individual, not the household, and to replace personal tax allowances and all benefits (including students' allowances) by a single system.[26] This would greatly increase transparency, and its advocates have argued that it would create a universal structure for decisions that would promote equality and sharing within household,[27] and responsibility and co-operation in the wider community.[28] But the political risks would be considerable, because the principle – an unconditional income guarantee for all citizens – is difficult to justify in terms of the liberal individualist tradition. The legacy of Thatcherism is that this ethic (and its perverse consequences) have become part of the institutional and cultural fabric of British social relations. To go with the grain of the practices revealed by this study would consolidate both injustice and inefficiency; to try to change them would be a bold and risky political strategy.

References

1. Department of Social Security, *Families on below average incomes* (London: HMSO, 1993), showed that the poorest suffered a loss of 14 per cent, while the average household gained 36 per cent in real income between 1979 and 1990. The equivalized post-tax incomes of the bottom fifth of households fell from 10 per cent to 7 per cent of national income between 1979 and 1988; the top fifth rose from 37 per cent to 44 per cent in the same period (Central Statistical Office, *Social Trends 22*, London: HMSO, 1992, Table 5.19). The real median net income, after housing costs, of the bottom fifth of individual incomes stayed constant at £81 per week (1992 prices) between 1979 and 1989; the average of all individuals rose from £159 to £207 in the same period, and the top fifth from £253 to £355 (*Social Trends 23*, 1993, Table 5.18, p. 77).
2. B. Jordan, S. James, H. Kay, M. Redley, *Trapped in poverty?* Labour-market *decisions*

in low-income households (London: Routledge, 1992).

3. Institute of Economic Affairs, *The emerging consensus* London: Institute of Economic Affairs, 1981).

4. A. Seldon & R. Harris, *Overruled on welfare* (London: Institute of Economic Affairs, 1979).

5. F. Hirsch, *Social limits to growth* (London: Routledge and Kegan Paul, 1977), Ch. 1.

6. Ibid., p. 5.

7. Between 1979 and 1992 the number of men in full-time jobs declined from 13,169,000 to 9,962,000, and the number of women in full-time jobs from 6,423,000 to 5,873,000. (Department of Employment, *Employment Gazette*, November 1980 and January 1993).

8. In the 1980s the net gain in the number of dwellings in the UK was around 200,000. In 1990, 156,000 households were accepted by local authorities as homeless (in priority need) (*Social Trends*, 1992, Tables 8.2 and 8.14).

9. In 1991, 32 per cent of unemployed men and women were in the age group 16–24, of whom 4 per cent of women and 6 per cent of men had degrees or equivalent (*General Household Survey*, 1991, Table 5.2). Graduate unemployment stood at 8 per cent in 1990 (*Social Trends 23*, 1993, Table 3.24, p. 47).

10. B. Jordan, "Democratic citizenship and community", Occasional Paper, Department of Economics, Politics and Public Administration, University of Aalborg, Denmark.

11. Hirsch, *Social limits to growth*, pp. 41–8.

12. The Retail Prices Index (January 1987 = 100) rose from 55 in 1979 to 125 in 1990. In the same period, the housing component of the index rose from 45 to 170.

13. Hirsch, *Social limits to growth*, pp. 5–12.

14. R. Harrod, "The possibility of economic satiety – use of economic growth for improving quality of education and leisure", in *Problems of United States economic development*, vol. 1, 207–13 (Washington DC: Committee for Economic Development, 1958).

15. Hirsch, *Social limits to growth*, p. 27.

16. C. Handy, *The age of unreason* (London: Hutchinson, 1990), estimates that by the turn of the century half the workforce (12 million people) will have "non-standard" contracts (part-time, short-term or irregular employment, or self-employment).

17. R. M. Solow, *The labour market at a social institution* (Oxford: Blackwell, 1990).

18. Ibid., pp. 47–9.

19. B. Jordan, *The common good: citizenship, morality and self-interest* (Oxford: Blackwell, 1989), Ch. 6.

20. M. Ball, *Housing policy and economic power: the political economy of owner occupation* (London: Methuen, 1983).

21. Ibid.

22. R. Berthoud & E. Kempson, *Credit and debt* (London: Policy Studies Institute, 1991).

23. The Labour Party set up a Commission for Social Justice in the autumn of 1992. The government instituted a radical ministerial review of the welfare state, and particularly social security, in April 1993 (*Guardian*, 23 April 1993).

24. British attitude surveys reveal that between 1983 and 1992 the proportion of British voters who said they wanted to reduce taxes and spend less on social services fell from 9 to 3 per cent, and those who said they wanted to increase taxes and spend more on education and social benefits rose from 33 to 65 per cent. However, in 1992

the British electorate returned a Conservative government for the fourth time since 1979, and a key factor in Labour's failure was the perception that it would increase taxation.

25. A. Coote (ed.), *The welfare of citizens: developing new social rights* (London: IPPR/Rivers Oram Press, 1992).
26. A. B. Atkinson & H. Sutherland, *Integrating income taxation and social security: analysis of a partial basic income*, London School of Economics, Number TIDI/123/July 1988; H. Parker, *Instead of the dole: an enquiry into integration of the tax and benefit systems* (London: Routledge, 1989); P. Van Parijs (ed.), *Arguing for basic income* (London: Verso, 1992); Netherland Scientific Council for Government Policy, *Safeguarding social security in the Netherlands* (The Hague: WRR, 1985).
27. H. Parker (ed.), *Citizen's income and women*, BIRG Discussion Paper No. 2, Citizen's Income, 1993; B. Jordan, *Rethinking welfare* (Oxford: Blackwell, 1987).
28. T. Walter, *Basic income: freedom from poverty, freedom to work* (London: Marion Boyars, 1989); B. Jordan, *The common good: citizenship, morality and self-interest*.

APPENDIX A

The Research Study

This study was the second part of a long-term research project, funded by the ESRC, on labour-market decision making. The intention was to gather data on higher-income households with children using similar methods to the ones we had developed in our earlier study of decision making in low-income households. We set out, as before, to find out what factors men and women said influenced their choices of employment, self-employment and non-employment, for what hours, at what salaries, under what conditions, and with what prospects of training, promotion, and so on. As before, we conducted individual tape-recorded interviews, followed by a joint interview, with a sample of couples (36 in all, though two sets were lost through tape-recorder failure), asking them about labour-market decisions and how (if at all) they influenced each other's choices, how they handled domestic tasks and child care, and how they set about providing for their welfare needs (e.g. pensions, children's education, health). The interviews were transcribed for analysis by the research team – an economist (Simon James), a social policy analyst (Bill Jordan) and a sociologist (Marcus Redley). The aim of the long-term project was to compare the two sets of data, though systematic comparison was postponed to a third project, planned to take place in 1991–3.

The focus of the second study, like the first, was a city (population just under 100,000) in southwest England. However, whereas the couples in the first sample were all drawn from one small deprived neighbourhood (a council estate), the couples in the second were selected from all over the city and surrounding villages (reflecting their greater mobility and the wider catchment area of employers of higher-paid labour in the city). We decided not to sample the occupations of people living in one neighbourhood, because (as one of the interviewees, an estate agent, pointed out in an off-tape comment) there is no one exclusively higher-income residential area in the city. Instead we sought interviewees whose occupations roughly tallied with the distribution of higher-income jobs in the city, thus reflecting the mix of professional, managerial, administrative and entrepreneurial rôles, of public and private sectors, agricultural, industrial and service occupations, and so on. After recruiting, usually by telephone, we sent a brief explanation of the research on headed notepaper.

As in the first study, we did not seek to discover respondents' earnings before interviewing them, but started from the assumption that certain occupations commanded average or above-average salaries, rather as we had assumed before that residents of the council estate were likely to have experienced poverty. Interviewees were asked to fill in a form giving details of their qualifications and earnings after their interviews. The interesting thing, of course, was to discover how earnings varied and how interviewees explained this variation. As before, the interviews consisted of open-ended questions, providing respondents with opportunities to expand on their reasoning over decisions. Finally, we understood the interviewees' accounts within the same broad framework in both studies – as attempts to give morally adequate versions of their labour-market decisions by reference to the standards that they considered applied to persons of working age with partners and children.

The team: power and gender issues

One important factor was that all the team were men. This meant that gender issues had to be addressed through the analysis of what happened in interviews or as arising within the accounts. There can be little doubt that issues of gender and power occur in every interaction in modern society; they are managed differently by all-male groups and by male interviewers than by mixed teams and female interviewers. The experience of working as an all-male team meant that the distinctions in status, influence, pay, working conditions, and so on between team members were not discussed in terms of gendered relations or experienced as being part of what it is to be an (advantaged) man or a (disadvantaged) woman. Issues of power, fairness in rôles and responsibilities, the division of labour and reward were mediated by age rather than gender factors, and any discomforts, guilt and unspoken tensions within the team thus had this different aspect.

However, the practice of a male interviewer asking women about their reasoning over paid work and the domestic division of labour in partnership raised other theoretical and ethical issues. In Chapters 2 and 3 we explain that we intend to analyze these interviewees' accounts of decision making as versions by social subjects (not asocial, disembodied beings or "cultural dopes") in a context of specific relations and practices. But the social norms, rôles and relationships revealed in the accounts can also be evaluated and criticized (in terms of power, exploitation and injustice), as we begin to sketch in Chapters 5 and 7. The problem posed by the situation of male interviewer and female respondent is what effect the wider power relations of gender have on the interview process: can the woman give an account of her reasoning to a man that is not influenced by male domination in society, male expectations of female subordination, male discourse about the formal economy and the household, and so on? Does not the interview process itself, and the interaction between interviewer and respondent, reveal power being exercised through a discourse of social science knowledge and academic enquiry? In Chapters 3, 4 and 6 we look at the interview interaction as an instance of a locally created discursive order, and in Chapter 7 we argue that power issues such as these are managed through ritual reciprocities within such an order.

Thus we recognize that gender-related power was an important issue in the study, and it is part of what we evaluate and criticize in the data. This was something of which we were very conscious in planning, in conducting the interviews, and in the analysis. In the first study, Helen Kay's awareness of ethical issues (on informed consent as well as on gender and power[1]) led us to think carefully about this[2] and to have it in our minds during the interview process. We tried to enable and encourage women respondents to give their versions by framing questions open-endedly, and by not using language, or making assumptions, that would push them towards stereotypical constructions of the woman's rôle. We also tried to ask questions – usually towards the end of individual and joint interviews – that gave further opportunities for reflective talk about decisions, values and rôles, and for evaluating choices or relationships. However, in the interviews with women there was a difficult balance to be struck between providing openings for reflection and sounding challenging in the power-based way that men often address questions to women. Hence it was a matter for judgement, discretion and timing whether to pursue an issue or drop it, to frame a general question about rôle divisions or to move on to another topic. Where a woman was talking confidently and assertively it felt ethically sound to pose such a question in a fairly direct way; where she was obviously ill-at-ease or uncomfortable (for whatever reason) this was judged to rule out the further pursuit of this topic by a man (who could be perceived as using a powerful academic discourse of interrogation unfairly).

Of course, having a male interviewer also affected the interviews with male respondents. The best clues we have to this lie in aspects of the interaction with a few male interviewees, whose overtly sexist comments are analyzed in Chapter 3. Such comments were part of an approach to being interviewed that distinguished them from most of the other respondents; it allowed them both to emerge as "characters" and to appear to take the process less seriously. The subversive, mocking tone they adopted seemed to be addressed to the interviewer as a man – wink wink, nudge nudge – and hence explicitly to the gendered nature of interview interaction, an aspect consistently played down by all the "serious" respondents.

The interviewees

In the higher-income households, the lack of social distance between interviewer and interviewees contributed to a strong sense that there was much at stake in the interviews – that moral adequacy was a minimal rather than an optimal requirement of the accounts given of labour-market decisions. These respondents invested a good deal in the process of the research, both in terms of wanting to contribute "good data" and in terms of wanting to tell a convincing story about their labour-market decisions and their partnerships. The experience of interviewing them was characterized by a sense of investment – almost intensity of commitment – to "do well" in the interviews, to give us what we wanted, and to make a good impression, which we were drawn into reciprocating, as we strove to be good interviewers, both in terms of our skills in asking questions and enabling answers and in terms of the poise with which we handled the attendant social niceties. This put in far sharper relief the few interviewees who did not seem to take the process seriously (who were jokey, who exaggerated for effect, or who subverted partnership talk), or who gave brief, attenuated answers despite encouragement to expand and develop their accounts (see Chapter 3).

These questions led us to focus far more on the interaction between interviewer and interviewees in the theory and methodology of the second study than we had in the first. In Chapters 3, 4, 6 and 7, we argue that the interactive order, which has hitherto been a research topic only in a small corner of microsociology, is far from being a theoretical byway in the

235

study of decision making and its relation to social structure. What we have in the interactive processes of these interviews is evidence about just those informal structurings of the everyday world – those modes of moral regulation – that the research set out to investigate.

This involves us looking more closely at the respondents as *interviewees* and at the interview, not only as a research tool, but also as a piece of social interaction. Clearly the interview situation is a structured situation in which the parties have different rights and rôles; their communication is in part a function of these. However, it is also a piece of human interaction that is sustained by informal reciprocities and exchanges, and that generates its own momentum (or lack of it), order and "ethic".

Gathering the sample

Because the research was qualitative rather than quantitative, we were not required to gather a "representative" or statistically selected sample; the task was to find a group of interviewees that was relevant to our research questions and with sufficient diversity to allow a convincing theoretical account of reasoning about labour-market decisions among better-off couples to be developed. It is therefore pertinent to ask of our 36 couples whether they are "typical", and if so of what. Here we describe how we planned and gathered the sample, and what we achieved – the social and economic characteristics of the couples we recruited.

Before starting our search for willing interviewees, we designed some criteria for selecting the sample as a whole, so that its final composition would be "balanced" along a number of axes. The following considerations were used:

(a) *Income*: "Higher income" was taken to mean average or above average for the region (South West England).[3] Because of the known disparity between single-earner and dual-earner households,[4] this meant that we would seek mainly dual-earner couples, but we decided not to exclude single-earner ones. In some cases we tried to find couples through the woman's employment, thus recruiting couples where both had careers or the woman was the chief earner.

(b) *Occupations*: Our aim was to select men and women in a range of higher-income occupations – professional, managerial, commercial and entrepreneurial. We also wanted to include some "rentiers" (people with property incomes); in the event only one – Mr Larch, a landlord – was found. We did not actively seek people in skilled manual occupations: the city's lack of manufacturing industries meant that there were few of these in the district,[5] and we decided not to target this group.

(c) *Employment/Self-Employment*: With the growth of small businesses and self-employment in the 1980s,[6] we decided to aim at recruiting a number of men and women who were self-employed and/or employed others. We were particularly interested in the processes through which employees moved into self-employment.

(d) *Industrial categories*: We wanted to recruit people working in primary, secondary and tertiary industries, but in such a way as to reflect the distribution of employment in the city. Because the city's proportion of manufacturing employment has for many decades been roughly half that of the country as a whole, and less than half of the average for cities, we focused mainly on service workers – people employed in finance, insurance, legal and business services, retailing, distribution, estate agency, administration, education, health and community services. The secondary sector was represented mainly by professionals in the construction industry and craft workers. There was one farming household.

(e) *Private/public*: We recruited men mainly from the private sector; their partners were predominantly employed in the public sector. Women's (mainly part-time) employment was concentrated in teaching and health and social services, all predominantly public sector occupations. However, we also recruited a group of women with small businesses in the secondary industrial sector – craft workers.

Tables A.1–A.4 illustrate the distributions of interviewees under these categories. They show that half the male interviewees were in professional occupations, with the rest distributed evenly between managerial and entrepreneurial or commercial ones; that two-thirds of the men worked in the private sector, that over a third were self-employed, and that they were heavily concentrated in educational, construction, financial and legal categories. Among the women, half were in professional occupations; but, compared with the men, more were concentrated in clerical occupations; more were in manufacturing (craft), health and community services, and fewer in the financial categories; and more were in the public sector. This reflects the distribution of male and female higher-income employment in the city.

The processes by which these interviewees were recruited were varied. We started by contacting organizations – firms, trade associations, profes-

Table A.1 Occupational categories.

Men

Professional		Managerial		Commercial and entrepreneurial		Rentier	
Pine, Hazel	University lecturers	Willow, Yew	Insurance	Alder	Builder	Larch	Landlord
Hemlock, Fieldmaple		Linden, Elder	Accountancy	Hawthorn	Civil engineer		
Dogwood		Rowan, Quince	Estate agency	Lime	Consultant		
Oak, Teak, Maple, Pear	School teachers	Poplar	Construction		structural engineer		
Beech, Ash, Redwood	Solicitors	Cedar, Chestnut	Distribution	Birch	Brewer		
Palm	Barrister			Hornbeam	Craftsman		
Elm	Accountant			Mahogany	Farmer		
Box	Architect			Laburnum	Publisher		
Spruce	Quantity surveyor			Silverbirch	Estate agent		
Conifer	Scientist						
Sycamore	Police officer						

Total = 36

Women

Professional

Code name	Occupation
Ash	Accountant
Beech	Solicitor
Blackthorn	Employment consultant
Conifer, Hazel	University research assistants
Oak	
Dogwood, Birch, Silverbirch, Pine, Palm	School teachers
Elm	Nursery teacher
Redwood	Piano teacher
Fieldmaple	Trainee occupational therapist
Box	Social worker (untrained)
Pear	Drama therapist
Willow	Nurse/trainer
Hemlock, Whitebeam	Trainers/organizers

Managerial

Code name	Occupation
Lime, Sycamore	Retail

Commercial and entrepreneurial — Publishing and craft

Code name	Occupation
Laburnum, Alder	Crafts
Plum (Larch), Maple, Hornbeam	
Mahogany	Farmer

Clerical, etc.

Code name	Occupation
Teak	School secretary
Rowan	School meals assistant
Poplar, Quince, Cedar	Secretaries
Chestnut	Shop assistant
Elder	Typesetter

Total = 34 (2 women not employed)

APPENDIX A

Table A.2 Employment/self-employment.

	Employed	Self-employed
Men	22	14 (including lawyers)
Women	24	10

Table A.2 Industrial categories.

Category	Men	Women
Finance, insurance services	6	1
Legal & business services[a]	5	3
Estate & property[b]	3	0
Education	9	14
Health & community services	2	6
Construction	6	0
Manufacturing[c]	2	7
Distribution & retail	2	3
Farming	1	1
Unemployed/non-employed	0	2

[a]Includes printing and publishing (Mr Laburnum and Mrs Elder).
[b]Includes property-ownership (Mr Larch).
[c]Includes crafts – Mrs Laburnum counted as craft worker.

Table A.4 Private/public sector.

	Private	Public
Men	24	12
Women	19[a]	15

[a]Includes voluntary sector of community services (Mrs Quince)

sional associations, small business groups – and asking them to approach members with children living in the area for volunteers. This method produced a slow trickle of interviewees: some organizations (such as the local chamber of commerce and the businesswomen's league) gave no response; others (such as the small business and crafts associations) provided several names. This meant that our first group of 10 couples was slanted in the direction of self-employed and small business people, most of whom had recently set up and hence were active members of associations. We also recruited numbers of solicitors, chartered surveyors and teachers (school and university) – partly as partners of women in craft or small business work. As the sample expanded, we began to seek particular occupations not hitherto represented, such as insurance and estate agents, health service professionals, police officers and farmers. We also recruited through a "snowball": one person referred several people who were friends of hers, most of whom were known to each other and some of whom recommended others of their acquaintance. This meant that, in addition to having a main sample of households drawn from all over the city and district who had no relationship with each other, and some of whom were recent incomers, we also had a sub-group of fairly longstanding residents, who formed some kind of "community". This sub-group were also rather active politically: whereas most people in the sample gave no indications of their political allegiance or of being involved in local or national politics, the sub-group were mostly members of opposition (Labour or Liberal Democrat) parties, and some were leading local politicians.

In some households we recruited the woman first, and through her the man; in most it was the man who was first contacted, and he brought his partner into the research, after discussion. This was because the women's organizations we contacted were unable or unwilling to provide volunteers. Towards the end of the interviewing, we recruited three households who had recently moved to the city because the man's (insurance) company employers had relocated to the city. These recent arrivals complemented the two men who worked away from the city (and the one who planned to do so) but returned at weekends. It was particularly difficult to contact the very rich – company directors, top managers and people with property incomes – and these are scarcely represented among our sample. As can be seen from a breakdown of men's, women's and joint household incomes (as supplied by interviewees at the time we spoke to them) the range is quite broad, but they cluster around the £25,000–40,000 total household income, which for many metropolitan couples would be regarded as modest comfort rather than affluence (see Table A.5). Only one household earned £100,000; in that instance, the total represented the profits of the business (a farm), most of which were reinvested.

Thus, in the total breakdown of occupations, there are many professionals, managers and small business people, and few directors, property-owners and large business people. Although this reflects the distribution of occupations in the city, it is perhaps regrettable that we were not able to

Table A.5 Earnings of couples who completed the questionnaire (top 20).

Men	Women
Joint earnings over £40,000	
Mr Mahogany (farmer) £100,000	Mrs Mahogany (partner in farm)
Mr Willow (insurance manager) £40,000 +	Mrs Willow (nurse/trainer) £11,000–20,000
Mr Cedar (distribution manager) £40,000 +	Mrs Cedar (secretary) £2,000
Mr Quince (estate agent) £40,000 +	Mrs Quince (secretary) £2,000
Dr Pine (university lecturer) £30,000–35,000	Mrs Pine (school teacher) £11,000–20,000
Dr Conifer (scientist) £30,000–35,000	Mrs Conifer (researcher) £10,000
Mr Beech (solicitor) £30,000–35,000	Mrs Beech (solicitor) £11,000–20,000
Joint earnings over £30,000	
Mr Palm (barrister) £14,000	Mrs Palm (school teacher) £20,000–25,000
Chief Inspector Sycamore (police officer) £20,000–25,000	Mrs Sycamore (retail manager) £10,000
Mr Dogwood (teacher) £11,000–20,000	Mrs Dogwood (teacher) £11,000–20,000
Mr Ash (solicitor) £25,000	Mrs Ash (accountant) £5,000–10,000
Mr Redwood (solicitor) £30,000–35,000	Mrs Redwood (piano teacher) £3,000
Mr Box (architect) £25,000–30,000	Mrs Box (social worker) £9,300
Mr Yew (insurance manager) £30,000–35,000	Mrs Yew (housewife) £0
Mr Hawthorn (civil engineer) £20,000–25,000	Mrs Hawthorn (trainer) £8,000
Mr Hemlock (university lecturer) £20,000–25,000	Mrs Hemlock (teacher) £11,000–20,000
Joint earnings over £25,000	
Mr Rowan (accountancy manager £25,000–30,000	Mrs Rowan (school meals assistant) £2,900
Mr Elder (accountancy manager) £25,000–30,000	Mrs Elder (typesetter) £2,000
Mr Linden (insurance manager) £25,000–30,000	Mrs Linden (housewife) £0
Mr Oak (teacher) £20,000–25,000	Mrs Oak (researcher) £3,000–5,000

recruit some very rich interviewees for purposes of comparison. It might be that the defining characteristics of this group of accounts – making something of oneself and putting the family first – would not apply to those with much more income.

References

1. H. Kay, "Can respondents give informed consent in qualitative research?", paper given to Social Research Association Conference on Ethics, Policy Studies Institute, London, 10 October 1989.
2. B. Jordan, S. James, H. Kay, M. Redley, *Trapped in Poverty? Labour-market decisions in low-income households* (London: Routledge, 1992), Ch. 3.
3. In the South West region of England the average household income in 1990 was £317.40 per week (£16,404.80 per year) (Central Statistical Office, *Regional Trends* 27, London: HMSO, 1992, Table 8.2).
4. L. Morris, *The workings of the household* (Oxford: Polity, 1990), pp. 119–20; J. Brannen & G. Wilson, *Give and take in families* (London: Allen & Unwin, 1987).
5. The city's proportion of employment in manufacturing was half the average for British cities.
6. Self-employment is highest in South West England of all the regions in Great Britain: one in seven of the workforce were self-employed in 1991 (*Regional Trends* 27, 1992, p. 80 and Chart 7.1).

APPENDIX B

Pseudonyms and family structure

Couple	Children's ages
Mr and Mrs Alder	17, 15, 7
Mr (Mark) and Mrs (Megan) Ash	11 months
Mr and Mrs (Mary) Beech	7, 5, 1
Mr (Adrian) and Mrs Birch	16, 15
Mr and Mrs Box	18, 15
Mr and Mrs Cedar	10, 7
Mr and Mrs Chestnut	15, 11
Dr (Andrew) and Mrs Conifer	(Caroline) 10, 7
Mr (John) and Mrs Dogwood	(Harry) 4
Mr and Mrs Elder	10
Mr (Rory) and Mrs (Iris) Elm	9, 7, 2
Mr (Jonathan) and Mrs Fieldmaple	17, 14
Mr (Steve) Hawthorn and Ms Whitebeam	17, 15
Mr (David) and Mrs Hazel	11, 4
Mr and Mrs (Hilary) Hemlock	(Jane) 18, (Sam) 17
Mr and Mrs Hornbeam	8, 4
Mr and Mrs Laburnum	16, 14
Mr (Michael) Larch and Ms (Melissa) Plum	4, 1
Mr and Mrs (Liz) Lime	(Rachel) 20 months
Mr (Leo) and Mrs (Rachel) Linden	(Reub) 4, 1
Mr and Mrs Mahogany	12, 10
Mr and Mrs (Maggie) Maple	(Felicity) 7
Mr and Mrs Oak	18, 16, 14
Mr (David) and Mrs (Susie) Palm	(Rose) 16, (Beatrice) 14
Mr (Ronald) and Mrs (Frances) Pear	7, 4
Dr (Edward) and Mrs Pine	19, 17, 4
Mr and Mrs Poplar	two teenagers
Mr and Mrs Quince	(Maurice) 15, 13
Mr (Bruce) and Mrs Redwood	14, 11
Mr and Mrs Rowan	(Emma) 12, 10
Mr and Mrs Silverbirch	12, 9, 6
Mr (Tom) Spruce and Ms (Emma) Blackthorn	(Alex) 11, (Daisy) 10
Chief-Inspector and Mrs Sycamore	20, 17
Mr (Trevor) and Mrs Teak	17, 15, 12
Mr (Max) and Mrs Willow	15, 12, 9
Mr and Mrs Yew	5, 1

Index

INDEX

INDEX

UNIVERSITY OF WOLVERHAMPTON
LIBRARY